799.1 MOR
Morrow, Laurie.
    The woman angler

12/97

24⁹⁵

JUL 17 '00	DATE DUE	
NR 17 '01		
JY 25 01		
MAY 14 2005		

The Woman Angler

The Woman Angler

Laurie Morrow

St. Martin's Press ⚍ New York

Library of Congress Cataloging-in-Publication Data

Morrow, Laurie.
    The woman angler / Laurie Morrow.—1st. ed.
        p.   cm.
    Includes index.
    ISBN 0-312-15697-9
    1. Fishing.   2. Fishing—United States.   3. Women fishers—United
States.   4. Outdoor recreation for women—United States.   I. Title
SH441.M633   1997
799.1'2—dc21   97–1828
                                                                  CIP

First Edition: September 1997

10 9 8 7 6 5 4 3 2 1

Dedication

—

Tommy, Tom, and Winston Morrow.
(PHOTO BY LAURIE MORROW)

When I decided to write *The Woman Angler,* I had already caught a fish. It was, I thought, a very fine fish—but having never caught one before, I had nothing to compare it to. I hooked it on a hot, pretty day in the summer of 1995, all by myself, at the age of 43, in the presence of my husband and our two teenage sons.

The men in my family are avid fishermen. On occasion they go fishing—these occasions being every Saturday and Sunday between opening day of trout season in May, until October 1, which is opening day of grouse season. After that, I see them on occasion again, until Christmas

Eve when they nestle all snug in their beds, while visions of sugar-plums, rods and reels dance in their heads. Santa, invariably, delivers.

One day it dawned on me that I minded being left home all alone thirty-two weekends a year, so on this particular hot, pretty day in the summer of 1995, I announced to my family that I was coming along to fish with them. The boys—then ages 16 and 18—greeted the happy news with resounding disdain.

"C'mon, Mom, you don't know how to fish!" my oldest son, Tommy, protested.

"Yeah, Mom . . ." the younger boy, Winty, griped.

"Let Mommy come along, boys," my husband said.

"Aw, Dad . . ."

It'll be a lot of fun, I explained. *I'll pack a picnic,* I suggested. *It's a lovely day to be on the lake . . . what did you say, Winty? Tough! I'm coming! We're going to spend some quality, family time together, goddammit.*

So off we went to the lake—lugging all kinds of rods and reels and fishing stuff and slimy worms—piled into our boat, revved the motor, and took off.

"Here," one of my sons muttered, unenthusiastically handing me a rod when we got to where we were going. "Just hold on to it like this—okay, Mom?"

Okay. Like I don't know how to hold a rod . . . hold it here? Like this?

Within moments I felt a tug! I knew I had hooked a fish when I heard Tommy, in utter amazement, cry out: "Mom, you've got a fish on the line!" Winty jumped up, practically capsizing the boat. "C'mon, Mom, reel it in!" he shrieked. I sort of knew what to do.

It happened so quickly. All at once my fingers got tied up in wads of fishing line, the fish was leaping and splashing all over the place, and the boys were yelling: "Set your hook, Mom!" "You're gonna lose him!" "Keep your rod tip up!" "Don't reel in so fast," then finally, "Give me the rod, Mom, you don't know *what the heck* you're doing."

"I don't know *what the heck* I'm doing, *huh?*" I yelled back.

They were right, you know. I didn't know what the heck I was doing. Fishing wasn't as simple as I had thought. To make a long story short, Tommy and Winty reluctantly listened to their father and allowed me to land the fish. It was a thirteen-inch rainbow trout, pretty impressive for our neck of the woods. After it was all over, I don't know who was more tuckered out: the fish from fighting, me from fighting the fish, the kids from fighting with me, me from fighting with the kids, or my husband trying to keep the peace through all the hoopla. Things eventually quieted down, and after we finished pumping out the water that had flooded into the boat during the excitement, my sons allowed how Mom had managed, somehow, to catch a pretty nice fish after all.

And so I am dedicating this book to my sons, Tommy and Winty, for convincing me—as far as fishing was concerned—that I really *didn't* know what the heck I was doing; and to my husband, Tom, who, along with all the wisdom he has imparted to me in the course of a quarter-century of marriage, advised me to listen to my sons. Without my precious family, I would not have gone fishing—and this book, therefore, would most definitely never have been written.

—LAURIE MORROW
Freedom, New Hampshire

Contents

Acknowledgments

—

I have had the very great, good fortune of being vastly overwhelmed, confused, coddled, and humored by a great many people who, through their generosity and love of fishing, taught me how they cast a line and catch fish. As a result I have developed a technique that works for me, and that's as much as you should hope for out of this book, or any other book for that matter. Fishing is a very personal sport, but you need guidance in order to get to the point where you're able to go out on the water and enjoy the sport all by yourself. To those people who helped lead me on my own personal journey into the sport, I am enormously grateful. They appear here in the pages of this book.

Several others, however, remained behind the scenes of *The Woman Angler* and I'd like to tell you who they are. There is my St. Martin's Press "team," the people that made Steve Smith's and my book, *Shooting Sports for Women* (the first book ever written on the shooting sports especially for women) such an important and critical success.

Bonnie Ainsworth, my dear friend and typist, once again endured another manuscript for me with a quiet devotion that I appear to take for granted, but never could. I wish to thank her for pulling together all the loose ends, as always.

My old grandfather used to say if you could count the number of true friends that you have gathered in the course of your life on the fingers of one hand, then you hold in that hand the riches of the world. My agent, Susan Zeckendorf, is the pointer finger of my right hand.

Steve Smith, my writing partner and mentor was unable to help me with this particular book because he is allergic to fish, but if the truth be known, he prefers bird hunting and gun dogs. However, without his guidance, I never would have become an outdoor writer.

And last, but never least, I want to thank my husband, Tom Morrow, for patiently and repeatedly reviewing my manuscripts, and patiently and repeatedly enduring our marriage, lo these 25 years.

Foreword

—

by Gwen Perkins, Director of Women's Outdoor Programs, The Orvis Company

I started working for the Orvis Company in 1980. I was hired part-time during Christmas to assist with customer service. I liked it so much that after the holidays I applied for a full-time position and was assigned to manage the women's clothing department in the Orvis flagship store in Manchester, Vermont.

During those early days at Orvis, I met a guy I thought was pretty neat. Three months passed before I realized that Dave Perkins was one of the sons of the company's owner, Leigh Perkins. When Dave mentioned this one day, he couldn't believe I didn't know—and I couldn't believe I had been so naive. Dave was mad about fly-fishing, and if I was planning on spending any time with him it would have to be hip-deep in a trout stream. That's when I decided it was time I learned about fly-fishing—and more about Dave. As it turned out, the Orvis Company enthusiastically encourages its employees to enroll in the Orvis Fly Fishing School, so not only did I have an opportunity to become a student at the best fly-fishing school in the country, but I'd be learning on one of the most famous trout rivers in the world—the Battenkill River.

The Orvis Fly Fishing School gave me a baseline level of knowledge from which to start. I instantly fell in love with the sport, and went fishing every minute I could spare from work. Dave and I had fly-fishing "dates" and soon we were spending weekends camping and canoeing with our take-down fly rods strapped to our backpacks. The more we fished, the better an angler I became—and the closer Dave and I became.

One day Dave invited me to join him and his family on a saltwater fly-fishing trip to Christmas Island in the South Pacific. Traveling halfway around the world for serious, hard-core fishing was both taxing and unbelievably rewarding. It was a thrill to be in this incredible place with the man I loved. And with his family. It was then I realized that I was being "put to the test" to see whether or not I would fit into the Perkins Family of Outdoor Enthusiasts. I guess I passed muster because then and there, on Christmas Island, Dave proposed to me. He had written a prenuptial agreement which I happily signed: We would fish together "till death do us part."

Upon our return to Vermont, I quit my job at Orvis. All my life I have loved and worked with horses, so I devoted myself to equestrian training for competition. I gave lessons to novice and advanced horsemen and horsewomen, and boarded and trained horses that were destined for the show-jumping circuit. It was hard, hard work: Besides, there were always stalls to be mucked out, fences to be mended and painted, tackle to be cleaned, horses to be brushed and watered and fed, fields to be mowed. I am a chronic "over-doer" and like a fool I insisted on doing it all. Ten years of marriage and two children later, terminal exhaustion set in.

Dave knew I was a good teacher and, by now, an expert angler. He suggested I teach at the Orvis Fly Fishing School. The idea fit me like a glove. Dave and I continued to travel all over the world to fish. One day we were fishing in Alaska when some nasty weather set in. We had been scheduled to fish in a variety of locations that were only accessible by small plane. The fog was so thick that our travel plans were put on hold. All was not lost, though, because we were staying at a lodge situated on the banks of a stream-fed lake full of fish. By early afternoon, the fog had lifted. Several other couples were staying at the lodge. The wives were all anglers. When the weather improved, the owner of the lodge asked if the ladies would like to take a "women only" helicopter excursion to a relatively remote place to fish for Atlantic char. Every one of us grabbed our fishing gear, gave our husband a quick kiss, and made a beeline for the helicopter.

That afternoon was one of the most memorable fishing experiences I ever had. We all cheered as each of us, in turn, played and landed one of those formidable fighting fish. After we finally quit for the day, we built a small campfire and sat around drinking coffee and reliving the highlights of the day. There was so much camaraderie that it was hard to believe we weren't lifelong friends. It was then that I realized that women can have a lot of fun fishing together, just as men do.

On the trip I fell in love with Alaska. I wanted to go back as soon as I could, so my sister-in-law, Molly, and I got in cahoots and planned a trip by ourselves. Without husbands. And without children. We went to Crystal Creek Lodge in Dillingham, where the fishing is beyond fantastic—in fact, it is just about the best fishing I have ever encountered *anywhere*. Molly and I had the trip of a lifetime. But the best thing was sharing this incredible experience with my sister-in-law. Our male guides, however, were a little skeptical. They had never taken two *women* anglers out before—oh, they had taken couples out, but never a couple of women and nary a man in sight! Anyway, by the end of the day I believe they were as delighted with us and our fishing as we were with them and their guiding!

My trips to Alaska really fueled my desire to show other women how much fun and rewarding fishing can be. I knew my own story was not unique, but women anglers back then were few and far between. So I talked to Dave and the family about teaching a series of "women only" Orvis fly-fishing clinics around the country—and they backed me one hundred percent.

The concept clicked with interested women as well. Classes booked solid the minute we advertised them. It was incredible how enthusiastic women were to learn to fish. Everywhere I went I saw the same thing, again and again: Not only were women "naturals" at fly-fishing—the movement you use in casting is very fluid and graceful—but they also discovered something in fly-fishing that gave them both pleasure *and* a shot of self-esteem. Interestingly enough, the greatest change I saw was in professional women, such as judges, lawyers, accountants, doctors, teachers, and others. The moment they put on a fishing vest and held a fly rod, it was as though a weight was taken off their shoulders—and *did they have fun!*

At first my students were a little intimidated by what I call T.T.L., or "technical tackle talk." There is so much to learn about fly-fishing that the sheer enormity of stuff you can get immersed in might even have given Einstein pause. When you bring fly-fishing or any type of fishing down to its basic terms, however—as Laurie Morrow does here in *The Woman Angler*—then it's not only easy to digest, but you also can add to your knowledge at your own pace, as you spend more time on the water.

Virtually overnight, the Orvis Women's Fly Fishing Program became a huge success, thanks in part to Lori-Ann Murphy, Christy Ball, and Nancy Zacon. Today Orvis has a team of women instructors who teach "women only" classes. A lot of women are more relaxed learning from other women. This is particularly true, I think, in fly-fishing, which is a whole-body sport that emphasizes the use of your arms, posture, and stance.

Early in 1996, it came to my attention that the techniques used in casting for fly-fishing could be advantageous as therapy for women who had suffered the fear and brutality of breast cancer. That's how Casting for Recovery Program began. It is a special school designed expressly for recovering breast cancer patients. Orvis has consulted with oncologists throughout the country. They concur that fly-fishing proves to have both physical and mental benefits for most women who had fallen victim to this ravaging disease.

The light, repetitive motion of the casting stroke gives strength and flexibility to the muscles surrounding the area of a woman's body that are compromised by surgery. The elevation of the arm for the backcast may benefit women suffering from lymphoma. A recovering cancer patient who is deemed fit by her doctor to enter this kind of therapy is taught to cast with the arm *on the same side* as her surgery to strengthen the muscles and build circulation in the healthy tissues. For example, if the woman's left side is the side of her total or partial mastectomy, then she will hold her rod with her left hand and learn to cast from that side. At first I thought this might be uncomfortable for right-handed students, but oddly enough—and I found this to be the case with women in our regular fly-fishing classes—many students actually feel more comfortable casting with their nondominant arm. I believe muscle memory can be too strong sometimes and difficult to unlearn. When I am teaching someone who is continually fighting the rod, I suggest she try the other arm.

Whether a student has attended the nonprofit Casting for Recovery School or the Orvis Women's Fly Fishing School, there's a benefit in common to *all* women that I can't stress enough. These are the *emotional* benefits you'll enjoy from fishing. Fishing is a release. It is learning something new that's fun at the same time. And it's spending your leisure time *for yourself,* even if you're with family, friends—or simply alone for a few quiet hours. Being on the water (or in the water), feeling the current against your legs and the sun shining on your back, listening to the birds singing in the trees—these things and more add up to a wonderful awareness of nature and our place in it. You can't help feeling alive and vibrant, and I've heard many students say the words, "I feel alive." More poignantly, I have heard students from the Casting for Recovery School say, "I am *still* alive, I am *still* here, and I am going to make the most of today and the rest of my life."

The Orvis Women's Fishing Programs have changed my life and I know they've changed the lives of our dedicated fishing instructors. Speaking for myself, however, I have to say I must be the happiest person on earth. After all, I met my husband fishing and we're raising our daughters to fish. I've met many extraordinary people fishing at home on the Battenkill and all over the world. And I love to teach fly-fishing. I just plain love to fish.

Just as the Orvis Women's Fly Fishing Schools teach women to fish,

The Woman Angler will introduce you to our sport. It's written for beginning women anglers by a woman who actually began her fishing education with us at Orvis. May this book lead you to bubbling trout streams, blue-green tropical waters, and entice you to explore for yourself the beauty and majesty of the out-of-doors and the great sport that nature provides for us all.

Go Fish

No matter how much you fish, or how good an angler you are, the fish always seem to be smarter than you. They're clever little rascals, wily when it comes to the ways of mere humans, and as much as we want to catch them, they don't particularly want to be caught. Since water is their home environment, we who fish are the underdog, put by nature at a disadvantage. After all, fishing is hunting on water. And just like hunting, we are predators seeking our prey. How we do it is what matters. And that's what this book is about.

Casting a fishing line into a bunch of water without hooking a tree, a shrub, a fishing partner, dog, or backside (usually your own) takes a considerable amount of skill. Getting a fish to take your lure requires knowledge, and that's perhaps the most exciting part about the sport. Just as a bird hunter must know about the migration of woodcock, and the waterfowler the ways of ducks and geese, so must the angler know the habits and idiosyncrasies of the fish she is fishing. There are numerous species of fish. Each has its own quirks, but more important, each listens to an internal clock that has been ticking since fish first took to water. There's a ton of fishing equipment available on the market that you'll have to sift through when it's time to purchase your own gear. You should only invest in your own stuff *after* you've been given a few pointers, preferably by a qualified fishing instructor, and have had enough time and experience on the water to decide which type of fishing you want to pursue. You'll discover soon enough how expensive fishing gear can be.

I can't help but think there are lots of women who have little idea what is involved in the sport of fishing—or how much fun it can be. I expect you are one such woman. If so, I invite you to join me. My travels took me to places I had never been and introduced me to people that enriched my life. Along the road I learned a lot about fishing, and I discovered a direct and uncomplicated way of getting into the sport. Most important, I discovered some new things about myself. Once you embark upon your own road, I expect you will, too.

There are a few things you should know about fishermen. First, the word *fishermen* is not really exclusive to men. The term has, at least since the establishment of the English language, referred to men *and* women who fish. Therefore, for the purposes of this book, I refer to women who fish as *anglers, women anglers, fishers* . . . and yes, *fishermen.*

Now that we have established a working vocabulary, be forewarned: *Beware of all fishermen.* Fishing, like all outdoor sports, is full of dedicated, enthusiastic fishermen who are absolutely confident that the particular rods, reels, hooks, line, live bait, artificial lures, spoons, spinners, floats, sinkers, dry flies, wet flies, any myriad of other foils they use to snag a fish are tried and true and the result of years of experimenting with every old and new ruse that is "just the thing" to land that fish. Having had the benefit of dozens of very fine anglers to advise me, each with an utterly different opinion from the other, I can tell you that there *is* no tried and true way, old or new, that's "just the thing" to hook a fish. Ask a dozen anglers to show you their casting technique. No two cast alike. Ask two fly fishers, "What's best for brook trout?" and one will prefer a Royal Coachman to an Olive Nymph, a fast No. 6 rod to a

No. 4 with a slower action, a fly reel with drag or without, a fly line that sinks, or a floating line. And you might as well put on a pot of coffee if you ask a seasoned bass fisherman if she prefers ultralight spinning to regular spinning rigs, or spincasting, or baitcasting, because the answer is going to take awhile.

Among the first discoveries you'll make when becoming a woman angler will be the vast selection of tackle and gear on the market today. For example, there is no such thing as *just* fishing line: there's multifilament line, monofilament line, tripolymer, copolymer, braided line, hollow line, floating line, sinking line, and others, in varying diameters, sizes, and weights (called "tests"), and in a wide variety of colors. If you are fly-fishing, you'll need a leader, tippet, and backing to tie to your fly line before you begin to think about selecting one of countless types of artificial flies you'll select to "match the hatch." If you're bait casting or spinning, there are virtually thousands of live and artificial lures to choose from. Don't forget the gadgets and gizmos, fishing apparel, waders, vests, gear, and all the paraphernalia you'll need before setting one foot in the water or on a boat. Take up fishing without knowing what you're getting into and you'll find your head spinning . . . instead of your reel . . . and your checking account as empty as your creel.

Although debates among people who fish can get heated, it is the very camaraderie of the sport that draws sportsmen and sportswomen together like a magnet in pleasurable, if somewhat lively, chat. In fact, a long-established ritual is getting together with fellow anglers at the end of a day's fishing, and shooting the breeze over a glass of cold beer—the official beverage of anglers the world over (as opposed to Scotch, which is the elixir of bird hunters). Men and women who fish are held together by a common bond, which is a great, deep-seated love of the sport and the out-of-doors. For centuries this camaraderie has been referred to as the "Brotherhood of the Angle." In recent years, this sacred fraternity has graciously, albeit gingerly, opened its waters to the "Sisterhood of the Angle."

Now you're about to set out on your own journey. Along the way, speak to others who fish. Listen to what they have to say. Outdoorsmen and -women who fish are a special group. One might not loan you her lucky dry fly, or tell you the location of her secret trout pool, but I'll wager that no man or woman who ardently fishes is unwilling to share some knowledge based on time-honed experience. And if your husband or lover tries to give you advice—whether you want it or not—listen to him. Chances are he'll become your best fishing buddy. Your wisest bet, however, is to first find a qualified fishing instructor who can teach you the preliminaries. For most women, learning to use our bod-

Take classes from a qualified fishing instructor.

ies in a manner unlike any we're accustomed to requires a lot of concentration, patience, and practice. And you can really push the limits of patience if your man attempts to be your teacher. In my case, when my husband tried to teach me to fly fish, my greatest single achievement by the end of the day was *not* strangling him with fishing line. Therefore, the best course is to *take classes from a good instructor.* She'll answer your basic questions, show you the proper techniques, and point you in the right direction. She'll also help outfit you with the correct tackle you'll need. Consider what kind of commitment you want to make to the sport and how much time you are able to devote to it. Ultimately, it's up to you to get a sense of what sportfishing can offer you.

Fishing takes us out of doors. We get addicted to nature. Tossing a line into some water isn't what makes fishing a passion for so many of us. It's more. It's the delicious way the sun warms your skin as you stand knee-deep in a bubbling trout stream. It's the way an east wind chides you and tells the fish to never, never take your lure. And it's how you find yourself in the very scheme of things, a part of a time-worn equation. Whether you're a newcomer to the sport or a seasoned woman angler, a splendid water world beckons those of us who choose to cast a line.

The books that have been written about fishing over the last five hundred years have helped sportsmen and sportswomen gain the knowledge and wherewithal to enter into the sport with confidence.

They tell of the many species of game fish that populate our rivers, streams, ponds, lakes, and oceans. The more you learn about the game fish you're after, its habitat, and its life cycle, the better chance you have of landing your quarry. The bottom line is this: you'll decrease the odds that you'll be a nonproductive angler as you increase your knowledge and experience of the sport. The more you learn, the more you know, the less likely you are to become disenchanted with the sport. And fishing, more than almost any other outdoor sport, including hunting, is purely a sport of chance. Certainly there are "clues" that an experienced angler knows to look for: the color, temperature, and current of the water (called "reading the water"), the time of day, the type of sky, and the direction of the wind—and much more, but even the most expert of anglers cannot guess where or when a fish will strike. These we'll discuss as we go along. This book is designed to help you get into fishing with a minimum of confusion and a maximum of pleasure.

There are many types of fishing, and we'll take a look at some of the more popular ones. But as a woman and a beginning angler, I find there are two types that suit me best: fly-fishing and ultralight spinning. Most women I've fished with feel the same way. The grace that fly casting demands and the ease of ultralight spinning complement the anatomy of most women. Although deep-sea fishing and the huge, heavy rods and reels that large game fish demand are a supreme test of strength on the high seas, bringing in a fighting trout or a contentious salmon can be an equally formidable task. For many women—and increasingly more men—the skill in handling a light rod, line, and small lure doubles the challenge of the sport and heightens the contest—and still has all the right stuff to land a good-sized game fish in the most sporting way possible. The fisher has a responsibility to pursue her quarry fairly and, once hooked, as quickly and humanely as possible.

Fishing is an approachable sport. Ease into it, learn it gradually. What you envision as a country outing in spring to get to a trout stream might become a private war against black flies, as you spray yourself from head to toe with pungent bug repellent and find yourself itching all the way home. Getting used to wearing a cumbersome fishing vest loaded with "essentials" you may or may not need but have, just in case, takes some practice. And, when day is done and your creel is empty, you become philosophical, which is easier than admitting the fish have you beat. But not always.

Fishing offers enormous variety and choices to the outdoorswoman. There are many different types of fishing you can do, countless places you can go to fish, a plethora of equipment you can choose from, and limitless personal pleasure you can garner from engaging in the sport. Once you get into it, you'll discover it's addictive. Be patient. Sometimes fishing can be so overwhelming that a woman new to the sport may find it simply too much to take in at once—and it is. She may become discouraged before giving the sport half a chance. To avoid discouragement, here are a few *do's* and *don't's* to observe:

- **Do not** walk into any fishing tackle shop or consult a fishing tackle catalog cold turkey unless you are in the company of a knowledgeable angler. The vast selection of gear will send you, literally, reeling.

- **Do not** fish with your husband or significant other the first time out on the water if you wish to stay married or significantly involved by the end of the day. (There are a few . . . very few . . . documented exceptions.)

- **Do** hire a qualified fishing instructor to show you the ropes—or in our case, the lines . . . reel, rod, etc.

- **Do not** buy any gear until you have consulted with your fishing instructor. Good gear can be expensive. Your instructor can tell you specifically what you need.

- **Do not** let some exotic place lure you into fishing there for the first time. Let the sport speak for itself—not through the deceptive haze of a Mai Tai swilled on some tropical island. Try fishing in your own backyard (if you happen to have a river running through it) or somewhere relatively nearby first. You'll probably be fishing within a hundred miles of home 90 percent of the time.

- **Do not** give up if you haven't caught a fish the first, second, or even third time out. You'll soon discover for yourself that the thrill of the sport is in the chase—not the catch.

We'll touch on these things and more in the following chapters. Ready? Good. Let's go fish.

C h a p t e r   2

—

An Introduction to Fishing

Fish is a four-letter word. Even Isaak Walton couldn't say enough about it in his bible of fishing books, *The Compleat Angler.* There are approximately 22,000 known species of fish populating the waters of the world. Some live in freshwater. Some live in salt water. Some live in freshwater *and* in salt water. Some are big, and some are small. Some are sport fish and some are not. Sport fish are clever; some are fast, and most are fighters. Since we confront fish in their native surroundings, not ours, they prove formidable opponents.

Methods of Fishing

There are several methods of fishing. The most popular use rods and reels with live bait or artificial bait (called a *lure*). The bait is attached to a hook that is tied to the end of a fishing line. The methods of fishing are *casting, still fishing, drift fishing, trolling,* and *ice fishing.* In *casting,* the angler pitches, or casts, a lure delicately into the water and carefully reels in, or *retrieves,* the line, in an attempt to tease or entice the fish to bite. She repeats the cast over and over again until a fish takes the hook, called a *strike,* and then brings in the fish by "playing" it while retrieving, or *reeling,* in line onto a fly reel. Fly-fishing is a form of casting.

Still fishing uses a spinning rod to throw out a line that has live bait or an artificial lure on the hook. The angler sits in an anchored boat or along the shore and waits for a fish that's attracted to the bait to strike, then reels in the fish with a spinning reel.

Drift fishing is when a boat is allowed to drift freely with the current. The lure is dragged behind the boat as it floats downstream. Any kind of rod and reel can be used in drift fishing, but you might need devices like a spinner to keep certain kinds of fishing line from twisting, depending upon the current and the speed of the boat.

Trolling is a form of fishing in which the bait is trailed from a rod that's held or attached to the stern or starboard side of a moving boat. You can troll in any water, but trolling is most common in deep-sea fishing. Heavy rods and reels are used for deep-sea fishing, since the fish can be enormous.

Ice fishing takes place in the cold climates during winter, through a hole cut in the ice. Equipment used for ice fishing is distinctly different from anything else you'd use during spring, summer, and fall.

Before we discuss some of the methods of fishing we'll be doing, let's first take a look at our quarry. The type of fish you choose to catch will determine the method of fishing you need to learn and the type of gear you'll need to buy. There are two basic types of fishing: saltwater fishing and freshwater fishing. Saltwater fishing takes place in salt water—oceans, seas, coastal waters. Freshwater fishing takes place on freshwater—rivers, streams, lakes, estuaries, and ponds.

Saltwater Fishing

There are four types of saltwater fishing: shore fishing, beach fishing, boat fishing, and big-game fishing.

Shore Fishing

Shore fishing is done from rocks, piers, wharfs, and jetties. Depending on where you're fishing, you'll be after saltwater species that include snapper, cod, pollack, hake, perch, catfish, mullet, mackerel, and many other varieties. Shore fishing is for fairly advanced fishermen. It's not the place for the beginning angler to start, but you should know what it's about. A shore fisherman has to know how to maneuver her rod and steer her lure away from obstacles. Because of where she is fishing, in possibly rough waters and offshore breezes or wind, she's in constant danger of snagging her line. She must know how to unsnag her line without cutting bait. Because she is standing high up from the water, she must lift her fish to heights not like any other kind of fishing. In addition to restricted movement due to all that's around her, the angler is not likely to be back casting any great distance. The fish are apt to be big, so given the fish and the conditions, a strong saltwater rig that is geared to relatively short distances is what most shore fishermen suggest. This includes large hooks (1 to 8/0), strong line (20- to 40-test monofilament), a heavy saltwater rod (11-foot baitcaster), a reel that can do the job (a baitcaster with two retrieve speeds), and live bait (crab, squid, and worms are most popular.)

Beach Fishing

This is the kind of fishing you see in travel brochure photographs— wide, sandy, long-sloping tropical beaches, bright sunshine, big fish. This is a great way to start fishing, although it is a little exotic and not where most women have the luxury of beginning. Beach fishing involves distance casting. You want to get a lot of line out and you want your lure to go a specific place, usually on the fringe of a reef or underwater obstruction. These spots are known as "fish-holding waters" because—you guessed it—these waters hold fish. You're fishing for the relatively shallow-swimming saltwater fish, such as bonefish, groupers, sea bass, walleye, and tarpon, and the beginning woman angler should use large-capacity spinning tackle rigged with 12- to 18-pound mono-filament line. Fly-fishing tackle is also used for beach fishing, and you'll use a rod that's heavy (no less than #9) and long (no less than 10 feet). Anything less is possible only if you're an expert. The rule of thumb is: the larger the fish, the heavier the rod; the larger the reel, the bigger the lure and hook size, and the heavier the line. Seasoned anglers often break these rules and manage to bring in huge fish with very light tackle. But for our purposes, the gear should match the fish.

Not all beach fishing is idyllic. I remember the first time I tagged along while my Uncle Gerry went fishing on Jones Beach on Long Island when I was a child. He was fishing for blowfish, which are not particularly big, but the surf was treacherous, and the wind was gusty. Unc used heavy spinning tackle. He had to. Light tackle would have been virtually impossible to cast into those waves and high wind, and he seldom waded out past his knees on account of the undertow. On the other hand, if you're bonefishing on Christmas Island or in the Bahamas, the water is sapphire blue tinged with emerald green, the breeze is soft, and the beaches slope gently out to the crystal-clear horizon. Here—where nature is generally far more cooperative—fishing is delightful, and you can get away with lighter spinning tackle, providing it's appropriate for the size and type of fish you're fishing.

Boat Fishing

There are two types of boat fishing. One is *inshore fishing,* which is done from flats boats or bass boats in relatively shallow coastal waters or inland lakes. The other is *deep-water fishing,* which includes wreck fishing and is done farther out at sea, although not as far as you're apt to go for big-game fishing.

Again you'll be using spinning gear, a relatively short rod, and heavy monofilament line. For the woman angler who is interested in saltwater fishing, this is a terrific way to start. Unless you hook the boat, your guide, the others in the boat, or yourself, you're pretty much free from obstacles. The spinning tackle is a delight to cast, and you'll get the hang of it quickly. Once you learn the basic knots, you can tie on your own artificial lures.

Big-Game Fishing

Big-game fishing is not the place for the woman angler to begin—unless she has a husband or friend who has a lot of experience . . . and his own boat. It is one of the most exciting sports you can hope to get into, but it is also expensive. The gear is among the biggest, heaviest, and most costly. The boat, needless to say, has to be an oceanworthy vessel. The fish you're after are the biggest in the ocean: swordfish, marlin, sailfish, and barracuda. It takes strength more than skill to land these fish, and you need to be in the company of an Old Salt who really knows how to play them.

Freshwater Fishing

There are four types of freshwater fishing: lure fishing, bait fishing, pole fishing, and fly-fishing.

Just a few of the hundreds—if not thousands—of lures you can choose from. Baitcasting, spincasting, and spinning lures are meant to mimic bait fish such as minnows and other small fish and creatures.

(PHOTO BY DON HOFFMAN)

Lure Fishing

Lure fishing involves casting artificial lures into freshwater, and this is what you'll be doing most of the time that you're fishing with spinning tackle. Baitcasting and spincasting tackle also falls within this category; theoretically, so does fly-fishing, but that is in a class all its own. The fact is, spinning and ultralight spinning are what the beginning woman angler is likely to feel most comfortable with and can handle with ease and pleasure. On the other hand, fly-fishing is, in time, apt to be a lifelong passion. You'll be fishing for perch, pike, pickerel, and probably for bass, trout, and salmon. The latter three are the fish that I focus on in *The Woman Angler* because these are the most popular of the freshwater species and the most widely available in American waters.

Bait Fishing

This type of fishing uses natural or processed bait, live and otherwise, instead of artificial lures. The difference is purely in the bait. The fact is, at certain times of the year fish simply have little or no interest in feeding. Your choice of live bait over artificial lures is a last-ditch effort to entice some of these fish to take your hook. In the hot summer months, when fish are generally well fed and lethargic in warm water temperatures, you've got to dangle something mighty appetizing right in front of them. Although some people have been known to put live or processed bait on fly tackle, this is pretty much frowned upon and defeats the whole philosophy behind fly-fishing.

Pole Fishing

Pole fishing is fishing in its purest, earliest form. It was how people caught fish before the reel was invented. It's how young children still catch fish. Fishing poles manufactured today are not the kind of pole or stick Huck Finn or Tom Sawyer used, however; they are telescopic carbon-fiber poles that can extend up to 56 feet but are extremely light and strong. Most fishing poles are 16 to 23 feet long. There is no reel. Pole fishers use live bait and floats to keep the bait from sinking to the bottom of the water. This is not a popular type of fishing—but for centuries, it was all there was.

Fly-Fishing

Fly-fishing is where I began when I first took up the sport, and is the type of fishing that most women anglers seem to settle into. Fly-fishing is a tremendous sport. In the early hours of morning or shortly before dusk, when my soul's weary and a little worse for wear, I find myself picking up my fly rod and heading down to a little river not far from my home. It's soothing and tranquil to cast a fly line; it revives. Even now, after miles of water, and reams of paper writing this book, what do I do? I fish. I find my solace in fishing.

Fish

Like every living thing on the planet, fish are born into families. A branch within a family is called a *genus*. The families that make up the branches of the larger family are called *species*. Members of a family will have basic similarities, but even within a genus, one species can look and behave quite differently from another. Species are fish of a feather, so to speak—that is, of the same kind—and can breed only among themselves. Although there are other *genera*, or several genus, within a family, one genus cannot interbreed with another. An Arctic char cannot breed with a lake trout, even though they are members of the same genus. An Atlantic salmon cannot breed with a sockeye. This is nature's way of segregating the international community of fish. This may sound confusing, but hang in there. There are several reasons why it is important that you have a general understanding of fish before you go out and buy a rod.

Let's take, for example, the *Salmonidae* family (salmonids), whose three branches include some of the most popular types of sport fish: salmon (*Salmo*), trout (*Oncorhynchus*), and char (*Salvelinus*). All members of the *Salmonidae* family are spawned, or born, in freshwater, where they grow to maturity. As adults, they will live part of their lives in freshwater and part in salt water and migrate between the two. Their journey can take them upwards of 2,000 miles, always along the same route, as they commute between their saltwater home and their freshwater birthplace, where they invariably return—often to the very pool in which they were spawned. Other salmonids, however, such as landlocked salmon and lake trout, live their entire lives in freshwater ponds, streams, or lakes.

Salmonids come in different colors, too—brown, golden, silver, red, pink. As a fish matures, it changes color, and apart from its length, its color is one way you can tell its age. Those that enter rivers from the sea change color as well, going from rich hues to a dull, silvery sheen the longer they stay upriver. Some salmonids don't grow large, while others achieve enormous size. For example, five pounds is the usual maximum weight of a cutthroat trout, but its sibling, the North American rainbow trout, has been known to max out at 50 pounds. Their cousin, the kokanee salmon, will seldom exceed five pounds, but its sibling, the chinook, is the family heavyweight at 120 pounds. Obviously, you will not use the same size rod, hook, line weight, and lure to take a cutthroat as you would a chinook. You can use a lightweight rod and line for cutthroat, but you'll obviously need a much heavier one to land a chinook, or "king salmon." Knowing about your game fish tells you what equipment you'll need.

It is equally important that you learn about the lifestyle and habits of your quarry. After all, fish are game, and a good hunter knows where her quarry is likely to be at a particular time of the season, during every moment of the day. For example, Atlantic salmon are especially hungry in May but are not inclined to feed in August. In May you can be assured of hooking a fish on an Atlantic salmon river; you can tie almost any dry fly on your line and, likely as not, a fish will bite. In fact, you can toss your line into almost any part of the river, any time of the day. But you have to be either an accomplished fisher or extremely lucky to hook one in August. Presentation, or how you present—or place—your dry fly to a fish, is crucial. What dry fly will you use? What weight rod? You have to determine these things from the clues around you: the time of day, the temperature of the water, pools in which a fish is likely to lie, the direction of the wind. Fish have reasons for being where they are, feeding when they do, and spawning when it's time. The more you know about their behavior and life cycle, the better chance you will have of being a successful woman angler.

━━━

Spinning vs. Fly-Fishing

Both are for you, but which is for what?

Spinning and ultralight spinning tackle are altogether different from the rig you'll use for fly-fishing. So are the lures and the technique. In many cases, you'll be fishing for the same type of fish. That's right: Just about any kind of fish can be caught with spinning tackle or a fly rod and reel. It's where the fish *are*—where they're lying and feeding— that determines which rig will work best for you. In some cases, such as fishing on the famous Atlantic salmon rivers, the St. Mary's and the Miramichi in the northeast Canadian provinces, the law permits taking a salmon on a fly with fly tackle only. On the other hand, fishing in big bass lakes, particularly in the South, is almost always done with spin tackle. Before we take a good look at each type of fishing and the gear you'll use, let's look at the basic differences and similarities between spinning and fly-fishing.

Fly-fishing uses a fly rod, a fly reel, a fly line, and a fly. The variations, apart from the quality of the materials and the make of your fly equipment, are in the weight of the rod and fly line, length of the rod, the rod grip, the size and drag device of the reel, and the size and kind of flies you'll use.

That's not the case with spin fishing. There are three variations. The difference is actually in the construction and operation of the reel. The rod, line, and lures are the same with all types of spinning tackle: spincasting reels, baitcasting reels, and spinning reels. (Ultralight spinning tends to be the exception in that the very light rod designed for an ultralight reel is generally too light for any of the other types of spinning reels.) These photos show the basic differences, and when you visit your local fishing tackle shop, you'll see for yourself just how the types and makes of spinning reels differ.

Although you may eventually gravitate toward spincasting or baitcasting rigs, I do not recommend either for the entry-level woman angler. Spincasting is elementary, and although it is an excellent way to introduce a child to this type of fishing, my feeling is that a woman an-

Spincasting is excellent for teaching children—but the beginning woman angler may find the challenge of spinning tackle more satisfying.

(PHOTO BY DON HOFFMAN)

You may eventually get into baitcasting, but don't plan on starting out with this kind of reel. It requires an expert's hand—and it can be a bit too much to handle when you're just learning to fish.

(PHOTO BY DON HOFFMAN)

gler likes—and needs—a bit more challenge. Spinning tackle gives you the edge you'll appreciate. On the other hand, baitcasting is for the advanced fisher. Experienced baitcasters and instructors agree that baitcasting can be taught to a receptive student in a half hour—but it takes a whole lot longer to get the hang of the reel. You need to learn how to control your line with your thumb and regulate the baitcasting reel with split-second timing. It's far more important at the beginning stages to focus on how to properly play and land a fish than to find yourself all wrapped up in the equipment, and possibly frustrated by it as a result. It's spinning, then (and ultralight spinning tackle), that's for us—at least in this book.

Once you learn how to use spinning tackle and fly-fishing tackle, and to identify the conditions that warrant one over the other, you will broaden your fishing horizons. In fact, with the exception of big-game saltwater fishing and ice fishing, a spinning rig and fly-fishing gear will take you just about any place you want to go.

Spinning tackle is one of the best ways to go for the woman angler.
(PHOTO BY DON HOFFMAN)

Spinning Tackle

A spinning rig consists of a *spinning rod,* which holds a *spinning reel* onto which *monofilament line* is wound. Monofilament is fine and light, and good mono line has high tensile strength, which simply means it's strong and tough enough to support a fish up to a specific weight designated by the weight (or "test") of the line. Unlike floating and sinking fly lines, which are polymer coated and significantly thicker, monofilament line is not coated—in fact, the construction of monofilament line is similar to a hollow braid. Although the weight of a fly line helps you cast a practically weightless artificial fly any kind of distance, with spinning tackle it's the weight of the lure—around ¼ ounce, more or less, depending upon the type—and the mechanism of the spinning reel that enable you to cast and propel your lure out into the water. With both types of fishing, the line speed you generate from your casting technique, along with your wrist control and that little *snap* you give your wrist just before you release the line with your forefinger, enables you to launch your lure just about anywhere you want it to go.

Spinning gear is designed to launch a *weighted* artificial lure or live bait that's tied to a practically *weightless* line. It is ideal under the following circumstances:

When you want to fish deep lakes or distance-cast in salt water
where conditions are best suited to allow the lure to do most of the
work. The fish may be feeding on the surface, in which case you can
string a bobber on your line and choose a good top fishing lure. If the
fish are more likely to be at the bottom, you can rig your line with a
sinker, or use a weighted lure (see page 139, lures for spinning tackle),
that will take your bait below the surface. Many artificial lures incorporate flashy metallic tinsels that reflect light underwater and attract the
fish's attention. Many artificial lures used for spinning are designed to
mimic the appearance and motion of a bait fish. A sinking crankbait, for
example, is carved from balsa wood to look like a minnow. This type of
crankbait has a long, extended "lip" at the nose that is designed for
"deep diving": it draws water as it sinks and propels the lure downward
to a desired depth that's determined by the amount of fishing line released from the bail (a sort of storage unit around which line is wound
and from which it is released on the cast). When the angler reels in,
jerks her rod tip, and manipulates the line as she retrieves the lure, she's
attempting to give the lure some natural underwater movement that
may (or may not) attract the fish. It's *movement* that, more often than
not, will excite fish into taking your bait. If there's no movement, or the
movement isn't natural, or imitates an injured or sick bait fish, the fish
probably will ignore it.

Many anglers favor fishing with live bait, which does its own work
by swimming naturally through the water. Bass, walleye, sea trout, redfish, pickerel, perch, and pike are just some of the fish that you'll have
success catching with live bait. If you haven't mastered your fishing
technique on artificial lures, you'll find you'll work less and have equal
if not sometimes greater success with live bait. After all, it's the real
thing—not an imitation, which is precisely what artificial lures are.
Some of the best live bait to use are small fish such as common minnows (creek chub, golden shiners, fathead minnows, bluntnose and
mud minnows), carp, gizzard shad, white suckers, alewifes, croakers,
dace, and madtom. Handling small fish as bait amounts to impaling
them on a hook. Grasshoppers, crickets, and other assorted slimy creatures such as leeches, worms, frogs, and crayfish are also popular
choices. What you use, however, really depends upon the appetite and
gourmet tendencies of the fish you're fishing. For example, bullhead,
which is found in most lakes, rivers, and streams throughout the country, is a bottom feeder that tends to prefer grasshoppers, worms, and
crayfish while walleyes and pickerel relish minnows.

Wherever you fish, always ask the locals what type of bait to use
and whether to fish live bait or artificial. Go to a tackle shop near your

fishing destination and get the recommendation of someone there who's well acquainted with the local fishing. Chances are, he or she can tell you precisely what the fish are apt to take *that day*. That's how you can tell you're talking to an Old Salt or, at the very least, someone who is a seasoned angler. If you're fishing with a guide, he or she will provide lures and, in most cases, your rig as well.

When you are wading or standing in an open, rather than a wooded, place. The most effective cast in spinning is the simple back cast. Unlike fly-fishing, you bring your rod back once. The distance you achieve with your cast largely depends upon your arm and wrist action to propel the lure forward. You need to make sure nothing is behind you to get in the way of your back cast. Trees, heavy brush, and other natural and man-made obstacles will prevent you from bringing your rod back for a clean back cast. Although you can side cast with spinning tackle, you will not achieve the same kind of range and distance that you will with a good, solid back cast. Even though your rod may be a relatively short one, say five feet, remember that your line and lure are behind you before propelling into your forward cast. You'll need at least eight clear feet behind you to achieve this. If you're fishing in a stream or river, those eight feet of clearance may mean you have to walk toward the middle of the river, and that can land you in waist-high water, or deeper. Of course, you can cast upstream in situations like these, providing you're not near anyone. However, streams, rivers, and brooks tend to be shallow, so this kind of fishing is better suited to fly-fishing tackle—which we'll discuss a little further on.

When you're boat fishing in relatively deep waters and don't need to distance cast. You may want to cast your lure relatively close to the boat—say, within 20 yards—and let it gradually sink and rest where it can reach fish that are lying or feeding around the bottom of the water. At certain times of the day and times of the year, fish will stay in the shallows and feed on top of the water. Other times they'll swim out to deeper waters in the middle of the lake and "lie low." On cool early mornings and late afternoons you'll generally find lake fish in the shallows, but at noontime, when the shoreline waters have warmed up, fish will seek the cooler depths.

When you want to use live bait instead of artificial lures. In the summer, a tasty morsel may be just what it takes to hook an already well-fed fish or entice a lethargic one from a kind of stupor that sets in when the water temperature gets too warm.

If you're casting for distance out to a reef or underwater obstruction, where fish may be feeding on top of the water. You'll probably need to cast 30 or 40 feet, which is not as difficult as it sounds as you become proficient with your tackle and technique. Whether you're wading or boat fishing, you cannot come too close to the fish—they'll simply scatter and swim off when they hear or see something approaching them. In deeper, darker water, a shimmering "bass assassin" or silvery streamer lure that's tugged along by the angler with little jerks comes very close to mimicking a real fish. And if the fish are moving or actively feeding, time is an important consideration in presenting your lure. If the fish are moving along a reef, it's up to you to get that lure out there effectively, naturally, and as quickly and quietly as possible.

Fly-Fishing

Fly-fishing is ideal for stream, brook, and river fishing, and it is becoming increasingly popular for saltwater game fishing as well. For many anglers it's the only way to go—and more and more women seem to choose fly-fishing over any other type of fishing when they first get into the sport. Watching a crackerjack woman fly fisher is comparable to watching ballet—she is graceful and skillful, and able to "present," or land, a fly on a dime. Fly-fishing is, in fact, the most precise and exacting form of fishing. Over and over again you will hear the word *presentation* from fly fishers. I learned the meaning of presentation from my favorite fishing guide, Jerry Stewart, who guides for André Godin at the Miramichi Inn on the Little Sou'west Miramichi in New Brunswick, Canada. "Getting a salmon to take your fly," he'd say, "especially a bright salmon, depends almost entirely on presentation. You should be able to present your fly right on the tip of the nose of a salmon at forty feet."

You'll hear fly fishers referred to as elitists or purists, as though they are snobs. This certainly is true of any number of anglers, and that's nothing to be ashamed of. Sure, there's some method to the madness of a fly fisher. If madness is obsession, then most certainly fly-fishing is an obsession. There also are commonsense factors that make fly-fishing so desirable in many specific circumstances.

For example, freshwater that flows is generally shallow. Streams, ponds, and rivers are ideal fly-fishing waters. If the fish are feeding or resting on the bottom, your artificial wet fly still needn't go terribly deep to reach them. Ten feet is usually the deepest part of most streams; some are as shallow as four or five feet, especially in late summer, when the water is usually quiet and low. If I'm fly-fishing and fish do not appear to be rising to the top water, I assume they're lying low in bottom waters of a stream, or in underwater nooks and crannies along the stream's twists and turns. In instances where you'll want your lure to sink, you'll use a wet fly on a sinking fly line and pinch some nontoxic lead a couple of inches above your knot to help carry it under the ripples. The lead, line, and wet fly will gently sink underwater, carrying the fly to the river bottom, where it will be carried along by the current. For this reason, you'll cast upstream, ahead of the current, and let the natural action of the water generate some lifelike movement in your artificial fly. If the current is calm, give your line a series of short tugs as you reel in or gather your line, or little jerks or similar movements with your rod tip will also put some life in your fly.

Again, it's motion that's going to help attract a fish's attention. Just as a sinker attached to fishing line in spinning tackle adds weight to an artificial lure and carries it down toward the bottom of the lake, a wet fly aided by some nontoxic lead will carry an artificial fly to bottom waters in fly-fishing. Lures used for spinning are designed to look like small fish and crustaceans, which are appetizing to fish. Artificial flies imitate natural flies . . . and other small critters as well, which we'll discuss a little later. Spinning lures and live bait can be just too cumbersome to cast quickly and repeatedly when you're delicately trying to fish on top water just as, say, a big rainbow trout is rising for a hatch.

Some say it takes a thousand casts to catch a single fish. If this is true, a light rod and a relatively weightless lure will be a pleasure to cast, whereas a heavier rod with a weighted lure may become cumbersome. For this reason, ultralight spinning tackle is the solution; but when it comes to small rivers, streams, and brooks, you'll discover that a fly rod and reel is the best way to go.

Chapter 4

—

Words You Should Know

As with any sport, fishing has its own language. There are words, terms, and phrases that are used to describe the things you'll be doing, the gear you'll be using, and the fish you'll be catching. You should try to understand the vocabulary right off the bat. For this reason, a glossary of common fishing terms is located here instead of at the end of the book, where a glossary traditionally belongs. Read through the list. You needn't commit the definitions to memory. But do yourself a favor and get a sense of what these terms mean. You'll see them over and over again throughout the book. As you get more involved in your sport and spend more time on the water, you'll grasp your newfound vocabulary as effortlessly as you will the grip of your rod.

The Language of Fishing

angling. The taking of fish by rod in hand to which is attached an artificial fly or an artificial bait, or hooks for the attachment of live bait.

back cast. The backward motion of whipping the weighted fly line behind the angler, which creates "line speed." That, coupled with the smooth transition into the forward cast, or forward whipping of the line in front of the angler, pulls line length from the reel and propels the fly forward over the water, sometimes at distances of 30 yards or more from the angler, depending upon her ability and where she wants to position the fly she's casting (this is called "presentation"). Only with a fly-fishing outfit (rod, reel, line, fly) is it possible to do two or more successive back casts. The back cast pulls line from the reel. Speed and control of the line are crucial to all successful casts, no matter how long the cast may be.

blind casting. To continue your forward and back cast one or more times in order to build up line speed.

fly-fishing. Casting upon water and retrieving no more than three unbaited artificial flies individually attached to a line to which no extra weight has been added. Note: It is illegal to troll in waters restricted to fly-fishing only. Fly-fishing waters are restricted to casting from the banks, in the water, or in a boat that is anchored.

trolling. A type of fishing done by trailing a line rigged to catch fish through or over the water behind the boat.

wildlife. All species of mammals, birds, fish, mollusks, crustaceans, amphibians, reptiles, or their progeny or eggs which, whether raised in captivity or not, are normally found in a wild state.

Lures

artificial lure. Any fishing lure that imitates a natural bait or fish forage. Artificial flies, spinners, spoons, poppers, plugs, and jigs are types of artificial lures.

barb. The primary feather in the hackle of an artificial fly.

bass-bug. An artificial lure made of plastic, balsa wood, or cork that is designed to attract largemouth bass. Bass-bugs are used in fly-fishing and spincasting to imitate bait fish and frogs. In fly-fishing, a bass-bug is heavier than a dry fly and is usually tied to a weighted line called a **bass-bug taper.** In spincasting, the weight of the bass-bug can be buoyed by a bobber for shallow casts and weighted with a sinker for fishing in deeper water.

fly. A single, pointed hook dressed with feathers, hair, thread, tinsel, or any similar material to which no additional weights, hook, spinner, spoon, or similar device is added.

salmon eggs. The eggs of both Atlantic sea-run salmon and landlocked salmon, used as bait in fishing.

Legal Language

Know these terms before you fish.

bag and creel limit. The number and weight of any kind of fish permitted to be taken at a specified time.

closed season. It is unlawful to take certain species of fish during certain times of the year.

closed waters. Waters that are unlawful to fish at any time, waters that are closed by the state to fishing.

commercial fisherman. Any person who takes, possesses, lands, or transports on the waters of a state any marine species by any method for the purpose of sale.

fish hatcheries. Places where fish are artificially induced to spawn and grow in controlled captivity, until they are large enough to be introduced into waters that support the particular species. All waters within 200 feet of any fish hatchery or rearing station are closed to fishing at all times, unless provided by special rule.

illegal fishing. It is unlawful to fish other than by the use of a single baited hook and line, artificial flies, artificial lures, and spinners. Tandem flies, or fishing with more than one fly on a line, are allowed when trolling waters that are not restricted to fly-fishing only.

night fishing. You can fish in all waters open to fishing at night during open water season unless otherwise posted.

number, amount, weight, or **size limits.** It is unlawful to fish for or possess fish in violation of the number, amount, weight, or size limits as specified by state fish and game regulations.

open season. The time during which it is lawful to fish for or possess any fish, as specified or limited by law or rule.

possession limit. The number of fish a person is limited to take lawfully in any one day.

red tide. The accumulation of toxic dinoflagellates (one-celled planktonic animals) in the ocean. The toxins can be stored in the bodies of clams, mussels, and oysters. Humans who eat contaminated shellfish may become afflicted with paralytic shellfish poisoning (PSP), which can cause death through respiratory paralysis. Shellfish may only be taken from open areas. Areas that are closed due to red tide must be avoided by law. Your state fish and game department posts approved shellfish areas in its saltwater digests.

tag or label fish. A legal requirement to label the fish you take with the name and address of the person who caught them if you are at a sporting camp, hotel, or public lodging. Atlantic salmon must be tagged with special tags that are provided with your fishing license.

two-line restriction. A regulation that makes it unlawful to fish with more than two lines at any one time during the open water season.

total length. The greatest possible length of the fish with mouth closed and caudal (tail) fin rays squeezed together. For all fish that have a total length limit, the head and tail must remain intact while on or leaving the waters of the state for purposes of accurate measurement.

Fish

Atlantic salmon (*Salmo salar*). Known as the "king of freshwater game fish," these are famous for their fighting spirit and ability to leap many feet out of the water as adults, when they return from the sea to their native river and swim upstream to spawn. Atlantic salmon must be caught with flies (not even floatant is permitted on the fly). Separate regulations and limits govern Atlantic and all sea-run salmon fishing in the United States and Canada.

bass. Smallmouth and largemouth bass are the most popular game fish in America's freshwaters. Saltwater species include striped bass. These fighting fish can get quite large and are delicious eating.

big-game fish. Marlin, sailfish, tarpon, tuna, shark, and other large sport fish caught with big-game rods, big-game reels, and 20-

pound-test lines. These fish often can weigh between 100 and 1,000 pounds.

black salmon (or **kelts**). Adult salmon that have spent a sedentary winter upstream. They will not have eaten for many months, and consequently are emaciated and famished. They yield to the strong and rapid currents that result from full rivers engorged by spring runoff, and make their way to the bountiful feeding grounds in the sea. When they return after several months of hearty feeding, usually in summer and early fall, they are known as **bright salmon,** so-called for their shimmering color (see Chapter 8).

bluefish (tailor, rock salmon). A popular migratory Atlantic saltwater game fish that favors temperate, 60-degree waters, spending summers in Maine and Nova Scotia and winters in Florida. Young bluefish are called snappers; adult bluefish are known as choppers.

bonefish (*Alubula vulpes*). A popular tropical game fish known for its speed, wariness, and ability to appear seemingly invisible in the silver green-blue waters of the Gulf Coast, Florida Keys, South America, and the Caribbean.

fish. Members of any of the following classes: *Cyclostomata* (hagfishes, lampreys), *elasmobranchii* (sharks, skates, and rays), *piscis* (trout, perch, bass, minnows, and catfish).

marine species. All fish that inhabit salt water, and all shellfish, lobsters, crabs, shrimps, and clams found in the coastal and estuarine waters.

salters. Any species of trout that spends part of its life cycle in brackish or salt water.

trout. Brook trout, brown trout, rainbow trout, Sunapee trout, or blueback trout. **Brook trout** include brook, rainbow, brown, and golden trout, Loch Leven trout and all their hybrids. Trout are the fish of choice of fly fishermen and are found in most of America's freshwaters.

Waters

coastal and **estuarine waters.** Waters within the rise and fall of the tide, and water below any fishway or dam that normally divides tide water and freshwater, or any streams flowing into the sea.

great pond. Any natural body of water more than ten acres in diameter.

inland waters. All waters within the state above the rise and fall of the tide, except private ponds.

ten-acre ponds. All ponds of ten acres or less formed on brooks, streams, or rivers, and governed by the same fishing rules that apply to the brook, stream, or river on which the pond is situated, whether the pond is natural or artificial, unless it is a private pond.

territorial waters. Ocean waters under the jurisdiction of the state and which lie within a three-mile zone from the coast.

tributary. A brook, stream, or river flowing directly or indirectly into a lake, pond, or another brook, stream, or river.

Ice Fishing

ice fishing. The taking of freshwater fish during the open season through man-made openings in the ice by use of ice-fishing devices.

ice-fishing device. Any device used to catch fish through the ice, including a tip up, jig stick, rod in hand, or handline.

ice-in. A period when the surface of a body of water or a portion thereof is covered with sufficient ice to safely support a person.

Fishing Tackle

net (or **seine**). Any open fabric constructed of string, cord, thread, or wire knotted or woven together in such a way as to be capable of entraining or entrapping finfish.

rod blank. The fishing rod without any of its component parts, such as line guides. Graphite is the most popular material for rod blanks. Fiberglass and space-age materials are also used.

Fishing Lines

backing. A hollow-braided dacron line that is first knotted to, then wound onto, the reel, followed by fly line and then tippet. It is thinner than fly line, and is neither weighted nor treated to float or sink like fly line. Its primary purpose is to be reserve line for playing a hard-fighting game fish such as Atlantic salmon. Fish you can count on to play hard and put up a big fight often take the full 90 or 100 feet of fly line off your reel as you try to land them. Backing comes in two tensile strengths, or "tests": 20-pound test for freshwater fishing, and 30-pound test for saltwater fishing.

Fishing Hooks

barb. A barb is the sharp point of a fish hook. In fly-tying, it is a part of the hackle feather of an artificial fly.

barbless hook. A hook without a point, designed specifically to make catch-and-release fishing gentler on the mouths of fish than traditional hooks that have barbs with sharp points, which can tear and damage a fish's tissue.

hook. A single fish hook constructed with one, two, or three points on which an artificial or live bait is secured.

single-baited hook (or **single hook artificial lure**). Up to three hooks attached together or in tandem to the end of a line and baited as a single apparatus designed to catch only one fish at a time.

Waders

bootfoot waders. Waders with rubber boots attached, as one piece.

chest waders. Like one-piece overalls, these provide full-body protection from water, and they have self- or separate suspenders to keep them up.

hip waders. One for each leg, hip waders are like long stockings. They hook onto your belt and provide dry protection up to the thigh.

stockingfoot waders. Waders with feet like socks, worn with separate boots.

waders. A waterproof outer garment usually made of neoprene or nylon that keeps the legs and torso dry when wading into water.

A Beginner's Guide to Fly-Fishing

Fly-fishing can be an exhilarating, rewarding, and challenging sport for a woman. However, it can also be overwhelming and fraught with frustration—that is, if you get into it without a basic understanding of what's involved. The premise of fly-fishing actually is rather simple. The angler tries to catch a fish by "presenting" an artificial lure, called a *fly*, in a delicate and natural manner. She grips her fly rod and casts, which releases the fly line and builds up line speed and distance by back casting before dropping the fly gently on the waters. She must study the water first and observe what nature's insects—mayflies, caddis flies, stone flies, damselflies and dragonflies, ants, beetles, and chironomids—are up to. Chances are, these are what trout and other fish you're fly-fishing for are after. You'll be "matching the hatch"—that is, selecting an artificial fly that looks like the real McCoy. In effect, you're trying to fool the fish.

This is not as simple as it seems. Fish are finicky creatures. Even if you see dragonflies scooting about, a trout may have its heart set on a mayfly. In fact, it may be hungry for a certain type of mayfly. Take, for example, the Hendrickson. The adult is relatively small and used on a #14 size hook. It has three tails, a brown or tan body, and transparent, unmarked wings. The Hendrickson hatches in late April, and usually by the middle of May the hatch is over. Some years, the hatch only lasts ten days. It is the major hatch early in the season on waters east of the Mississippi. Like all mayflies, the Hendrickson hatches in slow, quiet freshwater, usually a stream, river, or pond. The life of an individual Hendrickson mayfly is only twenty-four hours long. We'll discuss the life cycle of the mayfly shortly. However, when there's a hatch going on, you need to know what's hatching. During these times, trout are on a feeding spree, and if you properly present the right artificial dry fly and mimic the movement of the natural fly that's hatching, during the time of day that matches the stage of the hatch, you've got a pretty good chance of hooking a fish. Easy, right? Well, maybe not at first, but it will become easier as you go along. And it will present to you a lifetime of challenge.

Fly Rods

If you are new to fly-fishing, any idyllic images you may have of Huck Finn and Tom Sawyer hooking great big fish on the Mississippi with their homemade twig-and-twine poles will be dashed the instant you walk into a fly rod section of a tackle shop or open a fly-fishing catalogue and see the vast assortment of fly rods on the market today.

Action refers to the nature (or "personality") of the rod. The rod's composition and construction give it *trajectory*. Trajectory empowers the rod tip to propel the fly line by building up *line speed* as a result of the back and forward casts (or as a result of a succession of several casts called *blind casts*). When desired speed and length of time are achieved, the angler efficiently settles the fly on the water, usually in a specific pool or at the top of a swell or current that will carry her fly even farther as it travels with it downstream.

Unlike the ultra-fine fishing line used in spinning and baitcasting, fly-fishing line is significantly larger in diameter. Its core is either hollow or made of braided Dacron®, and the outer finish is polymer or PVC coated. Fly line is tapered and is only a section of the total length of line that's wound onto your fly reel.

Backing, a strong but much finer line, is actually the first length that's wound around the spool of your reel, and may be 20 or 30 yards or more, depending upon the size of your reel and type of game fish you're after. Backing affords a great deal more length and is designed for fighting fish that run and take a lot of line once they're hooked. You'll hear the phrase "gone into the backing." This means that in the course of playing a fish, the fish has run with so much line that your fishing line is expended and you're now on your reserve—that is, backing. If a fly reel was wound entirely with fly line, its weight would make the reel too cumbersome and heavy.

Fly line is tied to the backing, and that in turn is wound onto the reel as a continuous piece. As you near the end of the fly line after the bulk of it is wound onto the spool of the reel, you'll see that that end is tapered. Often there's a braided loop at the end of the tapered line. Several yards of leader are knotted onto the loop. *Leader* is the third section of the line and the one onto which the artificial fly is tied. Leader is available in many sizes and tensile strengths. Each one is geared to the weight range of the fish you're fishing. Leader is very fine and invisible to fish. You'll tie on your fly with a special knot, cast the line, and place the fly. The fly will appear as if it's floating freely, and you've plenty of line to use to play and land your fish.

Unlike spinning line, fly line is weighted. The weight of the line is, in part, responsible for the distance you achieve when you cast. The tension you put into your rod, which comes from upper arm and wrist action, is the power that propels the line forward. How you propel that line varies depending on technique, but it's the action of the rod that helps you achieve control and distance. To determine what kind of action will work best for you depends entirely how you work the rod. Your fishing instructor will help you understand what you're experiencing when you try out different rods. You have to try rods with different actions to determine what feels best to you.

There are three kinds of rod actions: fast, medium-fast, and progressive. A rod with a "fast" or stiff action is exactly that: the rod is stiff. A fast-action rod in the hand of a strong, experienced angler can achieve great distance. She can present a fly on a dime because a fast rod can offer exacting control. However, in the hand of a beginner, a fast rod is simply too much equipment. Besides, these generally are the most expensive rods you can buy.

For a beginning woman angler who has a natural aptitude for fly-fishing, a medium-fast action is about as much as she should handle. I find a rod with a medium-fast action has just enough stiffness to keep me confidently in control of my rod tip. It is a "slower" rod than a fast action—which simply means when you bring your rod tip back, the tip will not get to the back cast, or two o'clock position, as quickly. A medium-fast action also gives you a little more play in your rod, and a chance to make up for mistakes in your cast by virtue of the fact that your rod tip is moving in a great arc and therefore a more relaxed manner. (See Chapter 7 for more on casting technique.)

A "progressive" action is the slowest action. Compared to a fast-action rod, the progressive rod has much more bend to it, both on the back cast and forward cast. It moves through the air in a greater, somewhat more relaxed arc. And the rod tip will go from the ten o'clock to two o'clock position with far less effort than a fast-action rod. A progressive action may not propel line as great a distance, or with as much accuracy as either a fast- or medium-fast action. You can correct more mistakes in your cast with a progressive action, however, so if you are at all unsure about your casting technique, this may indeed be a good choice for you. Again, you'll have to try out rods with different actions to determine this for yourself.

Fly rods are made from a variety of materials—graphite, fiberglass, and composites. Traditional rods were made from bamboo or cane, and although some fly-rod makers still use bamboo, these invariably are the costliest fly rods on the market—$1,600 or more is not an unreasonable price to pay—and not intended for the beginning angler. Then there is the ever-evolving, new generation of high-tech innovations, such "MVR technology" (an Orvis trademark) and high-modulus graphite—space-age fibers developed to produce lighter, stronger, more responsive rods for the consummate angler. Look for a high-quality graphite rod. More than any other fly-fishing gear, a good fly rod is where you want to put your earnest money. It will be expensive—a good rod can cost you about $200, and a really good one will cost over $400—but you won't regret it. It will not only last a lifetime, but it will get you where you need to go on the water. Be sure to buy a rod that has at least a twenty-five-year full guarantee, or better yet, a lifetime guarantee. That way, if it breaks for any reason, it will be repaired or replaced at no charge. I had the great misfortune of breaking two rather expensive rods while fishing for Atlantic salmon, but am happy to say that both had full guarantees and were immediately replaced. Some fishermen say it takes a thousand casts to hook a fish. With that in mind, you need a fly rod that will make those thousand casts a pleasure, not a pain. Nothing will put

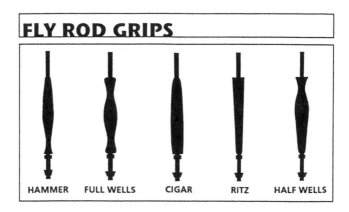

FLY ROD GRIPS

HAMMER   FULL WELLS   CIGAR   RITZ   HALF WELLS

T he grip you choose for your fly rod depends on two factors: what feels most comfortable to you and what is most effective for the type of fish you're fishing. (*BLACK'S FLY FISHING DIRECTORY*)

you off fishing faster than a rod that makes your muscles ache by the end of a day on the water.

The weight of the rod that you select depends largely upon the fish you want to catch. Experts like the late Lee Wulff and his wife, Joan, advocated the use of very lightweight rods, reels, lines, and minute flies to land extremely large fish. In this instance, their supreme skill and years of experience was what successfully landed the fish, not their fishing rig. Watch an instructional video from Joan and Lee Wulff's Royal Wulff Productions library (see Directory) and notice Mrs. Wulff's reserve and control. Her movement, coupled with a natural grace augmented by her years as a dance instructor, will show you precisely why fly-fishing is considered one of the most graceful of all outdoor sports.

Fly Reels

A fly reel, unlike a spinning, baitcasting, or spincasting reel, is basically a line collector. Its sole purpose is to gather and release the line that you cast and retrieve. The part of the reel that gathers your line is called the spool. You determine how much line to release from the spool by pulling it out by hand, then allowing the weight and the speed of the line to propel it forward from the motion generated by casting. When you want to retrieve your line, you lightly put pressure on the line with your

TYPICAL REEL

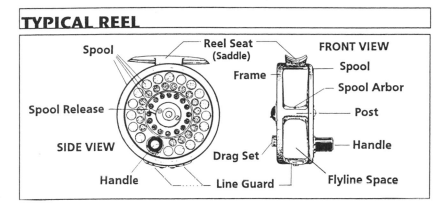

The fly reel basically is a line collector. It stores the fly line until you cast it; then you reel it back onto the spool, where it is stored until your next cast.

(BLACK'S FLY FISHING DIRECTORY)

fingers so that it collects tautly on the spool. If you don't, it will look like spaghetti and get tangled. With fly reels, you must regulate the pressure on the line with your finger. Keep an eye on what you're doing. In time, using your reel properly will come very easily to you.

Fly reels are usually made of machined bar-stock aluminum (which are the most expensive), machined cast aluminum (a little less pricey), or cast aluminum (least expensive). Some anglers will debate whether a more expensive fly reel makes for a better fly reel. Again, remember: a fly reel is basically a line collector and storage container.

A mechanism called a *drag system,* which is made up of discs stacked on a spindle, is a component of the reel and works much like brakes on a car. Its purpose is to start, stop, and feed line to the fish while the angler plays it and reels it in. You will hear references to rulon disc drag, spring and pawl drag, large surface disc drag, and sprocket and pawl. Beginners should look for a fly reel with disc drag in a moderate price range ($30 to $50) with an extra spool you can interchange to use a different line. An extra spool usually costs less than $20. Anti-reverse reels are primarily for big-game fishers who want the reel to turn in the "line-in" or retrieve direction. Without this function, large fish like bonefish and tarpon can run through all your line and all your backing very quickly, making the retrieve difficult. Anti-reverse reels have a larger drag surface and withstand the heat created from screaming reels as line feeds off at speeds up to 7,000 rpm. At this stage, you should not be concerned with this kind of reel, but don't refuse the opportunity to try one out. Down the road you may decide to buy one.

Fly-Fishing Lines

Fly fishers cast a weightless lure tied to a weighted line that's collected on a reel whose purpose is to retrieve fly line that is rigged on a long, flexible rod. Coupled with the line speed you generate from the back cast, the weighted line launches the fly forward and gives it distance.

Fly line comes in various sizes. The size you select depends on your fly rod. For example, the recommended fly line for a #6 weight fly rod is 5/6 or 6/7, depending on the action of the fly rod. Fly line that's too light or too heavy for your rod weight will not cast smoothly, so it's important that you use the right size line for your rod. Follow the guide on page 37 to figure out which line is appropriate.

There are three types of fly lines: floating fly lines, sink tip fly lines, and sinking fly lines.

Floating fly lines are used when you are fishing "top" water, or slightly under the surface of the water. As its name suggests, this line floats. There are many varieties of floating lines, and each has a specific characteristic that makes it appealing for certain conditions. For example, there are fly lines that are designed for heavy lures like bass-bugs and big streamers; lines that are wind-resistant; others that achieve distance in hot weather; and still others that are quick-drying so they maintain their ability to float. Even floating lines will sink, but because you are casting over and over again, in fly-fishing your line generally does not stay in the water for long. After you retrieve the line on your reel, you're ready to cast again. The casting motion actually dries the line out before you cast it forward again.

Sink tip fly lines are used when you want to reach fish that are below the surface, but not on top and not all the way at the bottom. A sink tip fly line allows the tip of the line to sink to middle water, but it doesn't sink the entire length. It is important that you keep your line tight and ready for a fast and fluid retrieve if a fish takes your fly. There's a little more underwater distance for you to retrieve, and you don't want to lose that fish you've been casting for all day long because you weren't in control of your line.

Sinking fly lines are meant for fishing bottom water. On hot summer days especially, when fish are lethargic and seeking relief in cooler waters way below the warm surface water, you'll need a sinking line to carry your wet fly down to where the fish are lying. It is unlikely you'll use a sinking line in the spring or late fall unless you're savvy to familiar waters and habits of the fish you're fishing. Fish are hungry in the

ROD/LINE USES & SIZES

Rod/Line Weight	Fish	Fly Sizes
1-2	Trout, panfish	#26 - #18
3-6	Trout, bass, panfish	#26 - #1/0
7-8	Trout, steelhead, bonefish, redfish, Atlantic salmon, bass	#20 - #1/0
9-11	Steelhead, Atlantic salmon, Pacific salmon, bluefish, small tarpon, dorado, stripers	#6 - #2/0
12-15	Tarpon, billfish, tuna	#2/0 - #8/0

There are many different weights of fly-fishing line. Each has its own special purpose. What you choose depends on the fish.

(*BLACK'S FLY FISHING DIRECTORY*)

spring, and some kinds—not all—are frisky enough in the fall to want to take whatever's dangled in front of their nose. In these instances, sinking fly lines are probably a poor choice. But in the summer, when fish are not rising to the top water, you often depend upon sinking fly

LINE TAPERS

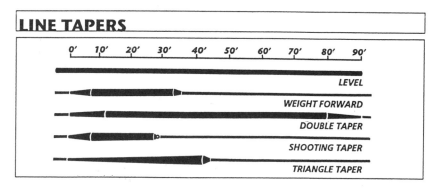

Fly lines come in various "tapers." Level taper is a good, all-purpose fly line. Weight forward is for short casts for large game fish, using large flies. Double taper line sinks slowly its full length and is best for salmon or saltwater fishing. Shooting taper lets the tip sink first while the rest of the line stays straight. Triangle taper is for saltwater shore fishing when the line must be stiff in hot weather, waves, and currents.

(*BLACK'S FLY FISHING DIRECTORY*)

lines to get to where the fish are, obviously, waiting for you . . . or so you hope.

The Leader

Unlike fishing line used in spinning, the fly line has a part called the *leader*. It is a thin, almost invisible length of nylon monofilament line that is tied to the fly-fishing line. Leader come in various sizes, and the size you use depends upon the weight of your line and fly rod. The thinnest section of the leader is located at its tip, and this is called the *tippet*. When you tie on a new leader to your fly line, the tippet portion is integral to the leader—between 20 and 36 inches of the flimsy stuff at the end (tippet thicknesses range from .005 inch to .012 inch). It's extremely flexible, drag-free, and so light that it enables the fly to land delicately and naturally on the water—providing you've achieved a delicate and natural cast, of course. With experience, you'll learn how much tippet you need to tie on to your leader.

The leader is sort of a means to the end. Let's backtrack a minute: The fishing line is thick because it is weighted. The polymer coating on your fishing line gives it that weight. And without a weighted line, you cannot cast effectively. Again, this is the major difference between spinning and fly casting. *In fly-fishing you cast a weightless lure tied to a weighted fly line. And with spinning tackle you cast a weighted lure tied to a weightless fishing line.* Fly-fishing line is visible. In fact, some fly lines are made in bright yellows, oranges, blues, and greens so you can see where your cast is going. If you can see your line, so can the fish. So you add an invisible building block to your line, and that's the leader. The leader is transparent and relatively thick at the loop end, which is where you'll connect it to your fishing line. After you've tied your leader onto your fly line (called a "loop-to-loop connection," which we'll discuss on page 52 under "Knots"), you're going to erase the leader's "line memory."

Line memory simply means the shape that tippets and leaders retain from being stored in a coil. Take a leader out of its package or cut a length of tippet from its spool. Hold one end and let it hang—don't stretch it. Looks like a coil, doesn't it? When you cast you don't want your line to look like a massive ringlet soaring across the water. So here's what you do:

Removing Line Memory

1. Wet your hands in the water.

2. Hold on to the loop end of your leader (or an end of tippet) with one hand.

3. Run the line between the thumb and pointer finger of your dominant hand, gently pull on the loop end in the opposite direction, maintaining pressure on the line, and pulling it through with the other hand.

4. Repeat two or three times until the line is straight.

It's kind of like pulling taffy. Just remember, keep your hands and fingers wet. Otherwise you won't create the friction necessary to remove the memory from the line.

Now, you're probably wondering, *What does she mean by "a spool of tippet"? I thought the tippet was part of the leader.* Well, it is, but the more you change flies—which you'll do often—the more you cut off some tippet. You tie your fly onto the tippet, that gossamer-sheer end of the leader. When you change a fly, you remove it by cutting the fly from the tippet with a little scissors or pincers.

Then you tie a different fly onto the tippet. *Cut a fly off, tie a fly on.* In doing these simple steps, you've probably lost somewhere between two and four inches of tippet. The more often you replace a fly, the more tippet you use. The leader is graduated in thickness—thick at the loop end, fine at the tippet end—so the further you go up the leader, the thicker it gets. You can't tie a small fly onto the thicker portion of a leader. Instead, tie a fresh length of tippet onto your leader using a "clinch knot" (page 45).

How much tippet do you tie onto a leader, you ask? (I know—it sounds like we're getting into rocket science here, but relax. You'll get the hang of it.) First, take out a spool of tippet that matches the number of your leader. Grab the loose end and pull. Holding the spool with one hand and the end in the other, spread your arms their full width. Pretend you're describing the huge fish you just caught: Spread your arms wide, and practice saying, "It was *thi . . . is* big." That's how much tippet you'll need—about four or five feet.

When you buy fishing line, stock up on several packages of leaders and corresponding tippets in the sizes you're most likely to use. This is inexpensive and essential fly tackle. Because a tippet is so fine (though not fragile—it is designed to be strong enough to withstand even the feistiest of fish), take special care when handling it.

TIPPET SIZE	DIAMETER	FLY SIZE	POUND TEST
0X	.011	#4 - #6	6.5
1X	.010	#4 - #8	5.5
2X	.009	#4 - #10	4.5
3X	.008	#6 - #12	3.8
4X	.007	#6 - #14	3.1
5X	.006	#14-#20	2.4
6X	.005	#18-#26	1.4
7X	.004	#20-#28	1.1
8X	.003	#20-#28	.75

Care of Tippets and Leaders

1. Store your tippets away from fluorescent light and sun. The nylon monofilament used in the manufacture of tippets is vulnerable to ultraviolet rays. The best place to store your tippet for practical as well as convenience reasons is in a pocket of your fishing vest.

2. Tippets can melt. Do not leave them on the dashboard of your car or other places that get very hot.

3. Always check your tippet to make sure it has no knots or abrasions. Knots and worn areas of a tippet or leader create a weakness that can easily break once you've got a fish on your line.

4. If you have old tippet from last season, check to make sure it is not brittle. If it is, throw it away. A good rule of thumb is to get fresh tippet for opening day.

The chart above tells you what size tippet you'll need for the fly size you're fishing. The larger the number, the smaller the size of the tippet. The larger the number, the smaller the fly size.

Determining what tippet size you'll need may seem a little confusing, but it makes a lot more sense once you get to know the fish you're fishing for and the size of the artificial flies you'll be using. This all will come easily to you in time. During these early days, consult with your fly-fishing instructor, fishing guide, or tackle-shop dealer.

HOOKS

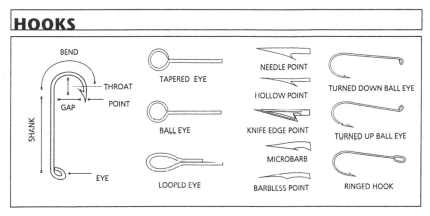

(BLACK'S FLY FISHING DIRECTORY)

Fly-Fishing Hooks

The flies you buy will be tied onto one of three types of hooks: the turned-down ball eye, turned up ball eye, or ringed hook. These can have several types of points and eyes. The chart above shows what these are. Get to know the parts of the hook. It's just part of the new vocabulary you're well on the road to acquiring.

Note: If you're fishing catch-and-release, unbarb your hook or fish with a barbless hook. To unbarb a hook, use fishing scissors, tweezers, or the pliers in your pocketknife or Leatherman™ to pinch the barb toward the shank of the hook so it does not catch the lip of the fish.

The Artificial Fly

History says the first fly fisher was the Roman poet Martial (A.D. 40–104), who is distinguished for having caught some kind of Mediterranean species of saltwater fish with a feathered hook. Another Roman named Elian recorded that Macedonian fishermen were catch-

ANATOMY OF A FLY

WING

RIB

HEAD

TAIL

BODY

HACKLE

Dry Fly

WING

HEAD

TAIL

BODY

HACKLE

Wet Fly

B   F   D

C

A = D
B = E
C = ¾ D
F = ¾ A

A

E

B

A = B

A

Traditional Fly Proportions

(BLACK'S FLY FISHING DIRECTORY)

ing trout on artificial flies a little later. References to trout fishing with imitation artificial flies are chronicled throughout the Middle Ages and the Renaissance. *Dapping* was the earliest fly-fishing technique. Line was tied to the ends of rods that were 20 feet long. An artificial fly was tied to the end of the line. The fly fisher suspended the fly over the water in hopes of teasing a fish into striking.

An artificial fly is an imitation of a live insect, small fish, or crustacean, including fish eggs, insects, mice, leeches, crabs, moths, minnows, and snails. Any fish that feeds on these creatures can be caught by a fly. Traditional flies are made of feathers, animal fur, and thread and can measure from a fraction of an inch to several inches. Artificial flies are used to catch sunfish, bass, trout, pike, bluefish, shark, bonefish, sailfish, salmon, walleye, bluegills, smallmouth bass, largemouth bass, baby tarpon, snook, and catfish. Fish that are plankton-eaters, such as shad, will sometimes strike at an artificial fly if surprised or angered. By law you can fish only with an artificial fly on certain rivers and waterways.

Selecting an artificial fly that has the best chance of attracting the fish you're after depends upon several factors that include the weight and size of the fish, the time of the year and the type of water you're fishing in, and what the fish are eating at the moment. Further on we'll discuss "matching the hatch." This means that the fly you select to fish with, say, a brook trout should be one that imitates the kind of real life fly that is currently hatching on the water. Each body of water has specific artificial flies that work best for the fish that inhabit its water world. Whether you're casting a fly into familiar or unfamiliar waters, discovering what attracts a fish is a large part of the fun and the addiction inherent in fly-fishing. It's also the most challenging—and can be the most frustrating. I have fished with anglers that have cast into the same waters for the same fish for over a half century. Invariably there will be days when absolutely nothing will entice a fish to bite. On the other hand, when the fish are feisty, seasoned anglers not only know exactly what to tie on the end of their tippet, but also where and how to present, or land, their fly in the most natural possible way. This is what defines an angler who understands the fish she is fishing and knows *precisely* what she is doing. It's what we all aspire to be.

C h a p t e r   6

———

Knots

The more I got into fishing the more I realized that not only is there a knot for everything, but seasoned anglers had developed their own *secret* knots. Although a few Old Salts tried to teach me their precious secrets, I have to confess I was all thumbs. It's easy to be a klutz when it comes to tying a fishing knot. The tippet is so delicate, and the fly so small, that "getting all tied up in knots" is what may happen to you, too, at the beginning. Knot tying got me all bent out of shape until I met an elderly woman who was a lifelong fly fisher. She said to me, "Ninety-nine percent of the time, I use the same knot. The fish don't know the difference."

That knot is the *clinch knot,* and it's what I always use to tie my lure or fly onto my tippet. I suggest you do the same:

Clinch Knot

Step 1. Insert 6 to 8 inches of tippet through the eye of the hook of your lure, threading from the back of the eye forward toward the barb. (If you're tying a fly, hold the fly in your left hand, pick up the loose end of

the tippet between the forefinger and thumb of your right hand—or reverse if you're left-handed—and wind the loose end of the tippet four or five times around the length, which you keep taut by holding it with the middle finger of your right hand.)

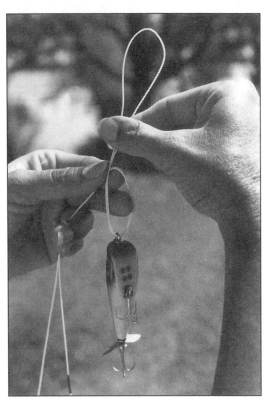

Step 2: Bring the loose end (or "tag end") of your tippet back toward your left hand, and thread it into the loop you've created next to the hook's eye.

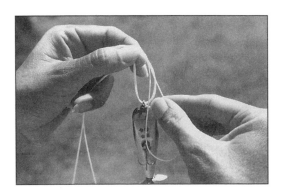

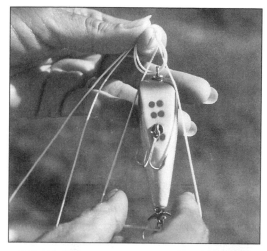

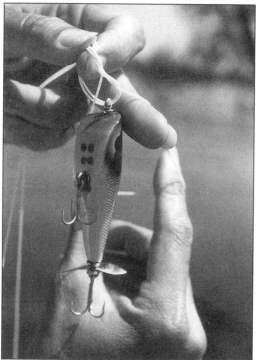

Step 3: Wet your hands and tighten the knot to the hook by pulling the fly in the opposite direction of the leader. *Do not* pull the loose, or tag, end of the line. Pull that knot nice and taut, but *be careful.* It is very easy to get overzealous and pull so hard that you end up jabbing the point of the hook into your hand. So do it gingerly, but firmly.

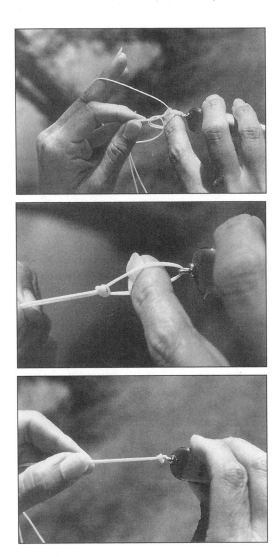

Step 4: With your fishing scissors or pincers, trim the tag end very close to the knot. Be careful not to cut into the knot.

Connecting Fresh Tippet to Your Leader

The next knot you need to learn is what you'll use to tie fresh tippet onto your leader. Say you've been fishing all morning. The fish aren't biting, or they are biting. Or you've cast into some trees behind you and you've lost a fly or two. Or three. You've changed flies so often that you've cut off a lot of tippet and you're now into the thickening part of the leader. So you whip out your spool of tippet, cut a nice long piece of length the width of your spread-out arms, and prepare to tie one end of the tippet onto your leader. How? Well, there's a special knot just for this situation. Like the clinch knot, it's firm, tight, strong, and keeps your line straight, so when a fish bites and you play it, there is no weakness whatsoever in your line as a result of the knot. In fact, this knot strengthens the line. This tippet-to-leader knot is called a *surgeon's knot*.

The Surgeon's Knot

Step 1. Lay an end of tippet next to the end of your leader so the two strands overlap about 5 or 6 inches. Tie an overhand knot in this doubled section by forming a loop and bringing end of leader and entire end of tippet through loop together. Keep loop open.

Step 2. Double the overhand knot by bringing the same double strands through the loop once more. Again, make sure to leave the loop open.

Step 3. Wet your hands—again, to create friction on the line—and tighten the knot by holding the double lines firmly between the thumb and pointer fingers of each hand. Pull *slowly, steadily, and firmly,* keeping even pressure on both double lines.

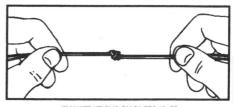

(ILLUSTRATIONS ON PAGES 49–52
COURTESY OF THE ORVIS COMPANY)

Step 4. Trim the tag ends of the leader and the tippet with your fishing scissors or pincers. Be careful not to cut into the knot.

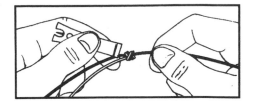

Tying Leader to Your Fly Line

When you take a fresh leader out of its package, you'll notice immediately that the butt end of the leader has a loop tied to it. Most leaders come this way, and if they don't you'll have to tie a loop to the butt end yourself. This is called a *perfection loop*. Although you may find it unnecessary, it's good to know—just in case.

The Perfection Loop

Step 1. Hold the end of your leader between your thumb and forefinger. Form a single loop by bringing the tag end *behind* the leader length, making sure that the tag end is on the right-hand side (even if you're a lefty).

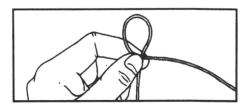

Step 2. Now make a second, smaller loop in front of the first one by bringing the tag end in front, then behind, the initial loop—think of it as "lassooing" the loop. Hold on, though. It can get a little dicey

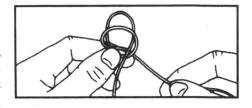

here because you have to keep *both* loops in place between your thumb and forefinger. But don't worry. You can do it!

Step 3. Now take the tag end between the forefinger and thumb of your right hand and pass it *between the two loops.* Hold *this* in place with the finger of your left hand.

Step 4: Wet your fingers. Thread the second loop through the first loop and gingerly pull on the second loop and tag end of the leader. The second loop will create a knot at the base of the first loop. You want to keep the loop relatively small—not minute, but about ¼ inch. If this knot seems tough to do, it is. Of all the knots, this is the one that takes lots of practice. That's why I'm always sure to buy packaged leaders that already have a loop at the butt end. Nonetheless, you should know this knot.

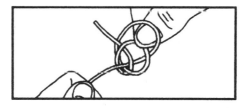

Step 5. Trim tag end as close to knot as possible.

The last knot we'll learn is the *loop-to-loop connection,* which you will use quite often, although not as often as the first two knots we've discussed in this chapter. This enables you to tie fresh leader onto your fly line.

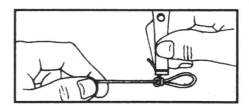

The Loop-to-Loop Connection

Step 1. Pass the leader loop through the fly-line loop.

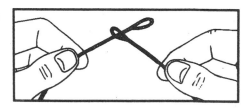

Step 2. Pass the fly-line loop through the leader loop.

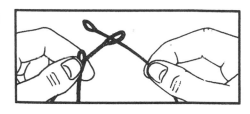

Step 3. Tighten by holding both lines between the forefinger and thumb of your left hand and your right hand. Pull. The correct loop-to-loop connection looks like a square knot when complete.

Chapter 7

———

Fly-Fishing Technique

Get it right the first time. That's about the best advice anyone can give you when it comes to learning fly-fishing technique. When I attended the Orvis for Women Fly Fishing School in Manchester, Vermont, several students had enrolled just to *unlearn* the technique they'd been using. As the Introduction makes clear, muscle memory is a heck of a thing to unlearn. That's why—*and I cannot stress this enough*—you should work with a professional fly-fishing instructor from the start. If you don't, it can get awfully frustrating if you don't achieve what you want in your cast. You don't want to feel defeated before you start.

Fly casting requires an entirely different presentation than spinning. Since the fly does not have the weight of a spinning lure, the angler depends upon the line speed she can create by casting her fly line 30 feet or more for distance casting. If she chooses to side cast (which is exactly what it means—casting from your side instead of over your head) to achieve a shorter distance, she'll know how to control the line without it puddling into the water like spaghetti.

It's important to avoid some common temptations, especially unnecessary motion. When you first cast a line, you may tend to thrust your arm forward, totally outstretched. You also may find you're using a lot of shoulder to bring your arm up for the back cast. If you're really into it, you may find you're pivoting your feet or taking steps. All this is unnecessary motion that actually *hinders* the casting action. The more unnecessary body movement you put into your casting, the more you take away from achieving the tension and arm/wrist action necessary to create line speed. Line speed is generated between the *back cast* and *front cast.* As you become accustomed to casting, you will incorporate a *blind cast* into your casting technique. This simply means repeating your back cast and front cast one or more times to generate more line speed and, therefore, greater distance. *Line speed* propels your line and allows you to present your fly any kind of distance. Your ultimate goal is to present your fly as delicately and naturally onto the water's surface as possible so that the fish think a real fly has landed on top of the water.

I am a firm believer that a picture's worth a thousand words, so this chapter is mostly photographic. The pictures I have selected show you several women's casting techniques. All are similar, and all use the following steps. Over time, you will develop your own style—not your own technique, but the manner in which you properly cast your line. Style is an individual hallmark; technique is not. Learn to do it right. Practice the proper technique over and over again. Commit it to muscle memory. But always remember that the way you ultimately will cast will take on your personal imprint—your own style.

Step 1. Pull 10 inches of fly line beyond the rod tip.

Step 2. Pull about 20 feet of fly line off the reel and hold it coiled in your noncasting hand.

Step 3. Using the forearm and wrist of your casting arm, point your rod tip at the 9 o'clock position and firmly bring your forearm up to 12:30, keeping your wrist straight and strong. The fly line will begin to form an arc.

Step 4. When the arc flattens behind you and becomes parallel to the ground, bring the rod tip back to 9 o'clock, keeping your forearm straight, and giving your wrist a slight "snap" just before you release the line. As you become more advanced, you'll repeat the cast one or more times. This is the blind cast mentioned above.

Step 5. Do not let the line slap the water. Your goal is to allow the line speed you've generated to propel the fly the distance, and allow the tippet to do its job. After a while, you'll get the hang of casting, and better control of your tippet. Again, the goal is to allow the fly to land as naturally on top of the water as if it were a real insect.

Remember, when you cast you are transferring energy from your forearm and wrist through the rod, and into the line. A weak or whippy wrist breaks that energy chain, and you won't achieve the distance you otherwise will if you keep your wrist fairly inflexible until the moment just before line release, when you give your wrist a determined "snap."

You may find that your instructor pulls the wristband of your sweatshirt over your wrist to block it from whipping around too much. You may get so caught up in trying to control your wrist that you don't pay enough attention to all the other things that are happening when you cast. Just remember, the entire casting motion only takes a few seconds. It's very hard to try to remember every step when you only have a few seconds to make them all come together in a fluid motion. Don't get too caught up in your wrist. It *is* important. It is perhaps the most important part of casting technique. But I have fished with old-timers and really expert fishermen who cast using nothing *but* wrist action, and they thrust their entire arm forward in the forward cast. It works for them.

As a woman angler, however, you'll hold the grip of your rod firmly in your casting hand, bring the rod tip back using only your forearm to the back-cast position, and return it, in the forward cast, relatively close to your body. Here's why. Most women have slighter builds than most men. They also have approximately 30 percent less muscle mass. You can get a fish on your first cast, or you can go all day with nary a bite. But the fact remains that by the very nature of the sport, you do an awful lot of casting, so it is essential that you put as little effort into the motions while still generating the most distance and line speed from your cast. And you *can* cast effectively, you *can* generate line speed and control with minimal physical movement. The secret lies in technique.

Say you've made a cast and the fly lands on the water. Let's say you tied a dry fly to your tippet. You may have moistened it with a little bit of *fly flotant,* a water-resistant emulsion that keeps a dry fly on top of the water longer. Let the fly remain where you cast it for a moment. Often, if you've cast over a hungry fish that's swimming "on top" of the water—that is, just under the surface of the water—you'll get a bite in jig time. If not, you need to put a little movement into your fly so that it attracts the fish's attention. You need to give natural motion to the fly. Concentrate on your rod tip, and regulate the line with your free hand. Gently and slowly pull in, or retrieve, the line with your hand, without winding your reel. By pulling the fly line with your noncasting hand, the fly will indeed take on the appearance of a live fly. As you do this, you are gathering the line in a coil with your noncasting hand until the next cast. When you've retrieved your line, and the fly is about five feet from the tip of your rod (about two-thirds of the way down the length of your fly rod, if you were to hold the rod vertical), then prepare to cast again. A good fly fisher can pick up her line right out of the water and practically cast on the nose of a fish.

There are a few factors you must always stay on top of after you've cast your line. The most important is to keep the rod tip down, close to the water's surface. The second is to *mend your line:* retrieve excess line and keep the line that you're fishing relatively taut. Once the fly is presented on the water, retrieve line that's bowed over the waterline or creates a bend along the length of your rod by pulling in line with your noncasting hand and keeping it neatly coiled. You'll continue to do this as you retrieve your fly line in preparation for the next cast—unless, of course, you happen to have hooked a fish, in which case the rules change completely.

Before we talk about how to play a fish, there's one other important thing you ought to do when you cast, especially if you've cast upstream in fast-running water: remove the *bow* from your line. The current will carry a line the instant your fly feathers on top of the water. Sometimes your cast will lay your line across the water in a bow similar to a C shape. If a fish happens to take your fly at that moment, you may have great difficulty setting your hook because you will have to compensate for all the slack you've created in that C. If this happens, immediately bring your rod tip down a couple of feet above the water's surface and manipulate the line so that you've removed that bow. The result will be an inverse C and that won't last for long. The current will straighten it out, you'll mend your line, and all will be well. Now you have a tight line.

Whether you feel a nibble or a jerk on your hook, be prepared. You're going to immediately *set the hook*—even if you're not altogether sure there's something on it. Chances are there is, and you don't want to lose any opportunities. All you do to set the hook is jerk your rod tip up until you feel pressure on the line. If there is indeed a fish on the other end, you'll know *instantly*. It is extremely important to keep tension on that line. If not, the fish likely will spit out the hook and swim away. The minute you think a fish has taken your hook, give it a swift, strong, upward jerk—about three or four feet above where your rod tip was positioned close to the water's surface—and reel in. When you reel, you must keep the line tight. If you don't—if there's any slack in your line—you may not have a chance to play your fish, and it's doubtful that fish will come back for more. In fact, you'll probably have scared any others that may have been in that pool, and you'll have to find another pool to fish.

Once you've set your hook and are sure you have the fish firmly on, begin to reel in the line. Do this, at first, as quickly as possible. When you've reeled in line so that your rod's at the 11 o'clock position, begin to bring the rod tip down to about 8 o'clock, reeling in even more rapidly, because on the downstroke you *must* keep your line taut. Reel in, moving the rod tip up to 11 o'clock; gradually bring your rod tip down to 8 o'clock as quickly as you can, maintaining line tension the whole time. Bring the rod tip up quickly, back to 11 o'clock, letting out a little line so the tension on the line won't break your tippet. With the line taut, return to 8 o'clock position. Repeat until you bring the fish to your side and it *pouts*. Pouting is when a fish gives up and lies on its side, resigned to its fate.

Some fish don't give in so easily. Bass, redfish, and salmon, for example, are among many sport fish that are famous fighters. It is not uncommon to play these fish for half an hour—sometimes more. When you've set the hook, the first thing the fish wants to do is get away from you. If it's taken a solid bite, you'll hear your reel screaming. As long as you're sure that the hook is firmly set, let the fish take as much line as it needs—providing, of course, your rod tip is up and you've maintained firm pressure on your line. As soon as you sense that the fish is tiring or taking less line, start to reel in quickly. Again, follow the 8 o'clock to 11 o'clock routine. Nine times out of ten, the fish will revive after a few seconds and you'll hear your reel scream. Again, let the fish take line, and don't be concerned if you notice you're out of fly line and into the *backing*, which is a much thinner line whose purpose, again, is to give you added distance in instances like these. A fighting fish will take a lot of backing, but your reel has been wound with plenty for instances such as these. Keep your rod tip up, maintain pressure on your line, and when the fish slows down again, reel in. You'll repeat this over and over again until you gradually bring the fish close to you. Even then, don't get overexcited. Don't reel in so hard that you're putting too much pressure on your tippet because it *will* snap if you're putting too much pressure on the line. You can get a sense of this from the way your reel is collecting line. If the line is too loose, you'll have wads of line lumped unevenly around the spool. If the line is being reeled in too tightly, you can see the line tighten on the reel. Either way, you're not applying the right amount of pressure. You want a smooth retrieve, and you need to guide the line evenly with the forefinger of the hand you're holding the grip with.

Finally the fish will be a little more tuckered out than you. It pouts, and you are ready with your net. Hold the fish head up, tail down, just above its gills, with your thumb under its lower jaw. Grab the base of the fly firmly between your thumb and forefinger, and in one determined pull, gently disengage the fly from the fish's mouth by following the direction opposite the way of entry of the hook. This way there's minimal tissue damage to the fish.

For more information on the proper way to handle a fish once it's been caught, see page 97.

The following photographs illustrate the technique you'll be striving to achieve. Remember, find yourself a good instructor. Then practice in your backyard without a rod. Just practice the motions, over and over again, until you've committed them to muscle memory. Your goal is to cast so naturally and effortlessly that eventually you will never have to think about it.

A Portfolio of Fly-Fishing Techniques by Professional Women Fishing Instructors

This fishing instructor teaches at the Orvis Fly Fishing School for Women. Notice how effortlessly she makes casting appear.

Take a look at where our angler's hand is in **photo 1**. She's brought it from the 1:30 position to the 10 o'clock position in her forward cast. Also notice how the line is starting to straighten out. That's a result of line weight plus line speed. Her wrist is straight, but she's just about to snap it. Her forearm is lined up with her rod as though it were an extension of it—which, in a sense, it is. She'll be bringing her arm down—not out. See how she's maintained a bent elbow?

Photo #1.

Photo #2.

In **photo #2,** she has completed her forward cast. Notice how the line has traveled through the rod guides and is straight and taut. Again, her arm is an extension of the rod, and her elbow is close to her body. She has achieved the maximum range in propelling her fly the distance, using a minimum of effort. She'll keep this up all day long without getting tired. You will, too, once you get the hang of it.

Photo #3.

Photo #4.

See **photo #3.** Our angler's got her rod tip down, now—only a foot or two above the water. See the slight bow of line along the rod? She's gathering it up, which is called *mending the line.*

Now our angler is ready for her fish (**photo #4**). Her line is taut, her hands are over the reel, and she's mended her line. But look! There's a slight bow to her rod. *Has she hooked a fish?* In a split second she'll jerk her rod tip up and set her hook. Our gal's gonna bring one in!

Photo #5.   Photo #6.

The thing you are aiming to achieve when it comes to technique is *maximum output using minimum energy.* Actually, that sounds pretty good for most things in life, but when it comes to fly-fishing, achieving that goal is certainly attainable. Our Orvis angling instructor is a good example of that. What's more, she's graceful. For the woman fly fisher, grace is a major part of the satisfaction you'll realize when you embrace the sport.

Now let's take a look at another instructor, Sarah Gardener. She's following the same technique as the woman we've just seen, but she's fishing with heavier fly tackle because her sport is saltwater fly-fishing. Her rod is a #9. (Our Orvis instructor used a #6.) Sarah teaches saltwater fly-fishing techniques in the Chesapeake Bay area of Maryland. She's got to cope with a heavier rig than our Orvis trout fisher, and that's because she's after bigger—that is, heavier—fish. Remember the rig you fish with must suit the fish you're fishing.

In **photo #5,** once again notice how the rod tip points to the 10 o'clock position. Sarah begins to pull line from her reel as she prepares to cast.

As her rod tip follows the clock to the 2 o'clock position (**photo #6**), our saltwater fly-fishing instructor uses her noncasting hand to pull more and more line off the reel. In a few seconds, the length of line she's pulled will travel through the rod guides in her forward cast.

Photo #7.

In **photo #7**, the rod tip is about at the 2 o'clock position. Our woman angler is holding several loops of fly line in her noncasting hand—about 20 feet of line, in fact. She's about to forward cast, and when she does, the weight of the line will propel her fly forward at that length *plus* whatever additional length Sarah realizes as a result of her back cast.

Now our angler is well into her forward cast (**photo #8**). Notice

Photo #8.

Photo #9.

how the line that she had collected in her noncasting hand has been re-leased and is traveling through the rod's guides and out into the water.

See **photo #9**. The rod tip is precisely where it should be, the line is taut along the fly rod, and our angler has mended her line. Now she's slowly going to retrieve line with her noncasting hand, all the while giving her fly a little action with the rod tip so that some big stripper swimming by will think her fly is real and take a bite.

I had the great good fortune to meet a number of women anglers along my own fishing journey. One of these women is Lori-Ann Murphy, co-founder of Reel Women Fly Fishing Adventures, a fly-fishing school and outfitting business based in Victor, Idaho, just outside of Jackson, Wyoming. Lori-Ann was the first woman angler to be an Orvis Endorsed Guide. That was back in 1989, and since then she has guided women and men all over the world. In fact, I met Lori-Ann at the Orvis Fly Fishing School for Women, and she and Gwen Perkins are jointly responsible for my utter addiction to fly-fishing. Lori-Ann has taught hundreds of women how to fish, including Meryl Streep on the set of the movie *The River Wild*, for which Lori-Ann served as the fly-fishing technical advisor.

Lori-Ann continues to serve on Orvis' Freshwater Advisory Team, and when she's not taking women—and men—on exciting freshwater and saltwater fly-fishing vacations to places like the famous South Fork of the Snake River or the Bahamas, she treks back to Manchester, Vermont, and lends a hand teaching at the Orvis Fly Fishing School for

(PHOTO COURTESY OF REEL WOMEN, INC.)

Women in May. From June through August, however, Lori-Ann heads west, where she conducts the Jackson Hole Fly Fishing School.

Lori-Ann Murphy (*without hat*) shows a student how to bring her rod tip to the 2 o'clock position. Notice the firm wrist and the way the student's fingers are wrapped high up around the upper portion of the

(PHOTO COURTESY OF REEL WOMEN, INC.)

(PHOTO COURTESY OF REEL WOMEN, INC.)

grip, not down by the butt. This gives increased leverage, especially when you give the wrist a "snap" before releasing the line in the forward cast. Also notice how both instructor and student are *looking behind to see where the rod tip is.* This is extremely important. Keeping your eye on your back cast allows you to see your fly line straighten, and to prepare

(PHOTO COURTESY OF REEL WOMEN, INC.)

your forward cast the instant your back cast line is parallel to the ground. In the bottom photo, page 64, Lori-Ann instructs her student to pull out line from her fly reel with her noncasting hand.

Lori-Ann guides her student through to the forward cast on page 65. The rod tip will quickly drop down to about 8 o'clock, where the angler will maintain it while mending, and then retrieving her line.

In the Directory, I've listed a number of fly-fishing instructors who can give you the guidance and confidence you need to learn fly-fishing technique. You can take classes. You can read this book and the dozens of other books that are available to the fly fisherman. There's only thing that can really make you a confident fly fisher, however—and that's practice. Think of the trout stream as your classroom, your fly-fishing instructor as your teacher, and the fish as the star you get next to the A+ on a test score. The feeling you'll get when you catch a fish is not unlike the feeling you got when you "aced" a test. If you can't relate to that, then maybe you'll relate to something one woman angler said to me: "Fly-fishing is better than sex." Of course, I expect that's up to the individual.

Fly-Fishing Terms You Should Know

Let's review some words and phrases mentioned in this chapter. They'll be pretty important to you, now that you're learning the language of fly-fishing. For a broader selection of fishing terms, see Chapter 4.

Match the hatch. In spring during a mayfly or other fly hatch, however, there's a great deal of activity on the surface of the water. Trout are hungry, and if you can present an artificial fly in a manner that will make the fish think it's natural food, then be ready: your fly will catch the trout's attention and it will bite. When you match the hatch, you're studying the water surface and the rocks and ledges along the river bank to see what kind of flies are hatching. Then you'll reach into your fly box and select an artificial fly that comes as close to the real thing as possible. Dick Pobst's book, *Trout Stream Insects* (New York: Lyons & Burford), is an excellent source of information on the entemology of fly-fishing.

What does a fly rod do? It casts, positions the line, and plays the fish. A fly rod should be an extension of your arm.

PARTS OF A FLY ROD

The Butt

Reel Lock

Reel Seat

Grip

Hook-Keeper Ring

Stripping Guide

Ferrule

Snake Guide

The Tip

The Middle

(BLACK'S FLY-FISHING DIRECTORY)

You do not cast a rod. You cast a weighted fly line and a weightless fly. The leader, tippet, and fly are components of the fly line, as are the many yards of backing that connect the fly line to the spool and allow you to have sufficient line to play a feisty game fish and allow it to run before bringing it in.

A fly rod is described by its length and the line weight it takes. An 805 is a rod that measures 8½ feet from tip to butt. If it is a #6 weight rod, it takes #6 fly line and is best for a specific range and weight of fish. The larger the number, the larger the rod. The smaller the number, the lighter the rod. A #10 fly rod is used for large fish such as salmon. A #2 rod, or "flea rod," is used for catching small fish.

Fly rods generally come in pieces. Most common are two-piece, three-piece, and four-piece rods. Two-piece fly rods are the most common. Three- and four-piece rods are convenient to carry when you're traveling. One-piece fly rods, less common today, are impractical to transport. In the day of the one-piece, bamboo was commonly used to make fly rods.

Know the parts of a fly rod. The lower section of the fly rod, including the handle, is called the *butt section*. The tip of the fly rod is called the *tip section*. The in-between section is called the *mid-section*.

There are several types of **reel seats.**

The *ring type* of reel seat, which is used for small reels and light fly rods, is made up of two thin metal bands that slip securely over the foot of the fly reel. *Do not* use reels that weigh over three ounces with a ring-type seat.

The *screw-locking,* or *down-locking,* type is a fixed metal hood at the bottom of the seat. This is the most popular type of reel seat.

Lastly there's the *reversed screw-locking,* or *up-locking,* type. It is the same as the screw-locking reel seat, but is enclosed in the cork grip. The screw band screws up toward the grip.

Again, always be sure your reel seat is the correct size for your reel.

Grips are constructed from cork that is turned on a lathe and then sanded. The type of grip you choose depends mostly on personal taste. Common grips are superfine, cigar, half wells, and full wells. At the bottom is a metal cap called the *end plug.* On some large saltwater and salmon rods, the plug can be replaced with a detachable butt extension called a *fighting butt.* The fighting butt can be braced against your stomach or belt to relieve the strain on your arms when you are playing large fish for a long time. The grip is made up of a frame and a filler. The reel seat holds the fly reel securely to the rod. The reel seat is a metal frame that holds the reel, usually a lightweight aluminum alloy. The filler is made from cork, walnut, maple, zebra wood, or other exotic wood. The reel seat in large saltwater rods is made from chrome-plated brass, necessary in holding heavy saltwater reels.

The hook keeper, located directly above the grip, is a small metal ring or hook where you hook your fly when you're not casting. When you're not fishing but need to move to a different spot, let out plenty of line, hook your fly hook into the hook keeper, then reel in the slack until the line is taut.

The stripping guide is the first guide above the grip. It is larger than the others that run up along the length of your rod. Guides hold the line to the rod during casting, direct the line along the length of the rod when *shooting,* or releasing more line while casting, and distribute the stress of the line along the entire length of the rod. Because the stripping guide receives the most stress, it is made from abrasion-resistant material, such as hard chrome or ceramic, and is larger than the other guides that run the length of the rod. These guides are bent pieces of wire called *snake guides.* The rule of thumb is that there are as many guides as the number of feet in the length of the rod. The last guide, near the tip of the rod, is called the tip-top. Fly rods with ceramic stripping guides tend to make the rod heavy and restrict the action of the rod.

Ferrules are the joints that connect rod segments together in two-, three-, or four-piece rods. All multipiece graphite, fiberglass, and boron/graphite rods have ferrules. In effect they are tapered sleeves constructed within the rod material itself, enabling each piece to fit snugly together.

Flies range in size from ⅛ inch to over 6 inches in length. The size of the fly and the air resistance it endures during casting will determine the weight of the line it needs to support it. *Rule of thumb:* The heavier the fly line, the larger the fly you cast. The less wind resistance there is, the farther you can cast. The lighter the line, the more delicate and accurate your presentation tends to be with smaller flies.

Atlantic Salmon Fishing

Yes, as everyone knows, meditation and water are wedded forever. . . .
Why did the old Persians hold the sea holy? Why did the Greeks
give it a separate deity, and own brother of Jove? Surely all
this is not without meaning. And still deeper the meaning of
that story of Narcissus, who because he could not grasp the
tormenting, mild image he saw in the fountain, plunged
into it and was drowned. But that same image, we
ourselves see in all rivers and oceans. It is the
image of the ungrapable phantom of life;
and this is the key to it all.

—Herman Melville, *Moby Dick*

Atlantic salmon fishing is called the Sport of Kings. This stands to reason, since the Atlantic salmon is considered the king of game fish. Fly-fishing for Atlantic salmon pits the angler against the fightingest of fish, and if—as consummate aficionados of the sport maintain—salmon possess real intelligence, then the sportsman enters a watery arena as the disadvantaged challenger. The Atlantic salmon is champion over its environment. Salmon know the nuances of their home stream: every rock and dark pool, the falls and ledges, and the routes the currents travel. They feel the warmth or chill of the water and the air above. They understand the east wind, which whispers a language even the sagest of fishermen cannot comprehend. Fishermen *see* and *hear* the wind. It gusts lustily over silvery, shimmering waters and darkens and corrugates the surface with rows of black ripples.

> *. . . and that if he be an honest angler, the East Wind may never blow when he goes a-fishing.*

> —Izaak Walton (1593–1683),
> *The Compleat Angler,* 1653–1655,
> "Epistle to the Reader"

Atlantic salmon almost never strike when an East wind blows, and no one knows why. It is part of the eternal mystery of nature, and the chemistry that has existed between living things and the elements from the beginning.

> *Say what some poets will, Nature is not so much her own ever-sweet interpreter as the mere supplier of that cunning alphabet, whereby selecting and combining as he pleases, each man reads his own peculiar lesson according to his own peculiar mind and mood.*

> —Herman Melville, *Moby Dick*

A salmon knows its time, its place, and how it fits into the scheme of things. It must be strong to survive. A youngster *parr,* if it survives its first winter, will become a *grilse* (or *jack*) and weigh up to nine pounds. A three-sea-winter fish can exceed 70 pounds. In fact, a 103-pound salmon reportedly was caught by poachers in 1901 in the River Devon in Scotland. A salmon must also be resourceful. Bears and hawks are among its natural predators—as are human beings. When an angler attempts to lure an Atlantic salmon, she cunningly connives to fool this remarkable fish with some feathers and thread wrapped around a hook tied to the end of a tippet—seemingly pitiful equipment against so formidable a fish. Needless to say, it takes more than an artificial fly to entice a salmon. It takes knowledge born of experience. Devout fishermen *commit* salmon fishing—for them it is an act of faith.

A fisher of salmon must be clever and thoughtful when stalking her quarry. She should have at least a basic understanding of the ways of this magnificent game fish. She gathers her clues from the season of the year, the month of the season, the day of the week, the time of the day. She checks the temperature and height of the water, and gauges how fast it is moving. When shoals of salmon rush downstream after their winter's dormancy, and later return to spawn, the angler perches on the riverbank, waiting. She suspects where salmon repose when the water is warmed by a hot summer sun, she seeks out cool, inviting, dark pools, knowing that's where they're likely to lie.

A basic understanding of your quarry, its environs, and habits will make you a better angler. Knowledge and skill enhance the thrill of landing a salmon. For example, in early spring svelte, sea-bound, "black" Atlantic salmon run downstream, ocean-bound for the bountiful food supply in the sea. Fishermen will fish from boats then because fast, high water from spring runoff and muddy river banks make wade fishing treacherous. Also, salmon will run with the currents, and currents generally gyrate down the middle of a stream. This is not to say that spring salmon cannot be found along the river's edge. On the contrary, salmon will rest in quiet waters. Casting technique and fly placement are somewhat secondary to selecting a dry fly that's apt to catch the fish's attention while racing, famished, for the plentiful feast that awaits it in the ocean. In summer and fall, anglers wade fish for "bright" salmon, which by now are well-fed and cease to eat when they return to the river. These fish are generally finicky and usually lethargic—until they strike. Then they are heavyweights, raring for a fight. Technique and fly placement are crucial to successfully hooking a bright Atlantic salmon, and often it's only the most experienced and talented fly fisherman who succeed in hooking one of these fish at all. For seasoned anglers, tying or selecting dry flies can border on religion. What will attract a salmon at any particular moment, in a certain spot? These considerations, coupled with the intrinsic grace of casting a line, are why I say salmon fishing is an art.

Equipped with appropriate rod, reel, and fly, the angler must be fit for a fight. Atlantic salmon are powerful athletes and surprisingly strong adversaries that possess a survivalist's sheer will to win. The angler casts, again and again, in a stretch of river here or a pool there. An intuitive salmon fisher has a sixth sense. She knows where the fish are.

There's never a question when a salmon strikes. You feel the hook set. Your reel screams. The salmon runs, frantically pulling yards of line from the reel and going well into the backing. Don't handle your reel—you can break a finger! Let the fish run . . . play it and pray it doesn't spit out your hook. Reel in a little, let it run, reel in a little more. Twenty, thirty minutes pass . . . the minutes feel like seconds. You bring it in, *finally*. The salmon lies on its side and flips up the tip of its tail like a white flag waving in defeat. It is *pouting*, which is precisely what it's called, and exactly what it's doing. You reach for your net . . .

Wait . . . We're moving ahead of ourselves. It's important to first learn a little about the Atlantic salmon—its life cycle, and what biological factors determine and support its survival. For the purposes of this book, we'll tackle up and fish for the most celebrated of the *Salmonidae* species, Atlantic salmon—the king of fish. But first let's meet some other members of this large and exciting family of sport fish.

The Salmonidae Family

Seven species of salmon that belong to two principal salmon families are pursued and prized in North America as sport fish: the Atlantic salmon and the Pacific salmon. All salmon are related to the trout, but the closest relation is the Atlantic salmon. The biological similarities end, however, when it comes to fishing for salmon. As noted outdoor writer A. J. McLane warned: "Forget what you know about trout fishing and learn salmon from a salmon fisherman, because salmon are for you the ultimate paradox. They neither hold where trout do in a stream nor do they act like trout when they respond—or don't respond—to your fly."

Biologically, there are key differences between the Atlantic and the Pacific salmon. The primary difference occurs in the spawning phase of their respective life cycles. The Atlantic salmon can spawn several times, but the Pacific salmon dies after spawning once. The Pacific salmon, at the peak of its growth, is substantially larger than the Atlantic salmon at the same stage. Although our discussion will focus on the Atlantic salmon, it's important to know at least something about their western cousins. The Pacific salmon provide highly invigorating and challenging sport in their own neck of the woods.

The Seven Species of Salmon

Atlantic Salmon

Atlantic salmon live in northeast U.S. and the eastern coastal provinces of Canada. They average 36 inches in length and weigh 10 pounds. They are neither as abundant nor as commercially important as Pacific salmon.

Pacific Salmon

Cherry salmon (masou salmon) are found in the coastal waters and rivers of eastern Asia. They measure 16 to 28 inches and weigh between 5 and 23 pounds.

Chinook (also known as blackmouth, king, quinnat, spring, tule, or tyee salmon) are the largest species of salmon: an average fish measures 36 inches and weighs 22 pounds, although they have been known to get up to 120 pounds. Chinook are considered the champion of Pacific sport fish.

Chum (also called calico, dog, or keta salmon) average 24 inches in length and weigh about 10 pounds.

Coho (also called medium red, silver, or silverside salmon) also average about 24 inches in length and weigh 10 pounds. The coho originally were introduced into the Great Lakes in order to control a small nuisance fish called the alewife. As a result, coho have become a man-made variety of landlocked salmon.

Pink (or humpback) salmon is the smallest species of salmon, and can grow to 20 inches and weigh 5 pounds.

Sockeye salmon (also known as blueback or red salmon) measure about 24 inches and weigh around 6 pounds. The landlocked variety of sockeye salmon is called kokanee salmon.

Life Cycle of the Pacific Salmon (genus *Oncorhynchus*)

Pacific salmon live primarily in the coastal waters of the north Pacific Ocean, though Pacific salmon also inhabit northern Asian waters. Like the Atlantic salmon, Pacific salmon are born, or spawned, in freshwater streams and live some part of their lives in the ocean. Pacific salmon have a different life cycle than that of the Atlantic salmon; essentially, a Pacific salmon spawns only once in its life and dies soon after it spawns. The Atlantic salmon does not die after spawning and, in fact, can return to the ocean and come back later to spawn in the stream as many as three more times.

The time of year salmon spawn—usually in the summer or autumn—is common to both Atlantic and Pacific salmon, as is their stamina and ability to fight against rapids, currents, and waterfalls to make their journey upstream, where they spawn. You can identify whether a salmon is en route to the ocean or returning to the stream by its color, weight, and shape. "Black" salmon—a fish that is ocean-bound after spending the winter in the river—has depleted its fat reserves and is hungry. "Bright" salmon returns from the ocean, stuffed from eating its fill, and ceases to eat in freshwater altogether, subsisting on its fat reserves. Bright salmon travel upstream to spawn or settle down for the winter.

All salmon will change, and lose, color and shape as they make their way upstream. Their flesh also loses flavor when they leave the ocean (which explains why commercial fishermen kill salmon in the ocean, before they enter freshwater tributaries). Males develop a hooked snout. Pink male salmon develop a humpback. Purple streaks line the sides of chum salmon, and sockeye salmon will turn a bright red. The largest member of the Pacific salmon family—the largest of all salmon, for that matter—is the chinook, or king salmon, and in Latin it answers to *Oncorhynchus tshawytscha*. It can weigh as much as 120 pounds. The average chinook is a substantial game fish—10 to 15 pounds—and bears a substantial similarity to its Atlantic cousin in appearance and coloration. Unlike the Atlantic salmon, both lobes of the Pacific salmon's tail are spotted, its head has fewer spotted markings, and it has a pronounced underbite. This is the Arnold Schwartzenegger of fish, enduring treacherous waters and distances in excess of 2,400 miles in the course of its annual pilgrimage between its feeding grounds and its spawning grounds, from Alaska down the California coast.

The coho, or silver, salmon (*Oncorhynchus kisutch*) is an equally important, but much smaller, Pacific salmon and can be differentiated from a young chinook because it has spots only on the upper lobe of its tail. Coho salmon have white gums, not black like chinook. A large coho is smaller than an Atlantic salmon of comparable maturity, and can reach a maximum weight of 33 pounds.

Other members of the Pacific salmon family are sockeye, kokanee, chum, and pink salmon. The sockeye, or red salmon, is not a popular game fish because it has no inclination to take bait or a lure. Neither does its slightly larger brother, the chum, though chum are apt to take light saltwater tackle and can provide frisky sport. The kokanee is popular and will readily bite just about anything an angler chooses to cast; however, the kokanee rarely exceeds five pounds. The pink salmon (nicknamed "humpback" or "humpy" because of its humped back) is also small, averaging three to five pounds. It is abundant in numbers and consequently an important commercial catch. A species of salmon in northeast Asia is the mau (*Oncorhynchus masou*), the smallest member of the *Salmonidae* family. It takes three or four years for a mau salmon to reach maturity, at which point it will weigh about ten pounds.

Landlocked Salmon

A landlocked body of water is precisely that: fresh lakes and stream water that is locked in by land, cut off from the seas or oceans. Landlocked species of salmon do not migrate, but instead mature and spawn in freshwater. Some varieties successfully introduced into waters include landlocked coho salmon, which are abundant in the Great Lakes. Native Eurasian species of landlocked salmon, such as the huchen and taimen, populate some French rivers, the Volga basin, and Siberian waters. Many coastal waters, lakes, and rivers are stocked with salmon. These will not thrive and reproduce successfully like the landlocked coho salmon, which were transplanted in the Great Lakes. Very few places (New Zealand being one) have succeeded in transplanting a permanent salmon population outside of its proprietary waterways.

Atlantic landlocked salmon populate waters in the northeast United States, eastern Canada, Australia, New Zealand, and Argentina. In Maine, I fish for salmon in Sebago Lake, home of the ouananiche, or Sebago salmon. Now let's get to know the Atlantic salmon.

Life Cycle of the Atlantic Salmon (genus *Salmo salar*)

Understanding the life cycles of the fish and animals you choose to fish or hunt—whether with rod and reel, gun, bow and arrow, or camera—is important to the outdoorswoman. It is especially important to the salmon fisher. Recognizing the stages of growth enables the angler to approximate the age of the fish. The color, shape, and size of the adult fish tell you where the salmon has been and where it is going. The time of the year and the hour of the day tell you what fishing techniques and lures are most likely to get the salmon to take your hook. Granted, there's always beginner's luck. But even the novice woman angler should go out for her first salmon with at least a basic knowledge of the fish. It will only enhance the challenge ahead. More important, you'll garner a great respect for the salmon you hook. That fish has gone through a great deal to get to that precise moment in its life when it is fighting you on an artificial fly. Here's how it all began. . . .

Spawning

In the fall, female salmon will swim from the ocean upstream to their native habitat, and spawn. Like many wild animals, such as deer, which live their entire lives within one square mile of where they are born, salmon will return to their home stream, even after journeys of thousands of ocean miles, to deposit their eggs. These fish know precisely where they belong: their instinct is like an internal homing device that signals them back to their old neighborhood.

When the female is ready to lay her eggs (roe), she digs several spawning beds about half a foot deep in the river bottom to insure that her eggs will be hidden from hungry fish. This is referred to as "cutting a bed" and can take hours, even days, until the female is content with her labors. While the male stands guard, the female lies on her side, flourishing and swishing her tail until she has dug a saucer-shaped nest deep in the gravel, where she lays her eggs. The male then fertilizes them with his sperm (milt), and the female covers the nest with silt and gravel. The couple will perform this procedure several more times within close proximity to the first nest, during which time the female will spawn between 2,000 and 10,000 eggs. Over 95 percent of salmon roe will be successfully fertilized by the male's milt. The area that includes all the beds the female has cut is called a "redd." During the winter months, the eggs lie dormant. Salmon eggs are a peachy-pink color, the size of a fresh green pea, and are suspended in a yolk sac that provides them with nourishment. They hatch after three to four months, come spring.

The Youngster Stages

The eggs begin to grow into baby salmon, or *alevins,* in the spring, when the water begins to warm. At this stage, the hundreds of alevins slip through the river-bottom blanket their mother had covered them with and, remaining together, seek shelter together in "schools." They feed on microorganisms such as plankton and small insects, and those that survive being eaten by fish and birds grow into *fry.* It is during the fry stage that baby salmon absorb their yolk sac. When it reaches about the length of a finger, the youngster salmon is known as a *fingerling.*

The "Teenage" Stage

The fingerling in turn grows into a *parr* and begins to take on its elegant coloration: a rosy belly and silver-gray back. Vertical bars, or "parr-marks," appear on either side of its body. A parr is easily mistaken for a brook trout. You can distinguish a parr from a brook trout by its tail: a parr has more of a forked tail than the "brookie." The parr will live in the river for more than a year, graduating to more solid food, such as insects and nymphs. The larger it grows, the farther it swims downstream, moving closer to the sea. By the time it reaches the estuary, its parr-marks have faded and the fish takes on its full adult coloration. When this happens, the fish is ready and waits for the tide to carry it out to sea. Now it is called a *smolt,* or *grilse.* Grilse will spend a year or more of growth at sea, and weigh between two and nine pounds. Most average around five or six pounds. In the ocean, they remain close together in schools. This is a dangerous time for grilse. Very few salmon survive this stage. Predators—diving birds such as seagulls and cormorants and other fish, like sea trout—will eat small salmon, leaving only a small percentage of the hatch to grow and eventually wend its way to salt water. Poaching, commercial fishing, polluted water, and man-made reservoirs plunder the lion's share of the salmon population. Conservation practices such as escapement and new designs for dams and fish ladders, coupled with strictly enforced salmon fishing regulations, have, in recent years, helped to limit and even abolish some of the flagrant practices that affected the survival of this magnificent fish. Nonetheless, those that survive know what to do and where to go when the time comes.

Adult Salmon

The point at which a grilse is considered an adult salmon has a lot to do with the river from which it comes. On the Miramichi in New Brunswick, a fish that's spent one year at sea, weighs over five pounds, and measures over 25 inches is called a "salmon." Chances are good that you'll catch a fully adult salmon in the Miramachi, but it's far more likely that you'll catch a grilse. Although this has much to do with survival rate and commercial netting in the estuary, a grilse usually takes the first fly, while an adult salmon is more cunning to catch.*

Note: Strict rules apply to each and every waterway for fishing that tell you what size a fish must be to be caught and kept, or released back into the river. Many rivers require

Some salmon will stay in the sea six months and others up to four or even five years before first returning to their river. They invariably will navigate back to the very stream in which they were hatched. Considering the incredible distances they travel—again, 2,000 miles or more—biologists seem to believe that the fish are capable of reading the currents and magnetic field of the earth in order to hone in on their home waters. By the time they do return, they will, of course, be large, fully grown adult fish. During their ocean stay, salmon eat shrimp, squid, and small fish. They cease eating altogether when they return to freshwater and live off the fat stored in their bodies. They do not eat again until they return to the ocean. One theory is that their sexual organs develop when they return to freshwater, and male and female salmon become totally absorbed in their mating rituals.

The rule of thumb is that the size of a salmon is proportionate to the size of the river. The Miramichi is a relatively narrow, winding river. A 30-pound salmon caught on the Miramichi is an extraordinarily large catch. On larger Canadian rivers, such as the Restigouche, a major-leaguer will weigh 40 pounds or more. The Canadian record for a salmon caught on a fly was 55 pounds taken in the Grand Cascapedia River in Quebec. Seventy-pound salmon are frequently caught in Norway.

Biologists conjecture that an identifying composition defines every waterway, and sections of that waterway. They maintain that the water's pressure, taste, smell, and the underwater landscape enable a salmon to determine its home—which would lead the layman to assume that salmon, therefore, have optic, auditory, olfactory, and other perceptive senses. Whatever guides them home, the salmon will return from the sea to the very tributary where they were born. Be it instinct, a miracle, or a mystery, it's simply the way of the salmon.

The fact that the salmon can absorb this information through its innate abilities, added to the general observation that salmon possess intellect, helps us understand just what we are dealing with when we fish for salmon. That is why I freely use the word *stalk,* which is a word generally associated with hunting wild game animals. Atlantic salmon are smart, defensive, and possess animal-like senses.

---

by law that you fish with a guide, and he or she will explain the rules before you even step foot in your waders. Whether or not you fish with a guide, it is your obligation to fully understand and follow the rules of the river. As a general guide, this book follows the Department of Natural Resources salmon regulations for Nova Scotia—but remember that rules and regulations will vary from province to province, state to state, and country to country.

Salmon Waters

You've chosen salmon as your quarry. Although you are not hunting with a rifle, shotgun, or bow, you *are* hunting with a rod, reel, and lure. You are hunting from a different angle: Pardon the pun, but you are, after all, a woman angler. And let me remind you once again: as you prepare to challenge the champion of fish in nature's arena, you're going in as the underdog. To get the edge, you now need to know about the salmon's natural environment.

The Seasons of the River

The time of year that salmon run upstream depends largely on the individual river, and the conditions in the river at a particular time. When salmon run it is called a *peak period*. Peak periods can vary from river to river, but the peak period of any given river never varies. Locals and fishermen who have been fishing a particular river for years and years can guess when a salmon run will begin and end almost to the day. A river like the Miramichi is called an autumn river, because the salmon will run upstream in the fall. Like everything else with a salmon, the time of its annual run upstream stays the same, year in and year out, almost to the hour.

When salmon run upstream, they must brave turbulent waters, such as falls and chutes, and obstacles such as ledges. If you have ever been caught in a strong current while swimming, you know how powerful the water can be. Imagine how it is for a salmon, racing against raging river currents and high waters! The salmon knows, by sheer instinct, to look for the quietest sections of the river, making its way over rocks and ledges, steering clear of fast water, and—when there is no choice but to jump—leaping staggering heights (one biologist measured a salmon jump of 11 feet 4 inches) as they continue on their journey. Salmon will run at night, at dusk, and at daybreak, but take the daytime to rest in quiet pools and reenergize for the next leg of their trip.

Black Salmon

"Black" salmon are also called "kelts," "spent fish," or "unclean fish" because they have spent all their food reserves and are emaciated. Their scales have a dull, silvery color. Black salmon spend the winter in the river after they spawn, and come spring, when the ice breaks and the waters begin to warm, they run downstream to the ocean. Many anglers feel that black salmon are not good sport fish, but the fact is they fight just as hard as when they are in peak physical condition after feeding for several months in the ocean. Granted, they are lean—almost emaciated—and the flesh is not as tasty, perhaps, as when they first return from the ocean. But you'd be foolish to expect a black salmon to give in easily. You'll be lucky to bring him in in under a half hour. The water is fast and furious during spring runoff, and you'll be fishing from a boat. It's often quite cold, so be prepared.

You can hook anywhere between a half-dozen and a couple dozen black salmon in one day, without too much concern about the fly pattern you use. Most of the fish you catch you'll release—they're either over 25 inches and must be released by law, or too small to keep. There is a difference in philosophy among some seasoned salmon anglers as to the merits of fishing for black salmon. Since only a few are kept and many more are released, there has been concern that the fish, having put up a tremendous fight in an already winter-weakened condition, may not have enough strength to survive in the ocean once it runs, or possibly even drifts, downstream. Black salmon that survive their journey to the sea and eventually return to the river, however, become the kind of trophy fish that every angler dreams about. On the Miramichi, for instance, there is speculation that approximately 12 percent of all black salmon that survive their ocean voyage will return to the river in trophy condition and size.

Bright Salmon

"Bright" salmon are summer and fall fish that return to the river in splendid, healthy condition. These are the way the fish are portrayed in sporting art. They are pink and plump, having spent several months gorging themselves on shrimp, squid, and small fish, and have achieved a length over 25 inches. Soon after they enter the river, however, their condition begins to deteriorate. This is when biologists figure that the fish are living off their reserves and focusing on their sex lives. They stop eating altogether, and if a perfectly placed fly happens to bounce off the nose of a salmon, it may bite purely out of instinct or curiosity, not out of hunger. Fishing for bright salmon is far more difficult than fishing for black salmon for this reason: the fish are not hungry. This is why expert placement of a fly is so crucial to successful fishing during the summer and fall. Even the best fly fisherman can easily walk away from the river with nary a bite.

Fishing the Miramichi

I woke up one day to discover that my son was a young man and that eighteen years had, quite unexpectedly, seemed to have slipped by in a New York minute. Soon he would leave home. I was not ready to say good-bye. I needed time to forge some more memories. And so, together we journeyed to the Miramichi to go Atlantic salmon fishing.

The drive from our home in Freedom, New Hampshire, to the Little Sou'west Miramichi takes eleven hours, but we were blessed with a beautiful spring day, and my son Tommy and I were excited about going to this legendary river to catch black Atlantic salmon. André and Susan Godin's fishing and hunting lodge, the Miramichi Inn, is famous the world over, attracting sportsmen and sportswomen from France, England, Germany, and just about every Canadian province and American state. We knew to expect a sportsman's paradise because friends of ours had highly recommended the place. But we weren't prepared for the warm welcome when, weary and worn, we arrived at dinnertime. André, Susan, and their chef, Patrice, greeted us as though we were long lost family. And the amazing thing was, we felt like we were.

The inn overlooks a portion of the Miramichi River known as the "Little Sou'west," a salmon-rich tributary that juts off the main river. Although small villages dot its banks, by and large the countryside is as untamed as the river itself. The Miramichi, as we would soon discover, has a life of its own.

Tommy and I were fed, shown our rooms, and tucked into bed. We slept, but we knew we would be up before dawn. We had come to fish. And the salmon were running.

It was still dark outside when André's strongly accented Quebec voice woke me from a deep sleep. "Breakfast! Time to get up and eat! The fish, they won't wait for you, you know." Tommy was already up

and dressed. Our guides, Timmy and Jerry Stewart, were already waiting for us. I gulped down a cup of coffee. I would wait for Patrice's
gourmet food until lunchtime. After all, my son and I had come to
fish—and as André said, the fish, they wouldn't wait.

A person who is not a resident of the province cannot legally fish its
rivers without being in the company of a licensed fishing guide. The
brothers Stewart were both licensed guides. So were their seven brothers, many uncles, countless cousins, and the one man they loved, perhaps, above all others—their father, known as "the fly man from the
Little Sou'west Miramichi." But he had died exactly a year before, and
by the end of my time on the Miramichi, I would mourn the opportunity to have met such a man, loved by so many and so well.

It was desperately cold when Jerry and Timmy stowed our rods and
gear into the back of their respective trucks. They had rigged our rods
while we were dressing. The brothers both agreed they had never
known late May to be so cold. They even had heard reports of snow. It
was dark and gray as the sun attempted to rise, but it, too, seemed re-
luctant to awaken. It was bitterly cold. The northwest wind shook the
trees, rustling limbs that had yet to even show a remote sign of bursting
into fresh, young shoots and green buds.

Tommy and I parted—he with Jerry, and off I went with Timmy.
Timmy is slightly younger than I—well, okay, five years younger. He is
the father of a relatively small family of three. The average family from
this neck of the northern New Brunswick woods numbers eight or nine
children, frequently more. This is Catholic country, so by and large the
children are the fruit of one marriage.

Timmy drove about three miles from the inn and parked his truck
at his home, which overlooks the Miramichi. We crossed the road and
he directed me down a steep bank to where his boat was beached on-
shore. It was a wide, wooden, flat-bottom boat and had the comfortable—and later I would add protective—bucket seat from an old truck
for me to sit in. Timmy was especially proud of the motor on his boat.
It was, he said, the best and biggest motor on the river.

We were going to be fishing from a boat, but I wore my neoprene
waders anyway. They are very warm, and I was very cold. That, plus a
couple of sweaters under a down vest and a heavy parka to top it all off,
restricted my movement, to say the least, but I did manage to get into
the boat.

Timmy revved the motor and over the din told me that we were going to go downriver to a little footbridge. Although many members of
Timmy's family owned river frontage, the sheer numbers of family
members—I think Timmy told me there were 86—made this part of the

river Stewart Country. The footbridge was the southern limit of what they considered their "territory." And everyone in the area pretty much agreed with that, too.

"The fish are really running," Timmy beamed from under the hood of his jacket. "They're hungry. You'll catch good fish today. But they'll be lean. That's how it is with black salmon. They've not eaten since the fall—some not since before summer," he continued with the kind of Scottish accent common among the non-French local population throughout the province. He stopped the boat and let out the anchor. I cast my line and within seconds felt a sure tug on my fly. Timmy had tied a "Black Ghost" salmon fly to my line. I would end up fishing nothing but a Black Ghost for the next couple of days.

"I think it's a trout," Timmy said as I played the fish, certain it was an offspring of Moby Dick.

"No, no!" I cried. "It *has* to be a salmon!"

"I believe it's a trout, Laurie." Timmy grinned. "You just keep your rod tip up, that's it, and reel him on in. There you go . . . He's pouting now . . . See him coming to the surface? Why, you've hooked a lovely rainbow."

I was delighted, salmon or no salmon, and I knew at that instant that I had questioned my guide for the first and last time. Soon I would learn that men like Timmy who were born and bred on the Miramichi understand the river and can read it like a book. They know the language. A good guide, like Timmy Stewart, serves as an interpreter for the people he guides.

Timmy pulled up the anchor and we made our way upstream. All the commotion involved in landing that trout meant that we had disturbed the waters. Most likely any fish that had been in the immediate area had taken off.

No one else was on the river except Timmy and me. Tommy and Jerry had gone farther upstream and were far out of sight. Once again Timmy revved the motor and went upstream about a hundred yards. Again he dropped anchor. He started to teach me how to read the water. I could see the current traveling rapidly down in an **S** formation, skirting rocks and boulders that dotted both shorelines. Where the water was darkest, it was deepest. Where there were white caps, the water was fastest. It was hard to say where the fish would be running, but chances are they would be traveling with the current. I cast and noticed that the wind had carried my fly farther than I had expected. It landed in whitewater, but nothing bit. I retrieved my line and cast again. And again. This time Timmy pointed to quieter water closer to the bank. "You cannot tell where they'll be unless you see them jump out of the water or get a bite. If you do, chances are his friends are not far off." At that moment a salmon jumped a foot out of the river, arching its spine, and diving back into the fast current. It looked all and all like the photographs I had seen in *Field & Stream,* and I stood in the boat, amazed and humbled.

Slowly Timmy pushed the boat here, then there, using his paddle as a pole. By now we were close to the shore, so the water was relatively shallow. Then we drifted a little downriver again and tried other pools that looked promising. No fish took my fly.

And then it happened, more suddenly than I had expected—and that's the thing. Until you hook an Atlantic salmon on a fly, you don't really know what to expect until you've experienced it. The fish took my fly with such force that I almost lost my rod. "Set your hook!" Timmy cried. "You've got a big one!"

I was unprepared for what happened next. My reel screamed as length after length of fly line flew out of the spool. Had I touched the reel I believe it would have burned me from the friction as the salmon ran fast and furiously away from the boat. "Do not touch your reel— don't touch it, Laurie!" Timmy screamed over the noise. "It can break your finger! Let him take your line, you've got plenty. Let him run. Wait for him to slow down a bit and then reel in. But not now . . . not yet."

It seemed like forever before the shriek of the line subsided a bit. "All right, now reel him in . . . Keep your rod tip up . . . Steady, that's it."

Whrrr . . . ! Again the line went screaming.

"Let it go, Laurie. Let go of the reel. He has to run. If you try to hold him he'll break your line and you'll lose him."

Again I let the line screech, again the reel seemed too hot to touch. I had been holding the rod with both hands and the fighting butt of my Orvis #9 was pressed against my hip. If I had thought my trout was a son of Moby Dick, by now I was convinced I had hooked Ahab's original antagonist.

Now the fight was on. The fish would stop running and I would reel in a little. Again he'd run, and again I'd reel in a little more line. Fifteen minutes, maybe more, passed before I had the faintest hint that my rival was getting tired. I should have been exhausted myself, but the adrenaline was pumping and I was totally caught up by the thrill of the hunt. Although the fish was neither a deer or a game bird, I was the hunter and it was the hunted. The victor would be determined by who was strongest—and who had the greatest will. I knew that I would triumph over the fish; I also felt the rules of the contest were fair. I had come to the fish in its territory, in its environment. I was the stranger, I was unfamiliar with this watery arena. I was terrified, but determined to see the contest to its end.

And so we struggled on for an eternity, but in the end my first Atlantic salmon surrendered. I had played it well. I had used my rod and maneuvered my line to my advantage. I had won the prize, which lay in the water alongside the boat. The salmon was silvery, majestic, fully a yard long. Thin from a long winter without feeding, he was, nonetheless, a substantial fish. "A three-year-old," Timmy beamed. "A fine fellow."

Timmy carefully captured the salmon in his net and brought him into our boat; and even more carefully he removed the hook from the noble fish's mouth. Salmon fishing is, as I said, "the sport of kings." It is wiser to acknowledge that salmon, especially fine salmon like mine, are kings of the waters.

The law forbids the keeping of such large fish. Later I would catch several grilse, Atlantic salmon that were fully a foot shorter and two years younger than this king that I had caught. Were there no such a law, had I a choice in keeping the fish or not, I cannot say. All I know is that my salmon gave me a far greater gift than my pitifully inadequate words can express. Along with the memories, that salmon—the first salmon I ever caught—has a special place in my heart.

I released my fish and he swam away, swept up by a strong current in high water, on a bitterly cold spring day. He will live as long as I do, in my mind's eye, as one of the most beautiful creatures I have ever beheld.

So caught up was I in my own little drama that I did not hear Tommy and Jerry come alongside us in their boat. Tommy was beaming. He had caught and tagged two grilse, and he had caught a trout. I could tell from the expression on his face, however, that there was something more. Tommy, too, had caught a three-year-old adult salmon. Although we had not been fishing together, we achieved the thing I had hoped for—doing something we enjoyed, in a place that was astoundingly beautiful.

We returned to the Miramichi Inn at dusk. We were cold and hungry. Patrice had been cooking all afternoon, and Susan had been baking all day. The aroma of baking bread hit us like a down pillow the moment we walked into the stunning timber lodge that André had designed and constructed in the course of 20 years. I went to my room, took off my outer clothes, and lay down on my bed. The next thing I knew, Tommy was shaking me by the shoulder. "Wake up, Mom," he said. "We've been calling you for ten minutes. Dinner's on the table."

I don't remember falling asleep. But I'll never forget my first of many dinners I've since enjoyed at the Miramichi Inn. In fact, you're in for a real treat: Chef Patrice shares his recipe with us for Salmon Scallop with Lemon Pepper Sauce. (See page 90 at the end of this chapter.)

The following day, Tommy and I again woke up to André's kindly summons, and to our horror saw that the weather was even more intimidating that the day before. "Oh, no," Tommy moaned. "Another cold day."

We ate a delicious breakfast, marveling at the fact that we had room after stuffing ourselves the night before, and again followed Jerry and Timmy into their respective trucks. I took my now familiar seat in Timmy's boat, and off we went.

"The fish won't bite," Timmy shook his head. "The wind is coming from the east. Fish don't bite in an east wind."

"Why not?" I asked.

"They just don't. Some old folk say it has to do with the riffles on the water when the wind brushes against the current. I think it's something else. I think the fish listen to the wind, and the wind tells them secrets."

"What kinds of secrets?"

"Nothing we would understand. It has something to do with the river, though. She's alive to those of us who live here. There's something powerful in the river. Sometimes she's soothing, sometimes she's angry. But she takes care of her own."

"What do you mean?" I asked.

Timmy paused, as though thinking back into his past. But he reached a little beyond.

"Here's a story," he continued, "about a couple of men my father knew. They lived on the river. They were both born on the river. They were best friends as children, and they worked together as adults. Both were guides during the fishing season, and in the winter they timbered the woods.

"One day in early April, just when the ice was beginning to melt and flow downriver, the two friends decided to paddle upstream in a wooden canoe they had built. No one understands to this day why they did. They both should have known better. The river was high and running fast, and there were great chunks of ice that were being carried down with the current.

"Both men were excellent swimmers. In fact, one of the men was well known for his swimming ability. They got in the canoe and paddled upstream toward the rapids. Now, no one goes near the rapids, even in the summer when the water is low and quiet. They got within a stone's throw of the rapids when suddenly the canoe got caught up in the current and capsized. One of the friends managed to swim to shore, but when he got there, his friend—the good swimmer—was nowhere to be found. He ran as fast as he could for help, and the townsfolk searched and searched. After a couple of days, the search was given up. He had *drowned.*

"Weeks passed, then months. One day the body of the drowned man was discovered—washed up on the shore on his own land, in front of his own cottage—the house where he was born. People around here say that the river took care of her child, and brought him home.

"All my life I have lived on the river, and I believe what folks say is true. I believe the river takes care of her children. When I have worries, I come to the river. You can solve a lot of problems on the river."

In the middle of the afternoon of the second day, I looked up at the sky and said to Timmy, "I believe it's going to snow." At that moment the sky began to spit snow as if it were early December.

"I've never seen it snow this late." Timmy chuckled.

"My luck," I said, grimacing.

That day I caught a grilse, but it wasn't near the sport I had the previous day. Tommy caught a couple of nice trout. We returned to the lodge exhausted and happy, ready for another meal by Chef Patrice.

It was dark when, unexpectedly, Jerry and Timmy returned to the lodge. Both had talked at length about their father. He was a great fisherman, a lover of the woods, and most especially, a son of the Miramichi. Although he had a limited education, he was a great scholar of the ways of nature and the ways of his river. His legacy was his large family and the love that he and his wife had given every child and grandchild. I have seldom, if ever, met a family bound by such limitless love and devotion.

Delbert Stewart was considered one of the greatest guides the Miramichi ever produced. He tied flies. Not hundreds, but thousands of flies. His children estimated he tied 40,000 flies during his lifetime. Fly-tying was his hobby and his life—guiding fishermen like me—was his avocation as well as his vocation. Jerry and Timmy came after supper on our last night at the Miramichi to give me this poem. It was written by a granddaughter of Delbert Stewart, Janet Stewart Savard.

The Fly Man from the Little Sou'west

They called him the fly man from the Little Sou'west
Everyone knew that his flys were the best.
His talent to tie hooks was legend to all.
They wanted his creations for spring and for fall.

He would sit at a table covered with furs and thread,
With hooks, pliers, and a light by his head.
His hands prided in the jewels they made,
To his family and friends these treasures he gave.

He was much more than the fly man we all knew,
He was father, a husband, and a grandfather, too.
He was loved by his wife, children, and friends.
We all mourned the time his life came to an end.

But his fly-tying hands have gone to rest,
Because God loves to fish and he wanted the best.

We love you, Fly Man, and always will.

Delbert Eugene Stewart (1924–1995)

Tommy and I would return to the Little Sou'west Miramichi that August. This time we brought my younger son, Winty, and my husband, Tom. We were after bright salmon. And we knew that fishing for bright Atlantic salmon in August required the expert casting and the most delicate presentation. We accepted the challenge. We couldn't wait. But that's another story.

Chef Patrice's Salmon Scallop
with Lemon Pepper Sauce

The Miramichi Inn
Little Sou'west Miramichi
Red Bank, New Brunswick

Clean a whole salmon and cut at a 45-degree angle perpendicular to the spinal cord, just behind the head. Use a long-nose pliers to remove the spine and take out the bones. You can use frozen salmon if fresh is not available.

3 tablespoons chilled butter
⅛ cup chopped scallions
1 cup dry white wine
½ cup fish juice
juice and zest from three fresh lemons
crushed seasalt, to taste, or regular salt
crushed black peppercorn, to taste
1 cup whipping cream (about 250 ml.)
fine cognac
minced chives (to taste)
salmon caviar (optional) as garnish, about 1 tablespoon or
    to taste

The Sauce

Melt the butter in a saucepan over medium/low heat. Add scallions and sauté. Add white wine and heat, stirring occasionally, until the mixture is reduced by half. Add fish juice and lemon juice. Again reduce the mixture by half over medium/low heat. Add the lemon zest, seasalt, and pepper to taste. Next add the cream, but make sure it does not boil. Let the sauce reduce some more. When it coats the back of the spoon, it should be ready. Make sure it is not too runny, not too thick. Splash a dash of fine cognac into the saucepan.

While you are preparing the sauce, steam the salmon fillets until the flesh is firm and white, but comes off gently with a fork. This will not take long, ten minutes more or less, depending upon the size and thickness of the fillets.

On plates that have warmed in the oven, arrange the salmon. Pour sauce over the salmon until the fillets are fully covered. Add a tablespoon of good salmon caviar, if desired, and garnish with minced chives. Serve immediately with a side dish of rice and steamed, fresh vegetables, preferably just picked from the garden.

▬

Fishing Facts You Should Know

Here are some important tips, rules, and techniques you should know before heading for the water.

How to Weigh a Fish

Measure the length of the fish.
Measure the girth of the fish at its widest point.
Multiply the length by the girth squared.
Divide by 800.

Example: The formula for an
18-inch fish with a 9-inch girth is:
$18 \times 9 \times 9 = 1{,}458$ divided by $800 = 1.82$ pounds

Landing a Fish Without a Net

This is a gentle and sporting way to catch and release a fish with a minimum of shock or harm.

1. Play the fish until it is exhausted and lying on its side.

2. Bring the fish near the boat or to your feet.

3. Wet your hands.

4. Maneuver the fish so you can securely grasp it.

When you scoop a fish out of the water with a net or with dry hands, or handle the fish excessively, the protective slime that coats the skin will rub off. A fungus infection spreads over the abrased area and, in time, will kill the fish. If you use a net, use one with Dacron® mesh, such as Orvis' Madison trout net. *Always* be certain your hands are wet before you handle a fish.

Fishing Seasons and State Rules and Regulations

Every state announces the dates its fishing season will open and close shortly before opening day each year. These dates differ from state to state and are determined by the state's wildlife service. Wildlife biologists monitor the health and size of populations and rate of propagation of the indigenous species of fish living in the state's native rivers, streams, ponds, lakes, and boundary waters, as well as its coastal waters and waterways, if a state abuts the ocean. Usually there is a general season for open fishing and separate, shorter seasons that pertain to certain species. When dates are determined, they are posted along with rules called "open water fishing regulations," in a booklet published annually by the state's Fish and Game Department or Department of Inland Fisheries and Wildlife. These annual fishing digests are free of charge and are available at most sporting goods stores, tackle shops, and from all places that issue fishing licenses. These booklets also contain a great deal of additional, important, and valuable information such as daily bag and minimum weight and length limits, provisions for fishing most rivers, lakes, ponds, and streams within each county, special regulations regarding boundary waters between states, and for states that border Mexico or Canada. In addition, boating laws are specified and helpful tips on methods of fishing, fish identification, catch-and-release fishing, and sunrise and sunset tables are also included in most digests.

Saltwater digests are available in states that abut coastal waters. These contain separate regulations for commercial and leisure sport saltwater fishing, as well as details on gear marking, reporting requirements, and tide tables, and some things that apply to saltwater fishing that do not pertain to freshwater fishing.

Fishing Licenses

Whether you are fishing in your home state or out-of-state, fishing regulations apply to you. You must buy a resident fishing license if you plan to fish in your state of residence, and a nonresident license if you plan to fish out-of-state. The only exceptions apply to resident owners of farmland and their minor children: they may fish without a resident license on waters located on, or running through, the land on which their home is located. I live on an old farm in the country, and a small stream runs below our lower field. I can fish that stream without a license, but if I fish off of my property, I need a resident license. One of our best fishing rivers, the Ossipee, crosses the border near one of the oldest bridges in New Hampshire, the Huntress Bridge. If I fish off the west side of the Huntress, I am fishing in New Hampshire. If I fish off the east side of the bridge, I am fishing in Maine. If I fish off both sides of the bridge, I need a resident license for New Hampshire and a nonresident license for Maine. It's not uncommon to find general stores located close to state borders that can sell you licenses for both states. License fees and requirements are listed in the front of state fishing digests. Fishing licenses are valid January 1 through December 31 of each year. They can be purchased from license agents, the Fish and Game Department, and some town or city clerks.

Resident Licenses

There are several types of licenses for residents. In order to qualify as a resident, you must reside in the state for six months immediately prior to application for a license and claim residency in no other state for any purpose, and you must be prepared to supply an acceptable proof of residency. Most states offer a lifetime resident hunting and fishing license for residents between the ages of 18 and 68. There is usually no specified fee for this type of license. Your license fee is determined by your age.

The most expensive annual license is a combination hunting and fishing license that is good for one calendar year. My home state of New Hampshire has something called a Super Sportsman's license. For $8 more, you can buy this type of resident license. Wildlife Management and Fisheries split your $8 contribution, and federal funding for management projects match your dollar with three of theirs. Therefore, your Super Sportsman license adds $32 to wildlife management and conservation. As with all licenses that include hunting, you must have a previous hunting license or a hunter's safety card, which proves you have successfully passed a hunter's safety course. Note that some states, such as Colorado, will not issue a hunting or combination hunting and fishing license unless you produce a hunter's safety card. A current or previous hunting license from your home state is not acceptable where mandatory hunter's safety cards are required.

If you do not hunt, you can buy just a fishing license. You can buy a fishing license that allows you to fish for all species. Another type of license restricts you from fishing for certain warm-water species; it's about $5 cheaper than an all-species fishing license. If you want to introduce the family to a day of fishing, you can buy a one-day, all-species license that's good for everyone, no matter how many are in your family—but it's only good for one day. There are special permits that you can buy as well. In New Hampshire, for example, the state offers an Atlantic salmon brood stock permit for $10. This entitles you to fish specific areas where a healthy brood stock population is controlled by the state fisheries department. A permit is required for children as well, but if your child is under 16, the permit is free. And if you have reached the exalted age of 68, you are entitled to a resident fishing license for free, providing you have been a resident of your state for over two years.

Nonresident Licenses

A nonresident can purchase a nonresident hunting and fishing license, a nonresident fishing license, a family fishing license, or an Atlantic salmon brook stock permit. Also available to the nonresident angler is a three-day, seven-day, or fifteen-day fishing license. If you have a child between the ages of 12 and 16, you can purchase a nonresident junior license for your son or daughter.

Catch-and-Release

It is an unwritten sportsman's creed to catch and keep only the fish you plan to eat—providing it's within legal limit. The fish you keep must be within the legal weight and length specified by state regulations, and you cannot exceed the daily limit of fish allowed for the species you are fishing. Keep in mind the following tips for the fish you decide to catch and release.

- **Play a fish as quickly as possible.** Once it is hooked, it expends a great of energy putting up a good fight. Do not tire a fish unnecessarily.

- **Release a fish as soon as you land it.** A fish should spend as little time as possible out of water. A fish suffocates when it is out of water for very long.

- **Be certain your hands are wet before handling a fish.** Dry hands can wipe the slimy protective film from a fish's body, permitting a harmful fungus infection to take hold that will kill the fish in time. If you catch a fish with a net, be sure the netting is fine and soft, not abrasive. Abrasive netting, like dry hands, can damage a fish's skin.

- **Handle the fish as little as possible.** Do not allow it to flop around on the bottom of your boat. Do not squeeze the fish. This can lead to injuries that will lessen its chances of survival when it is returned to the water.

How to Hold a Fish

Once upon a time, one way of catching trout in England was to tickle them on their bellies. This calmed them so much that they then could easily be taken out of the water. "Trout tickling" is no longer practiced today, but the fact is, there are ways you can hold a fish out of water once you have landed it. One method is to hold it around the middle and upside down. This calms the fish. Another way to hold a fish is head up, with your hand holding the fish gently under the gills. This also steadies the fish.

How to Remove a Hook from a Fish's Mouth

One of the most useful tools in fishing is a small pliers designed specifically to remove hooks from the fish's mouth. This is especially useful if the hook is deep down the throat of a fish, or hooked into the side of his lip. If you do not have a pliers, use your thumb and forefinger to loose the hook and gently wriggle it back until it pulls out. If you cannot disengage a hook, cut the leader as close to the hook as possible. It will rust or fall out by itself. On my first salmon fishing trip in New Brunswick, Canada, I caught and kept a nice grilse. When my guide and I gutted the fish, we were amazed to find a large, silver hook glistening inside its belly. My guide exclaimed he had never seen a salmon that had swallowed a hook whole in his many years as a fishing guide.

Once a fish is out of water, it suffers a bit of shock. There's a way you must return it to the water that will make it gentle on the fish. Hold the fish by putting one hand under its jaw and your other hand between its belly and tail. Lower it into the water and gently move its body back and forth, in a swimming-like manner. He'll catch on, and sooner or later swim away under his own steam.

Water Temperature

Fishing can be a four-season sport, but most anglers fish between April 1 and October 15 (depending upon the state you're fishing in and the species you're fishing), when the weather is pleasant and the fish are at their most energetic. There are prime times to fish, depending upon the species, but optimum fishing always happens when the water temperature falls between 58 and 63 degrees. Fish are cold-blooded animals. Their body temperature is regulated by the temperature of the water. When the water is cold, their body temperature is low and they tend not to bite. As the water warms, and their body temperature warms, they become revived and hungry. When the water is too warm, their body temperature rises and they become lethargic again. Then the fish will seek out the coldest water available, which is usually at the bottom of lakes and in deep pockets of streams. To reach them, you have to fish deeper, down toward the bottom.

In a way, fish behave a lot like people do. When spring finally arrives after a long winter, we break out of doors, kick up our heels, and frolic. Same with fish. They swim downstream at the first sign of winter ice-out and spring runoff, when the river waters are high and flood their banks, and the current sweeps them to sea and the banquet that awaits them after many months of not eating. Lake and landlocked fish seek the warmer top layer of water, which is also where hatches and other food is happening on or close to the surface.

The hot summer sun makes us lethargic and slow. Fish, too, become slow-moving and are apt to lay in the bottom of the water and seek deep, cool pools, dark pockets of water, or hidden places. Fish do not feed at all, or very little, during the summer and will only strike at a lure out of curiosity or some say out of anger, if perturbed.

In autumn, when the weather gets cooler, we busy ourselves as we prepare for winter. So do fish. Many species will spawn during this time of the year; other species make the journey upstream from the sea, where they will settle for the winter. Lake and landlocked species also perk up as the water cools down, and will begin to rise to shallower water levels again and have a renewed interest in feeding.

Chapter 10

Inshore Fishing

*Whenever I find myself growing grim about the mouth; whenever
it is a damp, drizzly November in my soul . . . I account it
high time to get to sea as soon as I can.*

—Herman Melville, *Moby Dick*

A Reason to Revel

Where does it come from, that desire to drop everything, grab a
rod, get on the water, and go fishing? For many women—and
many men—fishing is a passion, yet the sport can be secondary to
something deep inside; and sometimes it is not anything that can be put
into words. Perhaps it is a need to quench a fire that burns in the belly,
or to mend a wound that wants healing—or, quite simply, to soothe a
tired soul. The driving force that moves a woman to go fishing cannot
be put into words, nor is the reason the same for every woman.

Over the passage of time and knowing many people and places, I learned that, more often than not, the love for the sport was incidental to the need for the sport. It was not about catching fish. It was not about casting a line. It was the inexplicable desire to be somewhere serene where a woman could become part of something far larger than herself. To stand in a quiet stream, or look upon a boundless ocean to the distant horizon—this is as much a gift as a mortal has any right to expect. Should she cast a line and catch a fish, that fish becomes a token—something, if even for a fleeting moment—she can hold on to. There's wonderment in these private, precious moments. No matter how simple it may seem to stand in a quiet stream, or look upon a boundless ocean to the distant horizon, in its simplicity, the natural world that surrounds us has the power to turn our lives around.

And so I traveled my road, and listened to women anglers along the way . . .

"Have you ever seen the sun rise over Goose Island? Nightfall bows in deference to the dawn as the sun peaks over the horizon. First dawn is just a blush, then it ripens like a peach and bursts into an explosion of color. It kisses the treetops, reflects in the water, and tints the low-growing shrubs along the shoreline, all purples and pinks then white-hot yellows. This is the best time to go fishing. This is where I go alone and recharge my soul; and if I catch a fish, it's a bonus . . ."
—*"Carol," 64, widowed, proud grandmother of six, who successfully underwent bypass surgery two years ago*

"My career landed me smack in the middle of a man's world. My work consumes my weekdays and often cuts into my weekends. I've been married to a great guy for about three years. He loves to hunt and fish with his buddies. I never . . . well, seldom . . . stand in his way. Hunting and fishing are really important to him, and we made an agreement before we got married that I wouldn't butt in. One day a friend asked if I wanted to go fishing with her and her sister—you know, get away for a girls' weekend. 'Great,' I said. So I went fishing—and boy, was it a hoot . . ."
—*"Patty," 31, married, corporate consultant to the health industry*

"My mother took my brother and me fishing just about every day. Dad would get home late from work, so she figured fishing was as good a way as any for her to get us out of the house and into the fresh air. Often we'd come home with enough fish to fry for dinner. On weekends Dad took my brother fishing. I stayed home with my mom and we'd bake or sew or something—which I resented because I enjoyed fishing more than my brother Jimmy.

"When Jimmy got into high school, he discovered girls and so Dad started

taking me fishing instead. Soon Mom resented being left home alone, so she came, too. That was 25 years ago, and my folks have been fishing together ever since. That's why they have such a terrific marriage. They have something in common they each thoroughly enjoy, and being one another's best fishing buddy has given them a tremendous amount of pleasure, and taken them to places they normally wouldn't have seen.

"My husband's an avid fisherman—in fact, that's how we met. We get together with my folks a couple of times a year and go fishing together. I guess you can say the foundation of our family was built upon fishing."

—"Jill," 39, married, managing editor of a special-interest magazine

"The day after my graduation from high school I found out I was pregnant. My boyfriend and I were engaged, but when I told him I was going to have our baby, he broke off the engagement. He said a baby would ruin his plans for college. My parents sent me to my grandparents, and told all their friends I had gone off to college. I had the baby, and the day she was born I gave her up for adoption. Afterward, I did go to college, graduated with honors, and walked right into a terrific job. I threw myself into my career—it's pretty much what I live and breathe day and night—and over the years my work has helped me distance myself from my past. I've dated a lot of nice men, but I never found one I wanted to marry.

"One day I got a phone call. Even before she said who she was, I knew the voice on the other end was my daughter. 'This is Suzy, Mother,' she said, and I burst into tears of joy. Suzy was now 32, a nurse practitioner, and happily married with two children. She had been raised an only child. Her adoptive parents had been killed in a car crash the year before she got married. She'd been wanting to find me for a long time.

"When an adoption file is reopened after a period of years, the parties involved have to agree to go through preliminary counseling. Suzy and I agreed that this is what we both wanted. We decided it would be best to meet me without her family. 'How will I recognize you?' I asked. She said, 'I'll be wearing a sign that says: Are you my mother?' That's when I knew she was my daughter, all right!

"We decided we would do something we both enjoyed—and amazingly it was fishing. As a child, I used to go down to the river behind our house and fish with my grandmother's old cane pole. Even when life got hectic, fishing was one of the few things I'd choose to do on the rare times I managed to escape from the office.

"Finally the day arrived when I was to meet my daughter. I knew her the second she stepped off the plane. I don't know how to explain it, but it was as though we had never been apart. We got her bags, hopped into the car, and drove down the coast to a little cottage I rented. We didn't stop talking the

whole time. Fishing together, being on the water—that was a pretty special way to get to know each other.

"Well, that was several years ago. As if fortune wasn't already smiling on me, shortly after that my son-in-law was transferred to my city, so he and my daughter and my grandchildren live only a few miles away! I see them a couple of times a week. About a weekend a month, we pack up their van and go fishing. I bought some little rods and reels for the grandkids—they love having their own gear!

"Perhaps I'm making up for lost time, but finally I have a life. Fishing was a way I found the daughter I thought I had lost . . ."

—*"Donna," 50, executive vice-president of a major company*

"My sister, Betty, and I are extremely close, and when we were growing up we played a lot of tennis and went horsebackriding. I got married after college, but the marriage didn't last long. I was relieved to go back to living the life of an unhitched, single working woman! Betty got married and had three girls. I throw around my maternal instincts from time to time by taking the girls shopping or to a movie, and I baby-sit them whenever my sister wants to accompany her husband on one of his business trips.

"A year ago my sister was in a terrible car crash. She injured her back and can't play tennis or ride anymore. She gained weight and went into a mental funk. This guy I've been dating is really into fishing. He suggested I take my sister away for a weekend and go fishing. He made our reservations and arranged for a fishing instructor to teach us. My sister and I had never fished before. Outdoor sports meant going to a tennis court or a stable—not a lake.

"Our fishing weekend arrived, and my sister and I packed the car and headed off. She was frightened and convinced she wouldn't be able to fish. Our instructor was great. She explained you didn't have to use a lot of upper body motion to fish. In fact, too much upper body movement takes away from casting. You should have seen my sister's face when she realized she could cast! We had a wonderful time and caught some neat fish, besides. Every minute we were on the water I could see my sister's self-confidence come back. That weekend she broke out of her depression, and she's never looked back.

"These days she fishes all the time. It's helped her get her figure back. Her husband's delighted, and he's taken up fishing, and so have their kids. And best of all, my boyfriend and I frequently go away on fishing weekends with them. We have a great time! Know what? I think I'll marry this guy. Believe me, he ain't gonna be 'the fish that got away . . .'"

—*"Jennifer," 29, single, public relations director*

I heard stories similar to these when I traveled to Texas to fish with 40 women I had never met. The occasion was Gina's 2nd Annual All-Girl

Invitational Rockport Redfish Rodeo, a colorful, festive fishing weekend hosted by Gina Nesloney, a professional event planner. She organized a women's-only fishing tournament because she loves to fish, because she's a Pisces, and because she knew other women like to fish, too.

Fishing off the Barrier Islands of Texas

Rockport is located north of Corpus Christi and the coastal waters known as the Laguna Madre of the Gulf of Mexico. Long, thin fingers of islands skirt the coast and are among the best-developed barrier islands in North America. The barrier islands include San Padre Island, San Jose Island, and Matagorda Island. The terrain consists of broad, flat beaches, grass-covered sand dunes, and wind-blown plains called aeolian flats. Along the bay side of the islands are glacial formations called Pleistocene barriers. Deltas deposited by the Colorado River add land mass to the barrier islands, and periodically, loads of sediment and sand washed ashore on the mainland coastal plains are carried by longshore transport to the barrier islands, to compensate for erosion. A beautiful place to be on a warm tranquil day, angry weather can wreak havoc on these islands. Areas can be partially or totally submerged during hurricanes and other storm surges. As a result, many houses here are built on stilts. These topographical components produce abundant fishing grounds.

Subterranean formations such as reefs, timbers, and man-made obstructions are all part of the underwater landscape, and fish love them. Here you will find the many saltwater species that populate these waters on hot summer days when temperatures in the shallows can reach 90 degrees—or more. Just as it is difficult for us to breathe on a hot and humid day, it is also tough for fish to breathe the oxygen they need in the water. As water heats, the oxygen content decreases. Extremely hot water for a long period will suffocate fish and kill them. Finding cool water, therefore, is vital to the life of fish, and they will seek deep water or pockets of dark, cool shelter in relatively shallow water. Reefs and underwater structures are also where fish will find abundant food. Nooks and crannies afford them hiding places from predators.

The coastal plains of southeast Texas are topographically akin to the coastal plains of Mexico. Also related to this area is the ambiance, architecture, and general atmosphere of *fiesta* (spiced by hot food and strong tequila), reflecting close ties with Mexican and Latin American traditions. These are best experienced at the local tonks on a Saturday night.

This is where I—and 40 other women—came to fish.

Gina's 2nd Annual All-Girl Invitational Redfish Rodeo

The majority of women who descended upon the town of Rockport to participate in the Redfish Rodeo were Texas born and raised. All were credentialed professionals representative of a variety of fields, including medicine and law; most were wives, and the majority were mothers. These Texas gals wear big hair, great makeup, and (as the song goes) are "great balls of fire." Texas women can outdrink most men. Texas women can tell lewd jokes better than most men; and Texas women are particular about the cigars they smoke. These gals were hell-bent on having a rip-roaring ol' time. The sight has been known to make grown men shake in their cowboy boots.

Yet, there is a time and a place for fun and frolic—and for fishing. Fishing was serious business to these women. Most were proficient and dedicated anglers. Several were professional bass fishers. All were anxious to get on the water. So, one fine September Saturday, just as dawn

Gina's Second Annual All-Girl Redfish Rodeo took place during a hot September weekend in Rockport, Texas.

(PHOTO BY LAURIE MORROW)

was on the verge of peeking over the bedsheet of night, ten teams of four women anglers, each accompanied by a professional (gentleman) guide, stepped down into their assigned boats, and, at top speed, parted the waters as we made our way to where the big fish most likely would be.

Fishing requires skill and knowledge, but many a seasoned angler would claim that landing a good fish depends mostly on Lady Luck. These were the Rules of Gina's 2nd Annual All-Girl Invitational Redfish Rodeo:

- Each angler would be in possession of a current, valid, resident or nonresident Texas fishing license and a photo I.D. such as a driver's license. This is Texas law.

- Teams would report to their guide and his boat between 6:00 and 6:30 A.M.

- Team members were paid guests of the professional guides. Boat, tackle, and bait would be provided by the guide.

- All boats would return to shore in time for weigh-in at the Sand Dollar Pavilion by 2:00 P.M. sharp.

- Each team would present the three largest trout and the three largest redfish from their combined catch to the judges. If two redfish and six trout were caught, the three largest trout and the two redfish would be the sum total of the team's catch—no substitute of a trout for a redfish (or vice versa) was permitted.

Texas Fishing Regulations

It is the law in Texas that each angler has to be in possession of a current resident or nonresident fishing license (easily obtainable at local fishing tackle stores and stores like Wal-Mart, that carried fishing equipment) *and* a photo I.D., such as a driver's license. Although a resident or nonresident fishing license is required to fish by each state, carrying a photo I.D. is not, but it's not a bad idea. You must buy a license in the state you are fishing. For example, I carry a New Hampshire resident fishing license, which allows me to fish in my home state. However, my fishing license is not valid for any state except New Hampshire. In Texas, I bought a nonresident fishing license.

A Texas resident fishing license (at this writing) costs $19 for the year ($6 if you are over 65), $10 for a 3-day license, or $12 for a 14-day license. An annual nonresident fishing license is $30 for the year, and

$20 for a 5-day license. If you are saltwater fishing, you must purchase a saltwater sportfishing stamp ($7). Texas fishing regulations specify the daily limit for red drum (redfish): three fish per person. The fish must measure no less than 20 and not exceed 28 inches in length (see the explanation of how to measure total length on page 26). During the license year, two red drum over 28 inches may be kept. The first must be tagged with a Red Drum Tag and the second must be tagged with a Bonus Red Drum Tag. The reason fishing regulations protect redfish over 28 inches is so that bulls and spawning females can be conserved for propagation.

The Tournament Begins

The boats cast off, one at a time, and the air was charged with the spirit of competitive good will. "Hook the big one!" "Good luck!" "Go out and have fun." But "fun" can be a complex word when something coveted is at stake. As the sun began to rise over Goose Island, ten boats revved their motors and sped over the water and across Aransas Bay. Maybe it's a Texas thing. Maybe it's a gal's thing. But these women, to a one, were out to win.

Fish, Tackle, Techniques, and Tactics for Inshore Fishing

The great unspoken truth about fishing is that no matter where you go or how long you have fished, no two days on the water are ever, even remotely, the same. Much has to do with nature: the weather is never quite the same as it was yesterday, or the week before, or last season. The fish never behave quite like you expected. The water is a little colder, a little warmer, a little faster, a little slower; it's high tide or low tide or somewhere in between. The more time the angler spends fishing, the better she understands how to control her rod and reel. In time, the habits of fish suddenly make sense. You can read the water and, to an extent, the weather. Every day you're out fishing allows you to grow in your knowledge of the sport. It takes time, but you have to start somewhere! Let's see what's involved with inshore fishing by taking a look at some of the fish you're likely to hook, the tackle and techniques you'll use.

The Fish

About Redfish

"Redfish" is the generic word for red drum (*Sciaenops ocellatus*), or channel bass. Redfish have a reddish tint to their skin—hence the name. Drum is a saltwater species and a member of the *Sciaenidae* family, which consists of about 200 tropical and warm-temperate marine species that include sea bass, spotted sea trout (*Cynoscion nebulosus*), white croaker, and weakfish. Red drum is considered a large drum, although not as large as the black drum. Drum earned its name for the drumlike sound it emits. The fish's bladder is gas-filled, which gives the fish its buoyancy. When its muscles contract against the walls of its "swim bladder," it creates a drumlike sound.

Redfish are bottom feeders and eat crustaceans, mollusks, and mullet. The favorite choice of saltwater anglers for live bait for redfish is actually the smallest member of the *Sciaenidae* family—the croaker, which, like the drum, is named after the sound it emits. An adult redfish can weigh up to 40 pounds and is readily distinguished by the black spot at the base of its tail (some fish have more than one spot).

Angler Tudor Austin with a fine weakfish, or "speckled trout."

(PHOTO BY LAURIE MORROW)

About Weakfish

An angler can take up to ten weakfish (*Cynoscion regalis*) in one day. A fish cannot measure less than 15 inches, but there is no limit to its maximum length. It is especially important to set your hook firmly when a weakfish bites. Its mouth is very soft, or "weak," and can tear easily if the hook is in its cheek instead of solidly in its upper lip. Weakfish are silvery in color and covered with small black spots. An average adult weakfish will weigh under six pounds. Like the redfish, its teeth are sharp and are located in the back of its jaw, which enables it to tear the shells of crustaceans like shrimp, clams, and mussels. Mollusks, mullet, and golden and spotted croakers are also part of the diet of this bottom-feeding fish. Rockport fishermen call weakfish "speckled trout," which is how I'll refer to weakfish in this chapter.

About Croakers

There is no limit to the number of croakers an angler can take from the waters, which is lucky since croakers are what most anglers use when fishing with live bait. Although an adult golden croaker can grow to over a pound, croakers that are fingerling-size live in the shallows and therefore are easy to catch. It is best to catch live bait before even the slightest suggestion of dawn—say 3 or 4 o'clock in the morning. Who said fishing was easy! The angler has to adjust her internal clock so she can get up and on the water before sunrise. Fish feed early in the day and again later, in the evening. Freshly caught bait is one way of insuring a successful morning's fishing.

The Techniques

Inshore Fishing

Inshore fishing allows you to fish waters that you can't reach from the shoreline. You are within view of land, and sometimes only a few yards from it, yet you're not so far offshore as to be in the deep ocean waters frequented by larger fishing boats or commercial fishing vessels. Protected coastal waterways, estuaries, and saltwater bays and creeks can provide excellent inshore fishing.

You will drop anchor in relatively—and often very—shallow water. Because fish are sensitive to sound, the noises you make in your boat—shuffling around, closing a hatch, even standing relatively still while rigging your rod—can frighten fish from the immediate vicinity around your boat (some fishermen call this the "scare area").

Do not expect that fish will hang around your boat. If a fish jumps out of the water so near to your boat that you think it's trying to get in, chances are it is after a smaller fish—or, who knows, is trying to tease you. The rule of thumb for saltwater fishing is that dropping a lure off the side of the boat into relatively shallow water will probably be unproductive. Fish know you're there. Sound more than sight notifies a fish that there's movement on the water. Letting a hatch slam, shuffling about the boat, talking loudly, or playing loud music alerts the fish to your presence and is apt to chase it away from your vessel.

Uptide Fishing

Cast well away from the boat—30 or 40 feet—ahead of the current and let the drift of the water carry your bait along its course. This is called *uptide fishing*. "Read the waters" to determine the current. First, check the direction of the wind. This is done by watching the direction of the ripples in the water caused by an offshore breeze. If the water is quiet, the old-fashioned method of licking your pointer finger and holding it up in the air will do, too. Or, take an unattached piece of fishing line and hold it in the air. It will get caught up in the breeze and point precisely in the direction that the breeze is going. What's going on on top of the water, however, isn't necessarily what's going on underneath the surface. Tides and currents usually follow their own course. A piece of seaweed may be drifting by, or foam may be skimming the surface. Chances are, this is the direction the fish are swimming. In order to allow your line to drift, therefore, cast it as far above the current as you can. Watch your line (you'll be able to eyeball it by looking as far down from the tip of your rod as you can before you lose sight of the line). You'll even feel it pulling your rod tip. Rotate your body accordingly. When the line is about as far down-current as it can go, slowly reel in, keeping tension on your line, and cast uptide again.

You'll get a sense of the speed of the tide or current after a while. If your line seems to be moving more quickly than the tide, be suspicious.

It's likely a fish has taken your bait gently in its mouth and is running with it. You may feel no pressure whatsoever on the line, or the strength of the tide may mask any pressure the fish may be putting on the bait. But any second now it's apt to take a solid bite, in which case you want to be ready to set that hook firmly—and fast. Big fish run with bait. Little fish don't. So, be ready: this could be "the big one."

Bottom Fishing

The natural weight of the live bait on your hook—in our case, croakers—causes your lure to sink in the water. Weighted artificial lures, or lines that have sinkers and/or nontoxic lead or pellets tied to them, will slowly sink the lure to the bottom waters, if that's where you suspect the fish are lying—or if the boat's depth finder has identified fish at lower levels. These days, "fish finders" are common on most fishing boats. Bass boats, Boston whalers, flats boats—any boat that fishes deep freshwater lakes, coastal waters, and oceans—are likely to have this monitor, which bounces radio waves to the ocean floor and locates fish, the depth they are at, and the direction they are moving.

The line is taut from the weight of the lure when you are bottom fishing. Your bait is vulnerable to fish that may lunge for it and swipe it right off the hook because you tend to not work your line as much when you are bottom fishing as you would when you're top fishing. A lure is in motion to tease a fish. A fish has to manipulate itself and makes a lunge for a moving lure. You can't mistake the sharp tug you'll feel on the line when the fish closes its jaws over the bait. Conversely, a lure that's relatively motionless affords the fish the opportunity to swim around it, investigate it, prod it with its nose, and even nibble at the bait. Live bait can be pretty sorely nibbled or gnawed, if not completely taken off the hook; either way, you'll have to replace it with fresh bait. Fish are not attracted by dead bait. Remember, even though your line is taut as a result of the weight of your lure when you're bottom fishing, always be aware of where you've got your rod tip. If it's too high, you won't have the leverage to set your hook.

Top Fishing

If fish are feeding on the top of the water, you need to present your lure on top of the water. If you were fly-fishing, you would use a dry fly with flotant. If you were spinning for freshwater bass, you would attach a float to the line so your artificial lure would stay on top of the water. These are methods of *top fishing*. If you are fishing with live bait, however, you must depend upon your casting technique to keep the bait somewhere in the top three or four feet of water.

Throughout this book I recommend a spinning rig for the beginning woman angler for reasons discussed in Chapter 3. Using the same technique that Judy Wong demonstrates on page 135, attempt to cast your lure as far as possible to the area that your guide has pointed out. This probably will be a reef, underwater obstruction, or popular feeding area. He may point out a place where you *do not* want to present your lure, such as an underwater mass that's chockful of seaweed where you invariably will "hang up" or catch your line. After you have cast your line, slowly reel it in. This permits the live bait to swim and squiggle and naturally attract a predator fish. It also keeps the bait moving. Instead of sinking, you're pulling it along the top of the water. Gently jerk your rod tip up and down; move it from side to side. You must present your bait as naturally as possible. If you reel in too slowly, the bait will sink. If you reel in too quickly, the bait may not move of its own accord and you're simply dragging it through the water. This may alarm the big fish you're determined to catch.

Sometimes you'll see a small fish—or a school of small fish such as mullets—jumping out of the water as if it's being chased. Fish jump out of the water for all kinds of reasons, only a few of which we seem to understand. These little guys might be trying to get out of the way of a much larger fish intent on having them for lunch. Some fishermen accuse fish of having human attributes; they frolic, maybe play "tag," and chase one another in fun or perhaps in a rage of temper. Who knows? Whatever the fish psychology may be, the angler must act quickly. When you see a fish jump out of water, cast quickly a few yards ahead of its path. It won't wait for you, and it may not turn around if you cast your bait behind it. Seasoned fishermen try to cast their lure right on the nose of the fish—but this takes finesse in presenting the lure, reading the water, understanding precisely what the fish is thinking and, most important, unbelievable great good fortune. Many fishermen speculate, in fact, that during the time of the year when certain types of fish are less likely to feed, or not feed at all (such as bright salmon in the rivers in August), the only way to get a strike is if you literally cast so you bounce bait off the fish's nose. It may take a swipe at the lure or bite out of anger. Whether or not this is a fishwife's tale isn't important; it seems to work.

Too many casts to the same patch of water can make the fish suspicious or scare it away. The fish also may be preoccupied with keeping up with a school that's traveling to new fishing grounds, or journeying along its migratory route or to its spawning beds. You generally have one chance to make a successful cast—and you'll know almost immediately if the cast is good. A top-feeding fish will take the bait within seconds of it hitting the water. This is not necessarily the case with bottom fishing, where the lure has to travel 10 to 15 feet or more before it reaches the fish, and even then it may take time before a fish decides to take a swipe at the bait . . . if it takes the bait at all. It may not be hungry, curious, angry or any of the things that fishermen suspect make a fish take a lure. It may swim right past it, or prod it with its nose. It may nibble at the bait or ignore it with utter disdain. But if a fish takes a solid bite on your lure, be prepared to set your hook firmly, *pronto*.

Lures and Tackle

Inshore Saltwater Fishing Tackle for Redfish and Speckled Trout

Once again, keep in mind that in the early morning and early evening, redfish and speckled trout will stay in very shallow waters—as shallow as two or three feet—and seek underwater structures, such as reefs, where there is usually abundant food. As the sun rises high in the sky, it is likely these fish will travel farther offshore to find deeper, cooler waters. Open waters can yield a good catch in the early hours of morning, but by midday, redfish and sea trout will seek shelter from the hot sun under dark ledges and similar structures where more skill is required in placing your lure.

For bottom fishing, some anglers suggest using a 30-pound-class boat rod with a size 4/0 baitcaster reel, 30-pound monofilament line, size 4/0 hook, and artificial sinking lures. Some anglers use a surfcasting or baitcaster reel, 20-pound monofilament line, a size 4/0 hook, and an artificial lure such as a grip sinker. A woman angler intent on fishing all day may find both rigs unnecessarily heavy and cumbersome, even though she will cast less frequently when bottom fishing than she would when she's top fishing.

For top fishing and bottom fishing for redfish, sea trout, and speckled trout, I recommend a spinning rod with a spinning reel, 14-pound monofilament line, and a size 1/0 to 4/0 hook. I use a medium gauge, standard shank size 4/0 "salmon single" hook with a turned-up needle eye and hollow point. Do not even attempt to use a baitcaster reel unless you are an advanced angler with some experience using this kind of gear. You can use a spincasting rig, but I find that overly simple even if this is the first time a woman is out fishing.

Live Bait and Artificial Lures for Redfish, Sea Trout, and Speckled Trout

Although I used golden croakers for live bait, other bait that is used for these fish includes shrimp, crab, clams, mussels, worms, and pieces of squid, cuttlefish, crabs, and other small sea creatures. From June through September, it's very hot from the Carolinas to Texas. When the surface temperature on the water is over 70 degrees, fish can get pretty lackadaisical, especially if they are well fed. In the shallows, the water temperature can be almost as hot as the air temperature. Fishing with artificial lures is fine, but local anglers and fishing guides know that during this time of the year, these conditions require a tasty treat that is apt to attract the fish.

Handling Live Bait

Men tend to have the edge over most women on handling live bait. Squid, worms, sand eels, octopus, mackerel, maggots, casters, slugs, shrimps, prawns, eels, herring, crabs, clams and, in the case of the Redfish Rodeo, golden croakers are squishy things that move. These are among the many natural baits that fishermen spear onto the end of a hook to lure fish. Again, there are times of the year when live bait is the *only* way to fish. But in the summer months, when fish are well fed, they really are not as enthusiastic about striking at a lure as they would be when they are hungry and in the colder waters of early spring and winter and late fall. On the other hand, some anglers prefer to use live bait throughout the year.

Ideally, live bait should be caught just before you head out to fish. It must be stored in a cool, moist place such as a live-bait safe lined with moss or similar moisture-holding material. Usually made of cork, Styrofoam, or plastic, these handy containers provide a convenient and effective way to carry those crawly, squishy little creatures.

Some women may not have an aversion to handling live bait. I am not one of those women. Whenever it was time to put a new croaker on my hook, I looked to Gary, my guide, to do the honors. Guides will bait your hook and cast your line. These are only a few of the reasons why a woman angler who is new to the sport is wise to secure the services of a professional fishing guide. The more you get into the sport, the more you'll realize for yourself that fishing is more than tossing a line with a hook into a bunch of water and waiting for some fish to bite.

Artificial Saltwater Lures

During the cooler months, most anglers will fish with artificial lures. Fish tend to be more active. Some are migrating. The water temperature has dropped into the high 50s and 60s, when the fish are likely to actively seek food. (In very cold water, however—water below 40°F—fish are more likely to "rest" and not eat. As the water warms up again, their appetite revives.)

As with flies, artificial saltwater lures are meant to mimic the sea creatures that fish are likely to eat. Plastic squid, plastic eels, plugs, mackerel spinners, and rubber sand eels are among the countless artificial lures you can buy. Your best bet is to go to a local tackle shop and find out what lures are most successful in local waters.

Spoons are metallic blades that wobble through the water and draw fish toward the lure. There's plenty of light underwater, and it reflects and flashes off the spoon, causing a twinkle that attracts fish to the bait. Spoons are used with live or artificial lures.

Storing Artificial Lures

Tackle boxes come in all kinds of colors, shapes, and sizes. The best are made of sturdy plastic with heavy-duty hinges, and are lightweight. Lidded compartments and separators keep each lure in its own place, which is extremely important. With all the hooks, spoons, floats, and paraphernalia you'll begin to collect, you must keep your tackle separated and properly stored. Otherwise, I don't envy you the task of untangling it.

Fishing Guides

Unlike New Brunswick and other places where fishing regulations require that anyone who is not a resident of the province, country, or district must be accompanied by a registered fishing guide, it is not necessary to fish with a guide in Texas. But you should. As a beginning angler you are a stranger to these waters, and these waters can behave strangely. Tides, currents, abrupt weather changes—unfamiliar waters can be dangerous for any fisherman who is inexperienced in boating or not conversant with a particular body of water, be it inshore, offshore, stillwaters, or rivers. A guide knows the local waters like the inside of his or her own bathtub. He knows the fish and how to bait, hook, play, and catch them. More often than not, he knows where they were and where they're likely to go. Putting yourself in the hands of a professional guide can vastly increase your chances of catching fish and invariably insures your personal safety on the water.

Not all guides are good ones. Finding a guide is not difficult, but finding one that suits you is not unlike finding a doctor: you want to find someone you'll be comfortable with. Talk to friends who have fished where you're planning on fishing and find out who they recommend. Meet a prospective guide first. Ask him to show you letters of recommendation (many grateful clients often write to their guides). A guide should have a well-appointed, immaculately kept boat and supply clients with well-maintained, relatively new rods and reels. He should not look like Captain Ahab or Popeye, or smell of the local tonk, and he should not make overblown assurances that you're going to catch more fish than you can shake a stick at. If you are lucky enough to find a female fishing guide, all I can tell you is I've never met a woman (or, for that matter, a male) fishing guide I didn't like.

Without exception, outdoorsmen and outdoorswomen who dedicate their professional lives to fishing convey a love and enthusiasm for their sport that's contagious to those they teach or guide. They have a deep-seated respect for the game fish they hunt with rod and reel, and they are good and generous teachers. One such person was the guide that took me, for the first time in my life, on the coastal waters of Texas.

Sue King with Gary Clouse, our fishing guide at the Redfish Rodeo.
(PHOTO BY LAURIE MORROW)

Gary Clouse, Professional Fishing Guide

The guides at the Redfish Rodeo had been assigned to the various teams by a drawing, and our boat had the great good fortune of securing the services of professional fishing guide Gary Clouse. Gary has guided fishermen and fishing parties over the waters between Rockport and Corpus Christi full-time since 1981. My fellow teammates met Gary the night before to discuss tactics. He sweetly—but firmly—said, "We're going to have a wonderful time, providing you do what I say." He didn't mean this sarcastically, and explained that this was the suggestion he made to novice and experienced fishermen alike. "I know these waters, and I know where the fish are. If you cast where I tell you, and when I tell you, you'll catch a fish." It was only after we had been out fishing for a while that we realized he wasn't, so to speak, blowing up our skirts. When we did as he suggested, we caught fish. If we didn't, we caught no fish. It was that simple.

When my team and I joined Gary at the boat launch, he had already been up several hours catching golden croakers. We loaded our gear into his sleek 175-horsepower Mariner boat, and just as the sun began to rise over Goose Island, we took off at breakneck speed to the spot Gary thought we would catch our first redfish.

The Techniques

Casting Spinning Tackle for Redfish and Speckled Trout

Spinning from a boat is not unlike spinning from the shore. Turn to page 135 and review how professional bass champion Judy Wong demonstrates spinning technique. This is the same technique you'll use when spinning for redfish and speckled trout from a flats fishing boat. Spread your feet comfortably and balance yourself so that you are standing securely. When there's a little rocking from waves made by a passing boat or choppy water, balance yourself by shifting your weight from foot to foot to compensate for the boat's motion.

Practice how to work your reel. Remember, the wrist action you put into propelling your lure is where you'll get the distance you need to place it at least 30 and preferably 40 feet from the boat. When casting live bait, bring your rod tip back to approximately 2 o'clock. You can let the line rest there for a second while the bait straightens behind you. Keeping your forearm stiff and your wrist flexible, flick the rod tip forward to about 10 o'clock, with your forefinger gently holding the line. Do not stop before that point and do not release the line too soon. This will result in an abrupt stop to your cast and your lure will drop such a short distance that you'll have to cast again. Conversely, if your casting motion goes beyond 10 o'clock, you end up with a puddle of line on the water. If a fish takes your lure when your line is not taut, you will have great difficulty in setting your hook; in fact, the fish may manage to take the bait while you're crazily trying to reel in the excess line. For this reason, it is imperative that you immediately get rid of any slack in your line and keep it tense. Your rod tip should settle to about 9 o'clock, giving you ample leverage in which to bring your rod tip up and set your hook the instant you feel the distinctive tug that tells you a fish has taken your bait.

Setting Your Hook

As we discussed in our fly-fishing section, "setting your hook" is simply a determined upward jerk of your rod tip. When a fish takes your bait, or "strikes," secure your handhold on the rod, keeping the butt of the rod approximately waist-high. Your other hand should be on the crank of the reel as you prepare to reel in, or "play," the fish. Before you operate the reel lever, however, you must set the hook. Give a good, firm, upward yank of the rod tip—from 9 o'clock to noon. If the fish has taken a solid bite at the lure, this will firmly set the hook in the fish's upper lip. Where you position your rod tip is crucial to successfully setting your hook. Keeping a taut line is equally important—again, too much slack will not enable you to set your hook properly, if at all. You can use both hands on your rod when setting the hook for force, and if the fish is a strong one, you will need to use both hands. The hand that holds the rod should grasp the grip toward the top, not at the butt. Some anglers like to hold the rod above the reel seat while reeling in the line. This is a personal choice, but either way, your rod-holding hand should be far up on the grip so that you can tuck the butt against you when you are playing a strong, fightin' fish.

Playing the Fish

It is a common mistake to attempt to reel in a fish too quickly. As long as your hook is set and your line is taut, you must allow the fish to "take line" and run. Let the fish run—it will not take all your line. You'll know a strong fish is taking line and running by the screaming of your reel as the fish pulls more and more line in its attempt to get free of your hold. As the tension relaxes, quickly reel in some line—again, making sure your rod tip is up and there's tension on the line (but not so much tension that the line could snap). Again the fish will run; let it take some line. When you sense it is resting, reel in some more line. You'll do this again and again, depending upon the fish and how hard it is fighting. This is called "playing the fish." You'll know when the fish is all tuckered out because it will not run and you can bring it alongside the boat. Some fish will flip their tail up in surrender. This is called "pouting."

Landing Your Fish

"Pouting" means the fish is all tuckered out and ready to "land"—to be brought into the boat. Your fishing companion should by now be at your side with a soft net. In lieu of a net, grasp the line close above the fish's head and gently bring it into the boat. Do not underestimate your fish, however. It could thrash out at any time and break your hold. You must act quickly and confidently. Anything less may hurt the fish.

Whether you plan to release or keep the fish, you want to cause it as little distress as possible.

Removing the Hook

A hook set firmly in the upper lip of a fish is easily removed by grasping the hook firmly with your thumb and forefinger and, following the direction of entry of the barb, slipping the hook from the fish's mouth. If done properly, you will slightly tear the tissue of the fish's mouth which, in proper catch-and-release, will do the fish no harm and mend quickly. If the fish has swallowed the hook, or if it is caught deeply into the fish's mouth, you may have to use a pair of fishing forceps, tweezers, or rounded-point scissors to pull it out. This will cause more damage to the fish's flesh and for that reason you must do it gently. If you intend to keep the fish, be very swift in killing it or very certain that you return it properly to the water.

Catch-and-Release

Catch-and-release has gained in popularity over the years as a sporting way to play a fish and return it to its habitat. An appreciable percentage of fish do not survive after they are returned to the water, however. The primary reason is not because a fish has been hooked poorly, but instead because a fish is overhandled. It is absolutely imperative that you thoroughly wet your hands before you handle a fish. When you hold a fish, you invariably rub some off some of the protective slime that covers its body. If this film is rubbed off an area of the fish's body, the exposed area will be instantly susceptible to a type of fungus that will infect the fish and ultimately kill it. Another danger to fish is keeping it out of water for too long: it will actually suffocate.

Follow these steps to return a fish to water:

- Land your fish as gently as possible, using a soft-web net to limit abrasion to the body of the fish. If the hook is deeply embedded in the fish's mouth or cheek, or if the fish has sharp teeth, have a fishing forceps ready to remove it.

- Make sure your hands are completely wet before handling the fish.

- Remove the hook with one gentle jerk as soon as you have a secure hold on the fish. Hold the fish gently, without squeezing, just under the gills.

- Keep the fish out of the water for as brief a time as possible. Do not spend time rummaging for a camera or posing for that Kodak moment. The fish's chances for survival decrease as it spends more time out of water. The proper way to hold a soft-mouthed fish, should you wish to pose briefly for a picture, is to place your thumb gently under its lower jaw bone and support the rest of the jaw with your other fingers, as if you were cradling it. This paralyzes the fish, and it will stay virtually motionless. Again, don't indulge in time. Your priority is to return the fish to water as quickly as possible.

- When you return the fish to water, cradle it in your wet hands. Keep the fish upright in a firm but gentle hold, one hand under its head and the other by the base of its tail. Lower it into just enough water so that it is completely submerged. Move it gently back and forth. This forces water through its gills and revives it. Watch for its tail to swish back and forth. As soon as you see it regain strength in its upper body, it is ready to take off again under its own steam.

- A saltwater fish may have difficulty righting itself by the method described above. If you see its air bladder and gut lining projecting out of its mouth, the air bladder is distended. In order to save the fish and return it to water successfully, you'll have to do some prompt and delicate "surgery." Insert a thin-pointed knife, wire, or ice pick through the side of the fish immediately behind, and at the base of, the upper part of the pectoral fin. Done correctly, you will release the trapped air in the bladder and allow the fish to right itself, revive, and swim safely away. This problem is not unlike a distended stomach in sheep, cows, or horses that have digested too much gas-forming grain. A single, sharp blow to the stomach with a sharp-pointed tool will relieve the gas and prevent rupture. This is much more dicey in farm animals and needs to be done by a knowledgeable farmer or a veterinarian; otherwise incorrect placement of the puncture could kill the animal. Likewise, missing the gas bladder in a fish could complicate, not solve, the problem.

A Keeper

If you wish to keep a fish that's within the parameters of state fishing regulations, the kindest cut of all is to take it quickly with a firm hit to the head, either along the side of the boat or with a fishing club (also known as a "priest"). This is called *gaffing*. Immediately put the fish in a creel in a cool, moist place or in the fish well, if you are in a boat.

The Woman Angler Prepares Herself for Saltwater Fishing

F ishing on salt water is very different than fishing on freshwater ponds, streams, rivers, or lakes. You can't drink salt water. It dries your skin and can irritate it. And although sun reflects off all water, there are no shade trees to shield you from the sun's burning rays when you're on a boat in the middle of the ocean or on coastal waterways. Here are some important personal tips to observe when you go saltwater fishing.

What to Wear

When the temperature on the water is kissing the 100-degree mark, you might be inclined simply to wear a bathing suit on the boat. If you do, you run the risk of spending the night in the emergency room of the local hospital. If you are not used to the sun, and even if you are, bring a long-sleeved, lightweight, fast-drying fishing shirt or windbreaker and long tropical-weight pants. Wear shorts and a short-sleeved shirt or a bathing suit. You don't have to stay bundled up like a nun in a habit all day. It's fine to take in a little sun—but just a little at a time, and not most of the time. Late morning, high noon, and early afternoon are the most dangerous times to be exposed to the sun. That's when you should pull on your long pants and toss on your long-sleeved shirt.

Be sure to wear a hat. A brimmed hat is best, but is only good if you can tie it under your chin. If you have, say, a terrific straw hat but it has no ties, bring a long scarf that will go over the brim of your hat and tie under your chin. Most people wear a snug-fitting baseball-style cap on the water, but make sure the back of your neck is not exposed. Some fishing hats have front and back brims. If your hat has only a front brim, wear a bandanna around your neck to keep that vulnerable place from getting burned.

Good footgear is essential on a boat. The floor of a boat will get wet, so you'll need comfortable sneakers, Topsiders, or other rubber-soled shoes that will prevent you from slipping and falling flat on your bass. A pair of light cotton socks will prevent your shoes from chafing and will also keep your delicate ankles from getting sunburned.

Sunglasses: Don't Leave Home Without Them

Sunglasses are essential on the water. Your eyes can get sunburned, too: the reflective light from the water on the delicate cornea can cause discomfort and, in severe cases, damage, even on hazy, overcast days. Get yourself a pair of sunglasses with polarized lenses. You can spend under $20 for a good, dependable pair and you can certainly spend ten times that amount—or more. You'll obviously pay more for better lenses, but most of the cost of expensive sunglasses is figured into fashion frames. Although the choice of wire or molded plastic frames is up to you, the latter tend to be more durable.

If you wear eyeglasses, your optometrist can order prescription polarized sunglasses for you. He or she will recommend the type of lenses that are best for you, but if your prescription warrants, ask about thinner, scratch-resistant, safety lenses. You'll want a lens that is not heavy on your face, but more important, you need lenses that won't shatter if you are hit in the face, say, by a nontoxic lead sinker. Accidents do happen on the water; the better prepared you are, the better your chances are to get through the day safely.

Prescription sunglasses are expensive. If you wear eyeglasses, you can get clip-on polarized lenses instead. These, too, can be relatively expensive, but they are a good investment and something you'll wear all the time (I keep a pair in the car to clip on to my regular glasses when I'm driving, and another pair in my fishing vest). Another good precaution for eyeglass wearers is to attach a strap to your glasses. When you bend over the water, cast, or make a sudden movement, you can easily lose your glasses. A strap attached to the sides of the eyeglasses will insure that if they fall off your face, they'll land on your chest—not in the water. If you need reading glasses to see up close, which you'll do when you're tying knots, be sure to have a pair on hand.

Here's something many contact lens wearers do not know: many optometrists recommend you wear sunglasses with glass lenses. For some reason, plastic lenses actually do not afford absolute protection from ultraviolet rays when they pass through softwear plastic contact lenses. Again, be certain the sunglasses you buy have polarized, shatterproof lenses. If you wear contacts, bring a small bottle of lubricating eyedrops to keep your eyes moistened and prevent irritation. Also bring your storage container in the event you want to remove your lenses, and always bring a pair of regular glasses with clip-on sunglass lenses or prescription sunglasses, just in case.

There are several shades of sunglass lenses to choose from: purplish black, brown, amber, and an assortment of wild, fluorescent colors. Polarized lenses actually allow you to see what's going on underwater more clearly than the naked eye by minimizing glare. For bright sunlight, I recommend dark brown lenses. Amber is best for shady waters, such as rivers and freshwater ponds, since the lighter tint allows more brightness, but none of the glare, to pass into your field of vision.

Lastly, take proper care of your sunglasses. Store them in a padded case when not in use, and wash them with lens cleaner. If you have no lens cleaner, wet the lenses and wipe them gently with a soft, dry cloth. Never wet your lenses with salt water, and never wipe lenses down with a dry cloth—these will scratch the surface.

Makeup and Hair

I have seen Paris in April from the top of the Eiffel Tower. I have seen the first crocus of spring pop its head through the snow. And I have seen women with gobs of makeup, big hair, and three-inch red fingernails jump into fishing boats at dawn. If that's how you start each and every day, fine. However, minimal makeup such as waterproof mascara and a moist, natural-shade lipstick (preferably with sunscreen) is sufficient. The lipstick, actually, is important. Lips can get windburn and sunburn after a day on the water and may blister. Keep a good lipstick or lipgloss with sunscreen in your fishing vest.

If you have long hair, put it in a French braid, ponytail, or bun. If your hair is short, you're all set. If your hair is naturally curly, it will have a field day in the heat and humidity, so be resigned. If your hair is colored, be careful. I have seen blond color-treated hair turn green from too much sun, and henna-tinted hair turn orange. A hat will help. For short, fly-away hair, a wide fabric headband or terry-cloth sweatband will help keep the hair out of your eyes when you're not wearing a hat. Sea salt can really dry out your hair, so at the end of the day, be sure to give your hair a light conditioning when you shower or bathe. Likewise, use a greaseless, hypoallergenic face and body moisturizer to soothe your skin.

Sunblock

The importance of protecting yourself from the sun cannot be stressed enough. Buy a good, water-resistant sunblock for sensitive skin. Even if you do not have sensitive skin, the sun irritates the skin by the very nature of what it does—it burns the outer epidermis. Remember how your skin burns when you run into the ocean after you've been sunning on the beach?

Be kind to your skin, and invest in a lotion that is no less than SPF 15. This theoretically gives you 15 times the protection from the sun were you not wearing any lotion at all. There has been some speculation that lotions with higher SPFs—30 and higher—may not give you additional protection. The proportion of waterproof lotion lessens as the SPF increases, which means sunblocks with higher SPFs may not effectively protect the skin as long as one that's SPF 15. The best sunblock of all, of course, is full-coverage: lightweight clothing, a good hat, and a good pair of sunglasses.

Water—the Kind You Drink

There's another type of water you should be thinking about, and that's the water you keep in a cooler to drink. Over and over again I will stress how important it is to be on the water *with* water—drinking water, that is. Although you hope long hours on the water will yield fish, one thing that's certain is that long hours on the water will yield a ravishing thirst. In the course of a sweltering day, do not be surprised if you drink a gallon of water or more—in fact, you should drink this much to stay hydrated. Dehydration can be dangerous. So can overexposure to the sun. It can result in hypothermia, which, in extreme cases, can be fatal. Listen to your body. Maintain your body temperature, keeping it cool inside and out. You can't always jump out of a boat for a quick dip in the water. Poisonous jellyfish and other creatures infest many coastal waters, and if you are stung you run the risk of anaphylactic shock. It's a good idea to keep a hand towel or bandanna with your gear so you can wet it in the melted ice in your cooler, or with some of the drinking water you've brought along, and keep yourself cool. Applying a cool cloth to your forehead, temples, back of the neck and wrists alleviates the discomfort of severe heat. Drinking water—and lots of it—is essential.

Food

Make sure you pack a nourishing lunch for yourself and your fishing buddies, but when you do, avoid foods that can spoil easily, such as mayonnaise-based salads, soft cheeses like brie, milk-based products such as pudding, chocolate bars or any candy that is apt to melt, or any uncooked meat. Coolers equipped with ice packs will keep your food cool through most of the day. Good bets are deli meats, hard cheese like sharp cheddar and a box of crackers, fresh fruit, and peanut butter and jelly. Keep your meats and cheeses in plastic containers, and bring unopened jars of peanut butter, jelly, mayonnaise, and mustard. Not only can you make your sandwiches "fresh" on the boat, but your bread will not get soggy and you run less risk of food spoilage. If you bring a thermos of coffee, consider bringing a jar of nondairy creamer instead of a container of milk. Obviously, if the boat is equipped with a refrigerator or similar cold storage unit, you need not worry about spoilage. Otherwise, be cautious and only pack food that will stay relatively fresh as your cooler loses its cool when the day warms up. Don't eat heavy—and don't drink alcohol. One beer, perhaps two, is okay. Stick with water, soda, and juices. Save your serious drinking for the evening, when you're back on dry land and do not need to drive anywhere. That's the time to celebrate a good day's fishing, anyway.

Boat Safety

Your guide will point out the safety features and rules on board the boat. The boat will be equipped with a first aid kit, but if you are on medication, make sure you have a sufficient supply with you. Bring bug repellent in the event of mosquitoes or other biting insects. If you are allergic to bee stings, be sure you have a bee sting kit with you—your guide may not carry that as part of his kit.

Every person must have a life preserver, and although it is not necessary to wear it all the time, know where yours is located and keep it readily accessible. If there's rough water, or the boat is traveling at a fast clip, wear your preserver, especially if you are a poor swimmer. Standing in a flats boat can be a balancing act, especially if you run into choppy water or a boat passes you by. Sit if you do not feel sure-footed, and if you are standing, make sure your feet are planted securely on the floor of the boat. Standing on the bow of the boat or too close to the side can make you lose your balance; if the boat gets hit by a sudden movement, you are at risk of falling overboard. If for any reason you are alone on a boat, it is important that you wear a life preserver at all times.

Return to the Redfish Rodeo

Well, each of my three teammates pulled in some beautiful redfish and speckled trout that day. When we did what Gary said, we invariably caught a fish—most of the time. As the sun rose higher in the sky, however, the fish bit less and less frequently.

One of our teammates landed a monster 36 inches long—a real trophy fish—but she returned it to the water. That bull redfish would help replenish the waters with another generation of redfish. That's conservation-minded, even though we were all a little wistful to see it swim away. More and more people are taking fewer and fewer trophy fish in the name of conservation. To that end, wildlife artists will build a wood or fiberglass model or paint a picture of "the big one" that you let get away. Supply the artist with a photograph accompanied by the exact dimensions of the fish.

All in all, our team caught our limit. We caught a dozen lovely speckled trout. These fish do not have the fighting spirit that redfish do, so they are easier to play and bring in. Some of the trout were as big as the smaller redfish. Like redfish, the firm, white flesh of speckled trout makes them one of the most popular fish for eating.

The last fish we landed was a 27-inch redfish—an inch under the mark—and it was caught on the last cast of the day. Well, sort of. I caught that fish, and my last cast was my sixth or seventh "last cast." You, too, will discover that you can't help but say, "Last cast . . . one more time" a couple of times—or more, until your buddies pull you back into the boat and grab your rod from your hand. Well, time was running out, and if we didn't make it back to the Sand Dollar Pavilion by 2:00 P.M., we'd be disqualified. Gary turned his boat toward Rockport, and for the second and last time that day, we parted the waters at breakneck speed.

By now, everyone had gathered for the big weigh-in—anglers, guides, locals, and folks who just happened to stop by the Sand Dollar Pavilion to be part of the great excitement. There were banners and streamers and lots of country music and beer and noise and laughter. Our team didn't place, but we made a mighty fine showing with almost 20 pounds of fish, including three redfish. The winning team had fished hard like us, but Lady Luck was perched on the bow of their boat like a figurehead on a whaling boat. It was then I realized we hadn't been competing against the other teams. All of us were competing against the fish.

We ate mighty well that evening. The fish we caught were fried and served piping hot. A mariachi band serenaded us and wove lilting music through the star-crusted night as the 40 women anglers of Gina's 2nd All-Girl Invitational Redfish Rodeo mixed with invited guests under a star-encrusted Texas sky. Forty women came to Rockport to fish. They arrived as strangers. They left as friends. Some of them left their troubles on the water. Now you know some of their stories, and you know how they fished. Hard fishing with good people makes memories a shining thing—as shining as those stars in that great, big, starry Texas sky.

One Last Cast

F ishing for redfish, speckled trout, and sea trout off the Gulf Coast is an exhilarating experience. You can hook some mighty large fish, but the most "athletic" is the redfish. One longtime Rockport fisherman swears that the redder the fish's flesh, the more fight the fish will give you. When a redfish bites down on your bait, believe me, you know it. And when it starts to run with your line, you think you've got Moby Dick on your hook.

The biggest redfish I caught was that last fish of the day. It weighed nearly four pounds and measured 27 inches in length. It looked pretty and pink, and it was a fighter! The instant it took my bait, my reel started screaming. I needed both hands to set the hook. Then it tried to run away from the boat. I had to be careful not to reel in too fast or too much line, and I managed to keep my head enough to allow it to take line and still manage to keep my rod tip up and line taut. There were moments when I was afraid the line might snap. I had seen frayed lines that resulted from strong fish putting up a fight and anglers putting up too much fight. I knew if I reeled in too fast and overcranked my reel—instead of using my rod to play the fish and allowing it to run and tire itself out—I would snap the line.

It takes practice to know when the pressure on your line is just right—not too slack, not too tight—just as it's a delicate call to determine at what point you should reel in, and when you should allow your fish to run with some line. Eventually the fish will tire out, and although it will make you tired in the process, the secret is not to rush it—and to keep your wits about you.

I knew I had hooked a huge fish. I called out for Gary, and he guided me every step of the way in landing that brute. It took less than ten minutes, but time—and not the fish—slipped away. The fish would run . . . I'd pick up my rod tip to the 12 o'clock position and then, keeping firm pressure on the line, reel in quickly as I lowered the rod tip to 10 o'clock. The fish would run again . . . and again I'd let him take more line until it slowed down, and again I'd reel in quickly as I lowered my rod tip. When I felt it was losing steam, I used my rod to maneuver the fish closer to the boat, reeling in the slack as I could. Then I saw it. If I were to name it, I'd call it "One Eye'd Pete," even though it had both eyes. It just looked like a piratical Pete. Pete was big, and finally he pouted . . . and surrendered. Gary netted him, measured him, and then Pete and I made each other's acquaintance, face-to-face.

We kept Pete and had him for dinner. Was I sorry to kill such a mighty creature? Yes, of course I was. Fishing, after all, is a type of hunting—only the creatures that we take from nature are beasts of the land, while fish are beasts of the seas and waters. No hunter, be she a hunter of game animals or game fish, takes the life of a noble animal without a sense of remorse that far outweighs triumph. The following passage was written a long time ago by a fisherman who understood. His words, more than mine, convey what I think, and how I feel, about that glorious redfish:

> *Suppose the fish is not caught by an angler, what is his alternative fate? He will either perish miserably in the struggles of the crowded net, or die of old age and starvation like the long, lean stragglers which are sometimes found in the shallow pools, or be devoured by a larger fish, or torn to pieces by a seal or an otter. Compared with any of these miserable deaths, the fate of a fish that is hooked in his homewaters and after a glorious fight receives the happy dispatch at the moment when he touches the shore, is a sort of euthanasia. And, since the fish was made to be man's food, the angler who brings him to the table of destiny in the cleanest, quickest, kindest way is, in fact, his benefactor.*
>
> —Henry Van Dyke, *Little Rivers*, 1895

Chapter 11

—

Bass Fishing

An Interview with a Professional Bass Fisher

Emily Shaffer first picked up a rod when she was five years old. She went fishing with her brother and caught six brown trout. He caught a fit of jealousy and threw his rod into the water. You could say Emily was bit by the fishing bug from that point on. Although her father was a fly fisher, she preferred spincasting and continues to favor a Zebco 33 enclosed reel.

Emily continued to fish through her teenage years into adulthood. One day she met a guy at a fish weigh-in. They hit it off, and he asked

Emily Shaffer (left), with arguably the most influential woman in all of women's bass fishing, Sugar Ferris, founder of Bass 'n Gals and an inspiration to all women who fish.

(PHOTO BY LAURIE MORROW)

her if she wanted to go fishing. Their first date was early the following morning, before sunrise—and they have been together ever since.

Emily says she *caught* fish with her dad, but she learned *how* to fish from her husband. He taught her about the habits of fish—the actual science behind fishing and how the elements, water, temperature, and seasons affected their behavior. For Emily, pleasure came from the knowledge she learned and from going out on the water to fish; the reward was catching a fish.

Emily had met her husband in March; they married that September and have been married now for eight years. Before they married, Emily told her husband that she wanted to become a professional bass fisher and fishing instructor. She said if she couldn't make a go of it in five years, she'd "give it up, settle down, and have babies." Four years later, on October 25, 1995, she won the Bass 'n Gals Classic with the largest bass caught in a tournament that year by a woman—or a man.

Emily's husband had been a senior metallurgist at Nissan Motors, but by April of 1992 her fishing career was so promising that he quit his job to manage it. "We're a heck of a team," Emily said about her husband. "We're together twenty-four hours a day—and there aren't many people that can do that. We are best friends. I never dreamed I could be this close to someone."

Emily drives a Stratos 201 Pro-Elite bass boat, made by Stratos of Old Hickory, Tennessee. Her boat is powered with a 225 Evinrude Motor. The boat is equipped with a Lowrance Electronics fish finder. Her rods are made by All Star Graphite Rods. Emily is one of the 18 members of All Star's Pro Staff. She selects a different rod for every technique. For example, she uses All Star's F90H "flipping stick" for "flipping" lures, that is, a stick that's designed especially for throwing a jig or a worm in the water for bottom fishing. For fishing line she uses Strand Kevlar braided line. Her favorite bass lure is a Strike King bootlegger jig, which she uses on smallmouth, largemouth, and Kentucky spotted bass. For general bass fishing, the length of the rod she prefers is eight feet; and she likes a medium/heavy action, especially for bottom fishing.

All Star Graphite Rods developed its women's pro staff because they felt that women tended to promote their sport more enthusiastically than men. "Women seem more dedicated when it comes to supporting their sponsors," Emily points out. "Besides, women have a way of talking with kids. We on the professional circuit like to introduce fishing to the children. They listen to you and do what you show them. Kids are enthusiastic students when it comes to fishing." Emily has visited schools to talk to children about fishing.

"The thing I like about fishing is anyone can do it," she says. "You don't have to be athletically inclined; you may even be handicapped. I enjoy working with women anglers. I have found that women take a soft approach to the sport, even at the professional level. A lot of professional bass fishermen—I mean *men*—don't give you the time of day. Men are peacocks."

Peacocks or not, Emily makes an interesting point. "Men are confused nowadays. They were raised to be providers. Put a man and a woman together in a boat in a storm. The man becomes protective. 'Oh, I hope she's okay,' he thinks. When you put a man and a woman together in a boat in a fishing competition, the guy tends not to compete at his highest level. Some guys behave as though he's with someone who's second best. Put a man in the boat with another man, and they're out for blood. They don't realize we women are out for blood, too," Emily says with a laugh.

"It would be far more balanced if there was a tournament circuit where the competition in each boat was a mixed team—a man and a woman. Fishing, in a sense, is bred into men. Many men were brought up fishing and hunting. Women were not. On the whole, women as a group are just learning to fish; only a few have been lifelong anglers. In a way, I feel like I'm at a disadvantage because I have been fishing for only eight years. And I think the way some people separate the sexes into stereotypes is bad for the sport.

"Our generation of women has been able, often out of necessity, to leave the home. Our job is no longer only to be housewives and take care of the children, but we cook, clean, take care of our man, and work a nine-to-five job, besides going to PTA meetings, church functions, and community events. Women don't have a lot of time for themselves. So when a woman is treated like second fiddle after her husband's hobbies, it's hard. Men work hard, and to unwind they go fishing and hunting with their buddies for weekends instead of spending time with their families. If only they realized how much fun it would be to bring their families fishing with them. Honestly. I've seen more families grow closer together as a result of going fishing together. I know from my own experience that open communication is the only thing that keeps families and couples together. And fishing is a great way to communicate.

"You know how many women have been getting into fishing lately? *Thousands.* They get resentful that their husbands or boyfriends go off fishing without them. So one day they go out with their guy to find out just what fishing is all about. They cast a line and wonder, what's so great about this—until they catch a fish. The first time you've experienced that, once you see what it's all about, once you hook a fish, *you're the one that's hooked!*"

Women tend to be naturally good at fishing. Whether it's spinning or fly-fishing, the technique is a graceful one that works with our bodies and our builds. When a husband sees how good an angler a woman can be, and how much his wife enjoys the sport, he just beams. "You did a good job," he'll say, or "I'm proud of you."

"To successfully prove yourself in a man's world," Emily continued, "and have a man sincerely praise you and give you the recognition you deserve, well, that means everything. It makes you feel so good. It made me feel like I was an equal instead of excess baggage or a handicap, or a pain in the butt."

Between March and November, Emily does nothing but travel to different tournaments in Tennessee, Alabama, Texas, and Kentucky to compete, and she competes in local team tournaments with her husband, Larry. In January and February she attends boat and trade shows for her sponsors and gives lectures. Besides All Star Graphite Rods, her sponsors include Stratos Boats, Evinrude, Strike King Lure Company, Delco Voyager Batteries, Strand Line, and Dual Pro Battery Charger. Emily fishes strictly for bass, and in competition she only uses artificial lures.

When Emily lectures, she often discusses the basics of bass fishing and tries to prove to the weekend angler that you do not have to go into bankruptcy to enter a tournament. Fees vary from $50 to $300. "All you do is fill out an entry form, send it in, show up, and fish. Each circuit is different, some have cut-off times to prevent last-minute entries from a run of local or weekend fishermen that want to enter at the last minute."

What do you wear bass fishing? Emily wears a custom-made shirt with patches embroidered with the logos of each of her sponsors, a pair of jeans, and tennis shoes. "A shirt that allows you to cast and isn't binding is a *must*," she explained. "The fish don't care what you look like. They don't know if you're male or female. But people certainly do. I always like to look my best, wherever I go."

Why did you commit your life to fishing, Emily?

"I guess I love being out in a boat and experience what all you're experiencing. Like I said, if you get a fish it's a bonus. It's the hunt, it's the thrill of the chase."

What do you prefer to be called?

"Guys don't know what to call me. I do. I'm an angler. A woman angler."

But there was another reason, something far deeper than fishing, that inspired Emily to a life on the water. Emily's brother, who retrieved his rod from the water when they were children, ended up fishing with her throughout their growing-up years. But in his early thirties he died—from a drug overdose. "It was a drawn-out, tragic death, and watching someone you love die before your eyes leaves a wound that never will heal. You live with it always, but you learn how to deal with it, and get on with your life. One of the reasons I visit schools and talk to children so often is because I know that fishing can take the place of drugs. I know that being in the out-of-doors and doing something that makes you feel good will give kids the self-esteem they need to avoid drugs. I tell kids what happened to my brother and how it affected my family. Kids should know. I'm here to tell them what they'd be getting into, and show them that there is something out there that will give them a natural high, and a lot more besides.

"I feel fortunate, I think that I'm the luckiest person in the world, because I do have a great life, a great husband, and I'm making money doing what I love to do best. The only really bad thing that ever happened to me was when cocaine took my brother. Cocaine took someone I loved away from me. The way I give back what I lost is by talking to kids and teaching them, telling them: 'Don't fall into a trap that you'll get caught in. You'll never break out of it. You have the choice. You can be what you want to be. You can pursue your dream.' For every action there is a reaction. Fishing is an action; it gives you a real sense of your-

Emily Shaffer shows off her championship bass.
(COURTESY EMILY SHAFFER)

self—that's the reaction. Being on the water, well, you can understand a lot about yourself when you're out there, and about the people that come in and out of your life."

Bass Fishing: The Sport of the Common People

The President last night had a dream. He was in a party of plain people and as it became known who he was they began to comment on his appearance. One of them said, "He is a common-looking man." The President replied, "Common-looking people are the best in the world: that is the reason the Lord makes so many of them."

—*A dream recounted by President Abraham Lincoln to John Hay, 1863*

Bass fishing is unquestionably the most popular type of fishing in America today. The fish are terrific sport fish, the gear is always on the cutting edge of innovation, and the boats are fast and fun. That, plus the fact that there are bass in just about every body of water, means you're in store for some terrific fishing.

I have yet to take you through the casting technique for spinning tackle, however, and with the help of professional bass fisher and instructor Judy Wong of Houston, Texas, we'll do that now. When we photographed this sequence, we asked Judy to go through the steps on land. This way you can clearly follow her technique.

Step 1.

Step 1. Judy is standing with her shoulders squarely set over her feet. Her rod tip is pointed at the 9 o'clock position. She is holding her spinning rod and reel with her casting hand. Notice how her hand is high up on the grip.

Step 2.

Step 2. Judy brings her rod to the 10 o'clock position.

Here is an extended view of the 10 o'clock position. Notice that Judy's artificial lure dangles about one foot from the rod tip. That's about the right length to extend your lure. Too much line length results in whipping your lure; too little line and it can get caught up in the rod tip.

Step 3.

Step 3. Judy now has brought her rod tip back to the 2 o'clock position. So far, the rod positions are much the same as fly-fishing. The difference, of course, is you are not creating line speed . . . yet.

This is an extended view of Judy's back cast. Notice her wrist. Also notice how close her arm is to her body. There is no excessive body movement involved in her casting technique. But she's about to move into her forward cast—and that's where she's focusing.

Step 4.

Step 4. The forward cast. Judy's given her wrist a solid "snap"—and this wrist action uses the weight of the lure to propel itself forward the distance. The fishing line is weightless. It's simply following the lure. It has no line speed, unlike fly line.

Fishing on Fayette County Lake, Texas

One of the most famous brothels, the Chicken Ranch, used to be just "down the road apiece" from Fayette County Lake. The place got its name because clients would pay for the ladies' favors with chickens instead of money. This cherished institution about an hour and a half due west of Houston is, alas, no more, but the rolling countryside is reminiscent of the hills of Pennsylvania or Kentucky. It is a far cry from what you'd expect to find in Texas. Then again, everything's unexpected in Texas. That's what makes it such a great state—and a great place to fish.

These lures from Lur-Jensen & Sons are the kind of bait that attracts largemouth and smallmouth bass, white bass, pike, and saltwater species. These are used only on spinning gear, not fly-fishing rigs.

(LUR-JENSEN & SONS)

Sue King joined me for another outing, and this time we were off bass fishing on Fayette County Lake. Our guide was Judy Wong, a professional bass fisher, who also guides and teaches men and women the fine points of bass fishing. Judy learned to fish from her father—as did her brother, who accompanied us on our fishing trip. He brought along

We sped across Fayette County Lake to where the bass surely
were waiting for us.

(PHOTO BY DON HOFFMAN)

his Boston whaler, and that's where we deposited Don Hoffman,
our photographer, who took many of the pictures you see in *The Woman
Angler*.

The day would have been blistering hot had it not been for a cool
breeze that blew gently across the lake the whole day long. The water
temperature by midday was a sizzling 86°F on the surface, and by that
time we were well in the middle of the lake, tracking bass with Judy's
fish finder in her Astro bass boat. But we arrived early at the lake, before
the sun—and the electric power plant that hovers over the lake—
heated things up. We jumped into the boats and took off. We had some
serious bass fishing to do, and Judy knew precisely where we would
find the fish.

"Early in the morning like this," she explained, "bass tend to lie in
the shallows, around underwater obstructions such as fallen trees,
weeds, and the swampy shoreline. Bass are predator fish. They eat small
fish, and this is where they're likely to find breakfast."

We came to a cove and Judy shut down the engine of her boat. Attached to the bow was an electric motor, which slowly, quietly, allowed
Judy to propel the boat with the assistance of a foot pedal, closer to
shallows where we would take our first cast of the day. An electric motor doesn't scare the fish away as a loud motor would.

Sue chose the fishing seat attached to the bow of the boat and she hooked a nice bass on her first cast. She played him almost effortlessly. Later, when I hooked my bass, I realized that Sue's "effortless" technique was merely the result of a lifetime of fishing that began when she used to sit on her grandfather's knee with an old cane rod and catch fish in the pond behind his house.

The fish, however, were not biting as well as Judy had hoped. She changed our artificial lures—professional bass fishers, by the way, fish only with artificial lures when they enter a tournament—but the change didn't seem to do the trick. We visited different inviting coves that should have provided us with some sport, but our luck was thin there, too.

Soon we were skirting and skipping across the lake again at top speed, as before. Judy came to the middle of the lake and stopped. She checked her fish monitor, a device that sends sonic waves to the bottom of the water and records the movement and numbers of fish that are below, and the depth at which they are swimming. With a few words of advice and instructions to let our lures sink about 20 feet or so, we cast. And cast.

The sun was high and hot in the sky. I was grateful for the long-sleeved shirt I was wearing, even though the cool lake breeze was deceiving me into thinking I couldn't possibly burn. But I wasn't ready to tempt fate, and I stayed covered up under a hat, sunglasses firmly planted on the bridge of my nose, and kept ladling gobs of sunscreen on my exposed skin.

We visited inviting coves in search of bass.
(PHOTO BY DON HOFFMAN)

The day wore on. Sue got another bass, landing it as expertly as before and using her rod tip to direct the bass to the side of the boat. Finally it seemed about time to go in. And that's when I said that memorable line: "Just one more cast."

I let the lure drift down. Just as I was about to retrieve the line I felt a tug, and for the second time in my brief fishing career, the rod was nearly pulled right out of my hand. The line screeched and squealed, just as it had on the Miramichi when I caught that grand salmon. "Talk me through this," I yelled to Judy, and she and Sue together barked commands about my rod tip, telling me to reel fast when I'd drop my rod tip down, and to let the fish take the line and run without fighting him. It was a powerful fish, a fighting fish, and there was a moment when I doubted that I could land it. It was shortly thereafter that I sensed it was beginning to run out of steam. I played it, reeled in, allowed it to take more line, and repeated the routine until finally the bass came to the top of the water and pouted. With help we netted the fish, but it was too large to be a keeper. We removed the hook from its mouth, held it in the water until it revived, and watched it swim off with a whisk of its tail.

That day I saw bass leaping out of the water in schools. I saw them chasing their dinner, anxious to eat. I caught a fine bass, and as a result I caught the bass bug. Playing those energetic fish is a thrill. Again, it's all part of the chase, the hunt, and the quest we each undertake when we cast a line into water.

C h a p t e r   1 2

——

Return to the Miramichi

In August, the sky over the Miramichi is a vivid blue that is particular to that month and no other. It is kind of a cornflower blue . . . but not quite. Rummage through an artist's oil color box and cerulean blue would come close . . . but not close enough. No jewel or semiprecious stone captures the intensity of a clear blue August sky over the Miramichi—not a turquoise, an opal, or a sapphire. It hurts to look at the sky when it is purely blue.

Salmon will not bite under an August blue sky over the Miramichi. A thick rope of pines, birches, and alders binds the banks of the Miramichi as the breeze crescendos, crashes, and gusts, invisibly bending treetops and skirting across the water leaving whitecaps in its wake. It comes from the east. Salmon will not bite in an east wind over the Miramichi.

Miramichi waters are dark as onyx under the August blue sky, and the pools are deep. Sunlight plays across the riffles, a contrast of light against dark. The water looks cool, but this can be deceiving. When the sun blazes high above the river it warms the water, turning it temperate—pleasant for swimming. But salmon will not bite when the water is warm in the Miramichi, especially when it is heated by the sun under an August blue sky.

Last night the air was cool and today the water is cooler. The salmon like that. But if it were not for the August blue sky, if it were not for the east wind, perhaps the salmon would bite.

The salmon would not bite today. We fished the early hours of morning through midday, under that August blue sky. We cast dry flies, we cast wet flies, we cast into the wind and from behind. No salmon would rise. No salmon would bite.

My son Tommy and I had returned to the Miramichi to fish for bright Atlantic salmon. We brought my husband, Tom, and our younger son, Winty, along with us this time. They were entranced by the stories we had told them about our fishing trip in the spring, and they were anxious to see for themselves what fishing for Atlantic salmon on the Miramichi was like. The year before, our sons and Tom had fished the St. Mary's. That had been there in August, as well, and to the surprise of their guide, they each actually played a big salmon.

Unlike the thin, hungry black salmon Tommy and I had fished for in May, these bright salmon were stuffed to repletion—and totally uninterested in eating, let alone taking a bite at our flies. They had returned from their ocean feeding and were preparing to spawn and return to the headwaters of the river for the winter.

"Only the best anglers can catch a bright salmon in August," our friend and guide, Jerry Stewart, warned us.

"I have had the best in the world fish here, and even they do not get so much as a bump from the nose of a salmon in August," André Godin mused. Patrice and Susan just shook their heads as they stood over their pots and pans preparing for dinner.

For three days we fished. We got on the water early, right after sunrise. We fished until dark. No one got a bite. Except me.

It happened in the early afternoon of the second day. Jerry was sorely disappointed, but not surprised, that we had had no luck. He suggested every trick in the book. And then—as it always happens, when I least expected—a salmon chomped down on my fly.

I was so utterly startled, so absolutely thrilled, so bewildered and so grateful that this had come to me that I made just about every mistake in the book. I dropped my rod tip. I had slack in my line. I didn't listen to the fish or focus on its movements. In my enormous desire to land that salmon, I reeled in *too much*. I could feel the strain on my line. I knew I should have quit reeling and allowed the fish to run with some line. At the split second that I realized I had reeled in too hard, the fish took advantage of a momentary bow in my line as I down-reeled . . . and spit out the fly.

I don't know who was more devastated—me or Tom, Tommy, Winty, or Jerry. But at that moment a wise, kindly-looking old man came wading out into the water. The old man was one of Jerry's uncles. He motioned me toward a rock that was jutting up out of the middle of the river

"Have a seat," he invited.

"I'll stand," I said dejectedly.

The old man sat on the rock and leaned over his walking stick. He was well into his eighties, and his weathered face showed many fishing seasons.

"I was born on the Miramichi," he said, "and I've never been away from it. I have never traveled, have never gone out of Canada. I never wanted to. All I ever wanted was here, on the river."

He spoke about the fish and I listened. He watched my sons cast, and of the younger boy, Winty, said, "There's not much left to teach that young fellow. He's got it naturally. Now he just needs to learn the ways of the fish and he'll be a grand fisherman.

"I was the first man in the history of this river to travel its entire length in a canoe. I made the canoe myself," he said. "I've made lots of canoes. I made that one, over there." He motioned to a wooden canoe that was beached on shore. And then he told me stories of the river.

"Well, thank you for taking time to listen to an old angler." He smiled, and as he prepared to leave, I realized that our hour together had passed as quickly as a handful of minutes. "Here," he said, taking off his hat and removing a fly from inside the crown. "I tie all my flies myself. You try this one. It'll get you a fish."

As the old man made his way back to his canoe, Jerry waded over to me. "You know," he said, "that man's a legend here on the river. There isn't anything he doesn't know about salmon or this river."

If you've ever met a legend, chances are you won't realize how great that person is until after he or she has stepped out of your life. I met one, and for that brief time I spent with him he touched my life, and I'll never forget him.

That night Jerry came to say good-bye. We would be back, we said. We would always be back. In his hand Jerry held a little package. He handed it to me to open, but I already knew what was in it. Carefully wrapped up in tissue were half a dozen hand-tied flies. I said nothing, and neither did Jerry. I held in my hands a gift that I will cherish as a special token of kindness. I had fallen in love with the Miramichi. Perhaps I was her orphan, baptized by her waters, and the flies that were among the last that Delbert Stewart had tied were my christening gift.

> *Did you ever cast for salmon in the Spring,*
> *For the big, bright shining fish fresh from the sea,*
> *With the leaping strength and vigor they bring,*
> *To the swollen flood-fed river running free?*

> *That's the fishing that they called a "sport of kings,"*
> *When they fished in swollen rivers' springtime flow*
> *For the big, bright shining fish of other Springs,*
> *With the heavy rugged gear of long ago.*

—John Cosseboom, for whom the Cosseboom fly is named,
from his poem, "Old Time Salmon Fishing," 1925

I have left a piece of my heart by the river. I will return to retrieve it. Again and again I will return to the Miramichi, and there I will renew and refresh my soul.

All was not lost by not catching a salmon on the Miramichi that August. Patrice gave me another of his secret recipes, which he's allowed me to share with you.

Marinated Salmon

A Cold Salmon Appetizer

1 fresh, raw salmon, sliced thin
1 sweet onion, sliced thin
capers to taste

The Marinade:

⅔ cup olive oil
⅓ cup red wine vinegar
juice of one lemon
salt and pepper to taste

Stir the olive oil into the red wine vinegar. Add salt and pepper and juice of the lemon. Cover the salmon, onion, and capers with the mixture. Chill in the refrigerator for an hour. Serve on Breton or assorted crackers.

—

Chapter 13

Trout

Trinchera Trout

I had come to Trinchera Ranch in southern Colorado, in the heart of the Sangre de Cristo mountain range, two hours north of Taos, New Mexico. The 175,000-acre ranch now belongs to the family of the late Malcolm Forbes, but it was Mr. Forbes who saw gold in these mountains. Because the ranch is privately owned and managed, the streams have not been fished much over the years. There's been selective elk and deer hunting through an excellent program the ranch offers to paid guests. Now fishing is offered under similar terms, and anglers

The peaks look like sheets of gleaming stainless steel.
(PHOTO BY LAURIE MORROW)

looking for some worthy trout streams can stay at Trinchera Ranch to fish for trout. The accommodations and food are as superb as the streams.

The terrain varies from sagebrush flats to the kind of sharp, tall, rugged mountain peaks you associate with the younger Rockies that corrugate the West. In New Hampshire, where I live, the mountains are older, softer, and do not rise so sharply or dramatically, except, of course, Mount Washington, the tallest point on the eastern seaboard. Time and glaciers have polished the eastern chain, giving it a sort of patina. In the early hours of daybreak, however, the peaks of the Sangre de Cristos look like sheets of gleaming stainless steel.

Trinchera's fish are native and naive, and your fly is the first the fish you hook are likely to have ever seen. In the patriarchal waters of the Battenkill and Beaverkill, the trout are more worldly. There, a trout sees your fly and understands exactly what it is. That's an entirely different sport than you'd find in virgin waters like Trinchera's.

"I went up a stream here. I had a #16 Rio Grande King dry fly and wanted to see how many fish I could catch and release in one hour," explained Errol Ryland, a former Colorado Division of Wildlife Principal Biologist for the Southwest region. "I got sixty." Ryland later became Forbes's ranch manager. He was instrumental during his tenure at Trinchera in identifying the native Rio Grande cutthroat.

So I went fishing. The water was clear and fast-running in many places; still and dark where it bent around tight twists and turns, especially where the bank was high and lined with ledges.

It was a warm September day when first I cast a line. The winds were strong. The air was cold and crisp. I had a light line, a small fly, and even though I cast continually into gusts, it was effective. I could place a fly in the lull between breaths of wind. I fished deep, calm pools protected by curves of meandering riverbanks. It was on that day, my first at Trinchera, my first with a rod and a reel, that I hooked the Grand Slam of trout fishing, every angler's dream: a rainbow, a brook trout, a brown trout, and a Rio Grande cutthroat.

Does every angler remember his or her first strike? I'll never forget mine. The first tug on my line? I reeled in too fast and lost the fish. The second tug? I kept firm pressure and played the fish well and landed it easily. It was a cutthroat, and it twisted and fought, but I brought it in, admired the fish, and released it.

I used a Sage 379LL rod with a Lampson #1 reel, and a size 16 orange stimulator with a dry dropper. My fly-fishing guides, Tippie and Jack Woolly of Los Rios Anglers in Taos, New Mexico, had come to coach me.

As you have learned from this book, fly-fishing is indeed a passion for the serious angler. There's a mystery about it, romantically called "the lure of the angle." Fly-fishing is partly an intellectual challenge, and may or may not be a physically challenging one, depending upon where you fish. The sport pits you against the elements. Equipped with a rod and reel, you challenge nature, and if you win, your trophy is the fish you catch.

Overnight the temperature dropped a startling 40°F, and by morning a half foot of snow blanketed everything. It was the second week of September, and it looked like Christmas.

Considering the drastic and sudden change in the weather, Tippie Woolly suggested a Sage 279LL rod, again using a Lampson #1 light reel and this time a size 18 beadhead, gold-ribbed hare's ear nymph, which is a wet fly. The previous day the water was 58°F. Today it was 44°F, enough to make the fish too cold to want to bite. We tried several casts, but unlike the previous day, no fish was interested. Then we added some small Larva Lace™ nontoxic lead to weight the line, and a fluorescent orange strike indicator so we could see where the hare's ear had gone below the water's surface. All that day we had no luck.

The rest of the week I fished by myself. I would walk to a nearby lake, but it was hard to get to because the reeds were so thick and tall, and the land was so marshy. There I would find lake trout that were 18

Tippie Woolly suggested a light rod and a dry fly for the sudden change in weather.

(PHOTO BY JACK WOOLLY)

inches and larger. Behind the ranch house winds a stream. Its personality changes every 20 yards or so. All water offers its own challenges and promises. You can lose yourself in trout waters like Trinchera's. I did, and as the week warmed up I caught more trout.

The last fly I cast at Trinchera got caught high in an aspen tree on my back cast. I had to cut the line and sacrifice the fly, a small sacrifice for all the blessings I had received from the mountains. It was dusk and the sun was setting. I looked up at the gold leaves aflame against a blood-red sky. The sunset erupted like a volcano from the peaks of the Sangre de Cristo Mountains. I listened to the music of the rustling leaves and babbling trout streams. A bird called from somewhere not far. There, under the shadow of Christ's mountains, I learned to fish. I said a prayer to the holy hills, and returned home.

Fishing for Trout

The lure and legend of American fly-fishing is wrapped up in one family of fish—the trout. Trout is to the fly fisherman what bass is to the spin tackle fisherman. Trout is a daunting, taunting, personable fish—elusive and wise to the ways of the angler. Fishing for trout is like playing a chess game: it's all strategy. The pawn is the artificial fly (in this case, however, if the fish takes it, it's the loser and if it doesn't, the angler must resign herself to defeat). Even the most expert angler discovers fresh and exhilarating challenge in this most worthy opponent. The trout is the original American game fish, just as the whitetail deer is the original American game animal. Landing a trophy trout that's fought with a warrior's spirit at the end of a line after thrashing the peace of a sunlit stream is as great an accomplishment to a fly fisherman as is the successful pursuit of a wily, noble 12-point buck to the deer hunter.

It used to be that a trout stream was identified by the species that inhabited its pools and runs. This is no longer true. Today, three and sometimes four different species can be found in a single river or a lake. Many waters today are stocked with other species to augment the native stock in the interest of conservation and for the benefit of the leisure sport angler. Unblemished waters that exclusively supported their own native kind were compromised when two man-induced events occurred around the turn of the century, which virtually wiped out species-specific waters and tilted nature's pristine balance. One was the extraordinarily successful introduction of a significant quantity of European brown trout eggs into American waters by a German by the name of von Behr in 1883. These hearty fish transplanted so well that brown trout are probably the most abundant species of trout in American waters today.

The second event was western expansion and rural development. Clear-cutting to make way for crops and agriculture, the land-filling of wetlands, timbering and, of course, urbanization and pollution altered the course and quality of many of our rivers and lakes and warmed and muddied the cold, clear complexion of the waters in which trout once thrived. To compensate, fish hatcheries were developed so that waters could be replenished with fish, and while this worked quite well, the success of this strategy hinges on purifying and maintaining waters as closely as possible to their original, unadulterated state. In some cases, fish have been amazingly resilient and adapted to the change in their habitat, such as bass in Fayette County Lake, mentioned in Chapter 11. This large lake supports an enormous hydroelectrical plant that at times heats the surface temperature of the water to well over 90°F.

If America is a "melting pot" of nationalities, then today's trout waters have become a sort of melting pot of many different species and subspecies of trout. These transplanted fish are, in effect, immigrants—

such as the brown trout. Although sympathetic but nonnative species of trout, like von Behr's European browns, were successfully introduced into many, many rivers, lakes, and streams, there have been instances when the introduction of certain species of trout from one water system into another has backfired with tragic results. No one knows *who* did it or *when* it was done, but someone (biologists speculate probably around the 1940s) introduced trout from Lake Michigan into the Rio Grande watershed. Native Rocky Mountain cutthroats became infected with *whirling disease,* an apparently recent phenomenon so named because the infected trout actually whirls around in circles until it dies from exhaustion. There is no known cure, and nature may well defeat wildlife biologists in their attempt to remedy a problem that has blossomed over the decades to epidemic proportions. Some of the great rivers such as the Rio Grande and the Yellowstone are presently in grave danger as a result of this tragic, infectious man-induced disease. The most recent statistics cite 22 states that have confirmed the disease in their waters.

Species of Freshwater Trout

There are six major American species of stream trout: Eastern brook, rainbow, cutthroat, Dolly Varden, golden, and lake trout. These are divided into two groups: trout native to the northern United States, Canada, and the Arctic (technically known as "chars"), and those native to the warmer southern and central sections of the country (known as "true-trout"). Eastern brook trout, the Dolly Varden, and lake trout make up the char group, while rainbow, cutthroat, golden, and European browns are true-trout. Chars have finer scales than true-trout. There's a difference between the two groups in the physiognomy of their bones and teeth. Chars have light markings, sometimes red, against a dark body color, while true-trout are generally marked with black spots and have a lighter body color. Chars, as the northerly group, favor cold water and have been known to live as far north as the edge waters of the polar ice caps. True-trout favor warmer, southerly waters. Char spawn in the fall; true-trout, with the exception of browns, spawn in the spring. While this is the rule of thumb, it is not uncommon to fish for rainbow and browns in the colder northern waters, or hook a brook or lake trout in southern waters. Again, this is the result of transplanting and, to some extent, the trout's ability to adapt to unfamiliar waters.

Char: The Stream Trout Varieties

Eastern Brook Trout, An American Original

One particular species once dominated America's freshwaters and was the only kind of trout known to colonists and early settlers up until the mid-1800s. That is the Eastern brook trout. Affectionately called "brookies," this species is heralded as the *original* American trout and to anglers, the purist's trout.

Originally, the brook trout populated the Atlantic watershed of North America, from Labrador on south through the Appalachian Mountain chain to northern Georgia, and across the Great Lakes watershed as far west as Minnesota. A member of the char family, the brook trout prefers cold, clear northern waters. Although brookies were successfully transplanted years ago into more southerly, western waters in the Rocky Mountains and the Sierras, these are usually high mountaintop streams and lakes where the water is chilly, the way they like it.

The brookie is easily and uniquely identifiable by the light *vermiculations*, or vermicelli (wormlike) mottlings, along its back and its white-rimmed pectoral (front) fins. It has a cunning personality and is quite shy. It does, however, have one idiosyncrasy. Like so many of us, it has a weakness for eating. A brook trout will take a bite at almost anything that looks tasty all year long—even in the early spring, when icy-cold winter run-off waters fail to whet the appetites of other freshwater fish. These traits make the brook trout easy to catch and a favorite of the early-season fly fisherman.

The brook trout prefers intimate waters—quiet wooded streams, hidden ponds, and—like those I caught in Colorado—mountainside brooks. Do not underestimate a quiet, secluded pool. A formidable brookie is probably waiting for you there.

Dolly Varden, Western Cousin of the Eastern Brook Trout

Dolly Varden was the pretty, skittish, and coy leading lady in Charles Dickens's novel *Barnaby Rudge*. Dickens was not known to have been an angler, and would have been surprised and perhaps a little disappointed to know that "Dolly Varden" would become far more familiar to the world as the name of a fish than the name of his coquette.

The Dolly Varden populates the drainage system from northern California to the Arctic Ocean. Once prolific and abundant, this fish has suffered brutally at the hands of man. In the 1930s, commercial salmon fishermen accused the Dolly Varden of eating salmon eggs and threatening the population. Deaf to the cries of sportsmen, a bounty was put on the heads of the poor Dolly in Alaska—two and a half cents per tail—and virtually hundreds of thousands of fish were pulled from the water and left to rot on river banks. One fisherman claimed, with pride, that he personally had been responsible for killing 50,000 Dollies. As the waters became depleted of this fine fish, government finally took a closer look at things and came to the remarkable conclusion that the Dolly was not the *only* species of trout to eat salmon eggs. *All* trout eat salmon eggs. *Salmon* eat salmon eggs. The real culprits were bullheads and sticklebacks, who burrow into salmon nests and eat the fertilized eggs, not the Dollies and other fish, which eat eggs that float away, unfertilized, and therefore are of no significance in the life cycle of salmon but highly significant as a factor in the food chain. Finally the bounty was lifted off of the poor head of the Dolly, but not before the damage was done. Nothing was done to help the situation man had created, and the Dolly Varden was left to fend for itself. No conservation efforts were enacted to protect or help what was left of the population, or assist it to propagate and replenish its numbers.

Although the Dolly Varden is not the sport fish that brookies, rainbow, or cutthroat are, it is nonetheless a good fish. Almost any fish you catch is.

Char: Deepwater Varieties

The Lake Trout

Fly-fishing for lake trout is a challenge, since this deepwater variety of trout is a bottom feeder, a meat eater, and therefore to be sought in the cool chasms of lakes—sometimes as deep as 200 feet or even more. Heavily weighted spinning tackle, therefore, is far more effective in hooking this variety of trout than a weighted wet fly on a fly line, although fly tackle has caught some mighty fine Alaskan lake trout, which venture between fresh and salt waters. Its bailiwick is the southernmost range of char waters, a sort of beltway that extends from New England westward across the Great Lakes to Vancouver Island. Once known to exceed 100 pounds, the good-sized lake trout today runs a mere 12 pounds. The drastic decrease in average size is due to the fact that the lake trout is the only freshwater variety of trout that has commercial appeal. Millions of pounds of lake trout find their way to market each year, depriving the fish of the luxury of time in which to grow to its once formidable size.

Arctic Char

Arctic char is not a popular sport fish simply because it lives close to the Arctic Circle—a place so remote that only the most devoted sportsman must hanker to fish for this flashy, little-known fish. Exceeding 12 pounds in weight, the male of the species is a flamboyant green, orange, and red, while its mate is a classically tailored blue with white spots. Sometimes seagoing, this relatively unfamiliar trout is best known to habituate the Pilgrim River, north of Nome, Alaska. A northern variety of golden trout and red trout is classified in the Atlantic char family. These once were abundant in my own neck of the woods, northern New England. Sadly, these beautiful fish have suffered a fate similar to the Rio Grande cutthroat. Mankind got the notion that introducing landlocked salmon into Lake Sunapee, Rangeley Lake, and Sebago Lake, which are the native waters of these fish, would be a swell idea. It wasn't. Salmon soon dominated the waters once graced by the slim, graceful goldens and the handsome, blue-backed red trout. Although some have survived, the neighborhood just isn't what it used to be.

True-Trout

Brown Trout

Like many European immigrants, the brown trout has added a new dimension to its adopted country. From the time brown trout were introduced into American waters, it proved to be a highly adaptable fish. Changes in habitat, whether brought on by man or by nature, have hindered many fish—but not the brown. It hasn't appeared bothered by the muddying of once crystal-clear waters, nor has it wilted from warming trends in otherwise cool places. The introduction of other varieties of fish into the waters in which the brown live has not bothered this species one iota. If anything, it has continued to breed happily and healthily and so well that hatchery fish rarely need to be introduced into habitat with large populations of browns. As a result, the brown is responsible for maintaining an abundance of naturally bred fish in American waters, affording the trout fisherman ample and rather challenging sport.

Of all the trout, the browns do indeed present a challenge. These are suspicious fish, wary to the ways of the angler, and the fisherman that sets out to catch the elusive brown has to be wary, too. It is not beneath the seasoned angler to hide in the bushes or silently stalk this most worthy prey. In fact, the resolute nature of the brown often helps it grow to a ripe old age, and a good brown will weigh five or more pounds.

If given a choice, the brown trout will prefer a quiet river or stream, but because it is not fussy, it will do just fine in a landlocked lake, where browns often grow to be larger than those in winding creeks. It is particular about what it eats, which is mostly insects. The fly fisherman loves the brown trout. It grows to a good size, it provides a match of wits, and it eats flies. The trick is whether it will take the artificial fly that the angler presents to it. With the brown, presentation is absolutely crucial. The angler must cast her line so that she presents her fly on the water in the most natural way possible. Look for quiet, deep pockets by the water's edge. Look for dark, cool pockets in fast water thrashing along the river bank. That's where you'll find your brown trout.

Rainbow Trout

The rainbow trout is native to the Pacific watershed of North America, originally residing in California north to Bristol Bay in Alaska. Like the brown trout, the rainbow has transplanted exceedingly well into waters all over the country and to many far-off places, such as India, Chile, South America, and even Australia and New Zealand. In the 1880s, the rainbow was successfully introduced into the waters of the Ozarks, the Alleghenies, and Michigan—perfect waters for this big-swimming fish.

The rainbow is colorful like a rainbow and arches its back in the shape of a rainbow. It will leap out of the water, steal a kiss from the sun, and plunge back in with a light-catching array of color resplendent along its bowed back. A 16- or 18-inch rainbow is a nice fish.

The rainbow is a fast fish, a devilish fish, and the one most probably on the end of a line when you see a fisherman struggling with her pole as she is drawn closer and closer to dangerously fast water and defeat. I remember well the first rainbow I ever hooked. It was a quiet summer day, the kind when both you and the fish are too relaxed and carefree to be aware of much of anything except the quiet murmuring of the little stream and the occasional rustling of leaves from the canopy overhead. My rainbow struck like a bolt of lightning, exploded like fireworks, and leaped out of the water—then, with a sneer, dove back in and spit out my fly. The moment was blurred by excitement; the rest of the day was fraught with frustration at having been beaten by that cunning, arrogant rainbow.

This fish loves deep pockets in fast-moving streams and will rise to a dry fly as readily as it will to a wet fly, but it has to be presented naturally or it won't get the fish's consideration. Arguably the finest trout fisherman of all time once said, "With a big brown, the biggest part of the battle is getting him hooked; with a big rainbow it is keeping him hooked." Dan Holland certainly knew his trout.

Cutthroat

Earlier in this chapter, I write about catching Rio Grande cutthroat in the Trinchera in southern Colorado. If fishing can be considered a holy experience, taking a cutthroat from its native river—the river its species has inhabited since the beginning of time—is the answer to the angler's prayer. Western freshwaters were once full of cutthroat. Unlike other western fish, which primarily populated the Pacific drainage, the cutthroat populated this and a far greater range—watersheds on both sides of the Continental Divide, and from Mexico to Prince William Sound, Alaska. Today cutthroat are now the rarest of fish in their indigenous waters—again, a result of transplanting other species of fish into once-virgin waters.

When fishing for cutthroat, it's important to study the water and determine the hatch. If it's a caddisfly hatch, tie an artificial caddisfly onto your tippet. If it's a nymph, dry-fly fish with a nymph. Cutthroat are inclined to eat the insect that's mostly bouncing on top of the water during a hatch. If no discernible hatch is going on, you might do well to fish with a wet fly and perhaps add a little nontoxic lead to your line to get your lure into the cooler depths. There's some good-sized cutthroat in some of our western waters. You just have to know where to find them . . . and hope they'll answer your prayers.

Golden Trout

The true-trout species of golden trout evolved from the Kern River rainbow trout native to the western slope of Mount Whitney. Considered the most beautiful of all trout by many devoted fly fishers, the golden are as uncommonly hard to find as they are impressive to behold. Years ago, devoted anglers packed up mountainsides to release golden trout fry into high, clear ponds. There they have prospered, never getting very large, but keeping up their numbers the way nature intended. Some goldens have been transplanted to lower, warmed waters and actually have benefited by the longer growing season, getting larger than their mountaintop brothers and sisters. The purist, however, will pack his 3- or 4-piece travel fly rod and gear and trek up the Sierras to some high-up virgin pond. There, just south of heaven, she'll find a golden . . . and most probably, something more.

Steelhead

The leaping, athletic, hard-fighting steelhead more closely resembles the personality and habits of a salmon than it does those of its family, essentially the rainbow branch of the true-trout group. Just like a salmon, steelhead spawn in freshwater and mature in the sea. Like the salmon, the steelhead changes color when it returns to freshwater; unlike the salmon, it takes on a more pleasing appearance than its silvery sea luster—cherry-red gills complemented by bright rainbow arches down its side. And when compared to a nonmigratory rainbow, there's little difference except for its habits. Steelhead can reach incredible size—Corey Ford, the late outdoor writer, considered one of the highlights of his life the time he caught a 30-inch steelhead that weighed almost 13 pounds in the Russian River in Alaska. Like the Pacific salmon, steelhead spawn in the early spring (though they have been known to have both a spring and a fall run) and return to the river only for their spawning run. Within its family, the steelhead as a sport fish is the king of trout. Within the realm of fly-fishing, the steelhead is a prince among fish.

Grayling

The grayling is not a trout, but just as the steelhead is salmonlike, so is the grayling troutlike. If you come across one in the upper Missouri River watershed, you are fortunate. Grayling will jump out of the water with grace and fury, put up a terrific fight when hooked, and if not landed, come back again for a second round—something a trout would never do. Despite that kind of stamina, the grayling, though hearty, can't stand change. When the great white pine forests of Michigan were logged, grayling lost heart and within 25 years were virtually extinct. But you'll find them way up north where land hasn't been tampered with—in Canada and in Alaska. I've never had the pleasure, but I'm hoping to make its acquaintance one day.

C h a p t e r   1 4

Assorted Writings

The writings of authors of the past are usually dated, but those of
outdoor writers of the past never seem, at least to me, to suffer the
test of time. Seeing the great out-of-doors through the eyes of sportsmen and sportswomen who fished and hunted during decades before
us provides a perspective we are unlikely to see exactly the same today,
though the experiences are, of course, almost identical.

They say that yesteryear was a simpler time. Who knows? When it
comes to fishing, however, the gear most certainly was. Cutting-edge
innovations and modern technology were not in the vocabulary of the
angler. Bamboo, feathers, wood, cane—nature's products were the com-

ponents of rods and lures then, not man's artificial attempt to better what nature intended for us (although there's no question that graphite's pretty cool).

I have included three articles from a magazine called *Forest & Stream*. It is, alas, no longer in publication, and the kind of writers that wrote for this, and similar magazines, are no longer whinneying with us. They capture in their words a romantic view of the sport the woman angler will appreciate. More important, they speak in simpler terms that I feel will reach the beginner more easily than those she is apt to find elsewhere—although I myself, in this book, have attempted to keep it simple.

The Art and Science of Fresh Water Fishing

by Dr. George Parker Holden
Trout and Bass Habits, Lures and Use, and Some Stream
Entomology
from *Forest & Stream*, February 1928

A sentence in Lord Grey's *Fly-Fishing* that is much quoted by the experienced is this: "There is only one theory about angling in which I have perfect confidence, and that is that the two words least appropriate to any statement about it are the words 'always' and 'never.'"

The swift-water trout is likely to be lighter colored and slimmer than the denizen of the dark, deep, shaded pool which often is chunky and of very dark color—this referring to the same species in the same stream. Under certain conditions red-spotted trout may spend a good part of their existence, like salmon, in salt water—sea-trout (but it has been stated that the steelhead trout of the West is a sea-going rainbow); they then grow heavy very quickly and become lighter-colored, with faded spots. In lakes and ponds all trout and bass are largely ground feeders because they find most of their food near the bottom. Other interesting observations, by Mr. Southard (*Trout Fly-Fishing in America*), are as follows:

Trout rise most readily to the artificial fly when they have been and are feeding and almost gorged. (Apparently regard the surface fly as a delicacy or sort of dessert—see further explanation ahead, in discussing "bulging" trout.)

Large "rolling" (frolicking) fish are taken only on the sunken fly.

Use larger flies in early Spring, numbers 4 to 6, when the fishes' sight is poor.

September (when open season) is one of the best times for fly-fishing both in lakes and streams—the fish are nearing spawning time.

Spawning grounds are located mostly in the headwaters of smaller, tributary streams.

Winter Habitat (Nov. 1 to April 1). Spawning season over, in deepest water, burrow in mud. Dark coloration.

Spring Habitat (April 1 to June 15). Shallow, medium depth, along shore, on shoals or bars. Subdued coloration.

Summer Habitat (June 15 to Aug. 15). Medium and deep water, not so deep as in Winter; under-surface feeding, most shy. Bright coloration.

Fall Habitat (Aug. 15 to Nov. 1). Medium and shallow water, lightish bottoms. Brilliant coloration ("nuptial dress").

The spawning process is thus accomplished. The female scoops out a hollow in the gravel-and-sand mound, previously constructed by fanning with her tail and moving the larger pebbles in her mouth or with her nose, and then deposits the eggs. (At low-water these nest-mounds may be noted in the shallower parts of the stream.) The male, hovering near or paralleling his consort, ejects his milt upon them. Only a very small percent are productive, owing to destruction by minnows and various other spawn-eating creatures. While it long has been known that the male bass watches its nest vigilantly, it has been stated that both male and female trouts leave the eggs entirely unprotected after spawning. I have heard the truth of this idea of the male trout's indifference emphatically denied by a competent observer. Bass spawn in the Spring except in the more Southern sections, where they do so at varying seasons, and in the South they very generally are miscalled trout or green trout.

In lakes and fairly still water of streams trout stay in or near the shallow water they first seek in Spring after coming out of deep water, till they have finished "scouring" themselves on light, gravelly bottoms; then they "school," move to other shallow places and by the middle of June settle in some good place for the Summer. Sizable fish are more likely to retain their berths or remain in one vicinity in smaller streams; in large rivers, the currents varying considerably with floods, they wander more in "following their food." At times they move upstream in schools, with a rise of water, like salmon do.

Modifying the ancient dictum as to using small and dark flies in clear water and bright weather, and lighter and larger flies in deep and dark water and cloudy weather and for evening, Mr. Southard says that dark flies get more rises than light in the evening, except it be overcast and very dark, when the lighter patterns should be used. He recommends especially here dark flies having silver bodies, as Silver Doctor, Silver Spot and Silver Gnat; and he notes that very light-colored flies usually are less effective in rapid-stream fishing.

As a rule, bigger flies will catch bigger fish, though not always; and large trout are caught at night on flies as large as those ever used for bass or even salmon. With such a lure on the night of August 9th, H. B. Christian caught at Bradley's rock pool on the Neversink River a brown trout measuring twenty-five inches in length and weighing seven pounds. I first heard about this gigantic brownie—perhaps the largest fish ever killed with a fly on the Neversink—the following day from Christian himself, who sought the shelter of my "Big-Birch" camp in a heavy downpour near midnight. And when I was leaving Liberty for home one day later, the catch was confirmed by the baggage agent at the railway station, who said the fish had been brought to Liberty to be mounted; so anglers visiting this neighborhood may have the opportunity of verifying at least one big-fish story. How would you like to read an authoritative and complete autobiography of such a trout?

Wet or Dry Fly?—Hackles.—Considering all seasons, weathers and waters, both native and brown trouts, more fish will be caught on the wet than on the dry fly, but the latter way is likely to take larger brown than native trout, it is preeminently the late-season method for daytime fishing in much-fished waters, and it is the more artistic; here is the gist of the whole matter.

Good dry flies are: Alder, Black Gnat, Pale Evening (Watery) Dun, Whirling Dun, Yellow Dun, Spent Gnat, Hare's Ear Dun, Wickham's Fancy, Red Spinner, March Brown, Silver Sedge, May-fly (Green Drake), Cowdung, Cinnamon, Iron Blue Dun. In addition to patterns included in list Mr. G. M. L. LaBranche, our foremost American dry-fly expert, notes among his favorites: Gold-Ribbed Hare's Ear, Flight's Fancy, Willow, Mole, Black Hackle and Marlow Buzz, the latter two to simulate land flies blown onto the water; also he is partial to his Pink Lady. Mr. George A. B. Dewar, a prominent British expert in this branch of angling, some years ago published this preferred list (*The Book of the Dry Fly*): 1-Olive Dun, 2-Blue, 3-Red Spinner (small, the imago of the two foregoing), 4-Iron Blue Dun, and its imago, which is 5-Jenny Spinner, 6-March Brown, and its imago, which is 7-Great Red Spinner, 8-Yellow Dun (essentially a Summer fly—the Yellow sally is a flat-winged fly), 9-Red Quill, 10-May-fly (when the season is on, from last of May to Late in June—small-winged and darker pattern preferred), and its imago, which is 11-Spent Gnat ("the one succulent May-fly in its last and emaciated condition"), 12-Alder, 13-Sedge, 14-Grannon. Later Mr. Dewar revised and reduced this list, retaining those numbered above 1, 4, 9, 10, 12 and 13 to which he added Hare's Ear and the two fancy patterns, Wickham's Fancy and Governor, being thoroughly convinced of their value.

The Olive Dun he considers best of all through the whole season, and mentions that the Alder kills throughout the season also. The spent gnats and spinners come out in the evening largely, the Red Spinner being especially good in July and August. Sedge and Red Quill likewise are good evening patterns.

The famous "thirty-three" Halford patterns of the "new series" dry flies, described in *The Modern Development of the Dry Fly* (1904), are: Male and female Green May-fly (Drake), male and female Brown May-fly (Drake, or March Brown), male and female Spent Gnat, male and female Olive Dun, male and female Dark Olive Dun, male and female Red (Olive) Spinner, male and female Pale Watery Dun, male and female Pale Watery Spinner, male and female Iron Blue Dun, male and female Iron Blue Spinner, male and female Blue-Winged Olive, male and female Sherry Spinner, male and female Black Gnat, Brown Ant, male and female Welshman's Button (Coch-y-bondu, or Marlow Buzz), Small Dark Sedge, Medium Sedge and Cinnamon Sedge. Halford's *Dry-Fly Entomology* and the other books of his dry-fly series comprise the modern dry-fly fisherman's bible.

Close simulation of a natural insect is of more importance in fishing the dry fly—that is, for the artificial floating on quiet water—as no doubt it generally is taken for what it is intended to represent, and is subjected to more deliberate inspection by the fish than is the case with the sunken fly in swift or broken water, and is seized much more quietly than is the swiftly moving fly in fast water, for which the fish must dash.

The commercial "Dry-Fli" or white paraffin-oil may be sprayed on dry flies with an atomizer to assist flotation, or applied with a feather, etc. (Reference was made in the first chapter to Dr. Gove's "oil-dip.") The writer has found convenient the small tubular metal receptacle with a screw cap, known as the "One-Drop" oil-can, and a satisfactory substitute is a small medicine vial with an ordinary wooden toothpick inserted into the cork. R. L. Montagu said that a fly given a bath of "Three-in-One" oil and then allowed to drain for a time on a piece of blotting-paper "will continue to float bone-dry until the day's fishing is over." He found this oil equally as efficient as "odorless paraffine." Or common kerosene (preferably equal parts of kerosene and albolene) carried in a small wide-mouthed bottle serves for many anglers as "floatem" in which to dip these flies; though the oil need be applied only to the hackle. For the line, mutton tallow may be used, but equal parts of paraffine and white vaseline melted together is a preferable "deer-fat."

It is understood that the dry fly is cast up and across stream and allowed to drift down with the current uninfluenced by the angler, and cocked, with wings erect; and that four or five false casts are made into the air before permitting it to alight each time. These are best made to one side and not in the direction of the spot where a fish is rising or suspected to lie. Blowing upon the fly occasionally also assists in keeping hackle and wings in shape. While the fly is traveling downstream, the left hand is employed in gathering in the slack, to keep the line measurably taut in anticipation of the rise of a fish, and strike of the rodster which should instantly follow it. The great obstacle to the fly's floating down on the current in a lifelike manner, insurmountable at times, is the "drag," caused by the wind or current catching the loop of the line between the rod-tip and the cast and drawing the fly under, or moving it faster than the current. One way to combat it is to get directly below the point at which you want to cast and to cast straight upstream into the wind, or to lay the slack line directly downstream—"drifting" it—so that the fly will keep ahead of the line. Also, in casting across, a drag may partially be ameliorated by paying out some slack line as the fly is delivered, or, again, by dropping the line and leader on the water in a curve across and up the stream as already described in the "curve" cast. Especially in dry-fly fishing, except where the underhand (horizontal) cast is indicated as less likely to scare the fish, there is much advantage in keeping the rod-point high at the end of the forward-cast.

The fly thrown well up into the air drops altogether by gravity, and thus the fatal error of slapping it down on the water is wholly obviated:

There is more speed, hence certainty, in striking the fish:

In casting directly downstream, the lowering of the rod after the fly has alighted permits the fly to remain longer on the water before being pulled under by the current.

Angling does not differ from other things in life in that there is always something more to be learned in connection therewith. It would seem to be an anomaly to dry-fly fish in the rain; yet the writer has had the experience, late in the season, of fishing the sunken fly unsuccessfully under this condition while an experienced local fisherman alongside of him killed trout after trout on the floating fly. When "Pop" Yorks' eye meets this reference he doubtless will recall the August afternoon of the circumstance. He used a very fine and long leader, a number 12 fly and threw it very high in the forward cast so that the long drop to the water caused it to alight so gently that it floated, if not for long yet long enough to induce rises.

Fly Rod Lures for Bass and Trout

by O. W. Smith

from *Forest & Stream,* February 1928

Anyone who has kept tabs on tackle-making can not help being impressed with the great increase in lures designed for use with the fly-rod. It was only yesterday, so to speak, when small plugs, "bass-bugs" and "feather-minnows" appeared. I have received several sample lures for 1928, and, with few exceptions, they have been designed for use with the fly-rod. Why? Because anglers generally have come to realize that there is greater sport in using a measurably light fly-rod, also, chances for losing the fish. This is not saying there is no place for the casting rod, for there is, and I am wedded to its use; simply, for those who enjoy running a chance, the fly-rod offers untold possibilities. Not always is the fly-rod enthusiast in a mood for working with the rather difficult wand, and neither are the lures designed for use with it always winners. The successful angler is the one who can employ the most diversified methods, all else being equal—knowledge of water, fish-habits, etc., etc. There is more to this game than the uninitiated imagine.

In selecting a rod, much will depend, of course, upon the particular lure, more upon the angler's experience and ability. There is no great virtue in selecting a rod so light that the owner thereof is in imminent danger of a smash, though granted that there are thrills in employing such tackle. There is another side to this light tackle question, one not often touched upon. Why employ tackle so light that a hooked fish will depart, wearing a streaming line or gnawing hook? We hear a great deal about the virtues of a light line, but if the line breaks on a hooked fish, what of the fish's side of the question? Perhaps this has nothing to do with the subject being discussed, still, it is thrown in for whatever it is worth.

As I said a moment ago, there is no particular virtue in selecting a

rod light to the point of danger, though it should be light enough to afford necessary resiliency and action. It should not be too resilient, for
fly-rod lures are a bit heavier than simon-pure flies, and the fish—bass
and trout—which come to them are apt to be large. As to rod length I
would say approximately 9 ft., though if the angler has predilections of
his own he can vary 6 in. either way, 8 ft. 6, or 9 ft. 6. The weight should
be 5 to 5½ ounces. I doubt the wisdom of going down to 4 oz., that is,
for the average fly-man. Remember my assertion regarding the lack of
virtue in going to too hazardously light tackle.

I know there will be many to rise up and tell me I am all wrong in my
conclusions, but remember I am writing for the average fisherman, and
not for the specialist who insists on shaving away the ultimate ounce, or
for the big-fish crank who is never satisfied unless he has something
like shark tackle. I am trying to guide the average angler along the highway of safety and enjoyment. Remember the rod is of utmost importance and should be carefully selected, which brings up the matter of
material. My personal preference is for split-bamboo, especially in the
better grade rods, though I have no prejudices against solid wood or
steel, employing both upon occasion. I honestly think that where a low-
priced rod is desired, one will get better service from steel than a
cheaply made split-bamboo. For the latter pay $15.00 and as much
more as you can, if you want finest of action combined with maximum
of strength. I have never been a great advocate of solid wood fly-rods,
though, as said, and I have no prejudice against them. Always purchase
your fly-rod from a maker who has a reputation to sustain. Once more,
select with care, for a good fly-rod, one that "fits" you, is not picked up
every day. Know what you want, what you want it for, and how much
you are willing to pay, then take some reliable dealer into your confidence. So much, in brief, for the rod.

Reel and line are subjects we will dismiss with a paragraph or two
just because we should devote a whole chapter to them. I prefer a
single-action reel for use with lures of which we are writing, large
enough to allow the use of a large "core" of "filler," thus increasing the
speed of the winch. There is, to my knowledge, no good multiplying
reel suitable to the needs of the fly-rod user. The off-set handles of the
regular casting reels preclude their use for this sort of work: don't try
them even, for you will tangle your line around their protruding cranks
and get mad enough to upset your digestion for a week. For those who
like them, the automatics are wonderful for this sort of work, though
one needs to remember they weigh considerably more than the single
actions and should govern himself accordingly when selecting the rod.

The old rule is that the reel should weigh once and a half as much as the rod, a rule which forms a working basis, though I stretch it when using automatics. I must confess to a tender spot for these auto reels, so quick are they on the take up, so instant in control. With them, the playing of a goodly bass or trout is a very great joy.

The regular fly-line should be used, your favorite, in the size best suited to your rod. Do not undertake to handle these "new-fangled" lures with an undressed casting line. There is nothing which works so well as the regular enamelled, either in level or tapered, and here you must be governed by your own wishes. Some of my friends poke all manner of sport at me because I use the double tapered, but with it I think I get out my lures more easily and accurately. Don't know that one can say "naturally," for there is nothing in the skies above or the waters below that looks like a feather-minnow or bass-bug. But then, when it comes to that, what natural insect in anywise resembles the Royal Coachman, that widely popular trout fly? Fact is, a lure doesn't have to look like anything but itself in order to take fish—when it does. Thirty yards of line will prove amply sufficient for this work, as it does in regulation fly-fishing. There is much that might be said upon the subjects under discussion, but I promised to confine myself to two paragraphs, and have done so.

I hold no brief for any lure—and they are many—bass-bugs, feather-minnows, small plugs, artificial insects, etc., etc. Practically all are manipulated the same and therefore may be classed as one. I have some bass-bugs which have proven wonderfully successful, though I have not seen them on the market of late. Generally speaking, you will find those made of feathers or feather combinations the most popular, because they make a greater show in the water, though some of the fly-rod "plugs" are proving great fish winners. Perhaps the color combination is not important, but like every dyed-in-the-wool angler, I have my own favorite tints by which I swear; but I am compelled to add that my friend in the next boat, with predilections for other colors, is just as successful a fish-taker. Much depends upon the character of the water and sky, as well as time of day. I find there are days and waters where and when brown is the best color; though at some other time it may be that a shade of red will prove more taking. One should carry several colors, whether using small plugs, feather-lures or artificial insects; then he will be in a position to give the fish what they want; anyway, he can amuse himself changing lures. One of the newest lures of the type which the maker says "looks more like a bug than a bug itself," is almost irresistible when handled adroitly.

Perhaps I have not made the point I desired to press home all along, to wit, more depends upon the handling of this type of lure than upon the color or shape of the lure itself. I say this even though wedded to certain contraptions in certain shades, in which I am like the reader. Just the same, the man who knows the water, the habits of the particular fish sought, and how to handle his lures, is going to take more fish, even though he has not the best shade of color or shape of body, than will the man properly outfitted, but who is unacquainted with wise methods. Too many anglers depend upon their lures, their tackle and are woefully ignorant when it comes to fish-knowledge and skill in handling tackle.

I know a man who lives in a midwest city of several thousand, and probably every tenth man is a devoted and more or less expert fisherman. This city is very fortunate in location, being built around several lakes. Now those lakes were once famous fishing places, but with the great increase of population and anglers, they are "fished out." This man tells me that within two weeks after the bass season opens, the fish are "scared to death," seek the depths at the first splash of a plug. You see the great majority of those anglers are devotees of the short rod and multiplying reel—great and enjoyable implements they are too—and get out early and late, slapping and banging here and there, without much rhyme and with less reason. I have counted forty boats along a single weedy shore of one of those lakes. My friend waits until the fish are scared properly, then he and his wife—also an expert angler—set forth, usually early in the morning, casting carefully and craftily, taking all the time in the world, and taking fish. He insists that a dozen casts, properly placed, will bring a pair of bass even on his much-fished water. You see, the average angler fishes not wisely, but too well.

The secret of success in using these fly-rod lures lies in understanding, deliberateness, skill. Get away from the crowd, if possible, early in the morning or at the edge of evening. If fish are rising, you will have no difficulty. "Fish the rise," as our English cousins say of the dry-fly. Honestly, these modern fly-rod lures should be fished dry, almost. Select the spot for the cast with circumspection, if no fish manifest their presence, at the edge of a weed-bed, where the grass hangs down for the bank, close up to a snag, even a fence-post will offer shelter enough for a bronze-back. When the lure strikes the surface, let it lie quiescent for a little while, where the fish are "frightened to death." Then with a little twitch of the rod-tip, start retrieving, working along with many a hesitancy, many a stop. Whatever you do or don't do, don't hurry. In great deliberateness lies the secret of success. It is truly surprising how often a bass or trout will rise to these lures after five or ten minutes waiting on the angler's part. Having cast, won or lost, move on some distance before casting again, selecting the second location for the second cast with greater care, if such a thing be possible. Says my friend referred to in the foregoing paragraph, "Wife and I often limit ourselves to ten casts apiece, and often we don't use them all to secure a brace of bronzebacks." If they can do that on their much-fished water, you can do as well wherever you fish.

I have mentioned the method as achieving success with bass and trout simply because most of my readers fish for one or the other, but other members of the sunfish family—blue-gills, croppie, rock-bass, perch, and sometimes wall-eyes will rise to them.

They are universal lures as flies are universal; in fact, this is an exaggerated sort of fly-fishing. Don't think there is anything crass or uncouth about it, for, rightly understood, it is the sublimation of art. Naturally it will never supersede simon-pure fly-fishing, but for a change, and for our more common fishes, you will find it well worth investigating. I have said over and over again, and I want to repeat in closing for emphasis, understand the water, the habits of the fish you seek, how to handle your tackle, and above all, in the language of Henry David Thoreau, "Bait your hook with your heart. All else being equal, the secret of success, in fishing or anywhere, lies therein."

At the Falls of the Willamette

by C. M. Speare

from *Forest & Stream,* February 1928

That fishing trip to the Falls of the Willamette was sheer accident. A most delightful accident, if you will, but still an accident, for no plans whatever had been made for it.

In all the years that I had lived in Portland, only thirteen short miles away, it had never been my good luck to be able to fish there when the salmon were running. The busy season for me and the salmon run, invariably coincide, with the result that each year it has been my fate to be many miles away, where the salmon runneth not. Once, the first year of my residence in Oregon, I had been salmon fishing, but long since had all hope been lost of repeating the performance.

So faint was its memory that when I was scheduled to be near Oregon City and the Falls of the Willamette that day, the idea of fishing never occurred to me. Therefore I traveled to the meeting, took my allotted part, and started on the return trip, guiltless of any designs on the salmon. John, my companion, and an ardent fisherman, broached the subject casually as we came in sight of the falls.

"Let's go fishing for awhile," he suggested, "it's not yet four o'clock and we can get in a couple of hours before you need to go on." Totally unprepared for the occasion as I was, the idea yet made a powerful appeal. "I'd do it in a minute," I replied, "except that I've neither a license for this year nor a fishing outfit." "Those things are both easily overcome," he replied, "you go get the license—I'll borrow a rod and tackle for you, we'll rent a boat and go."

He did, I did, and we did—just about that fast. It was only a few steps to the old fashioned court house where the County Clerk with the skill born of long practice, deftly separated me from a five dollar bill in return for a combination Oregon hunting and fishing license, 1927 model. Across the street was a furniture store into which my friend vanished to re-appear in a moment with a salmon outfit.

A visit to his office for his outfit, a walk of two blocks, and we had our boat on the water in a scant quarter of an hour after the trip was suggested.

It was an odd situation—fishing for as gamey a fish as swims, with buildings lining the stream bank as far as we could see. Great paper mills were on our right and left as we looked up stream and almost overhead the great concrete Pacific Highway bridge spanned the river at a drunken angle. I say "drunken angle" advisedly for the bridge actually runs up hill, one end being many feet higher than the other.

Up stream the water thundered over the falls and all about us were boats, scores of them after the same game as we. The rocky walls of the river rose steeply above us—gayly decorated with a beautiful stone crop with the unpronounceable name of *Sedum spathulifolium*. Its soft gray-green rosettes of fat thick leaves were variegated with reds and bright green tones in bewildering array, for it is a most capricious and chameleon-like plant, for all its soft loveliness. Sword ferns and maidenhair hung in the crevices and everywhere blossoming dogwood and the bright greens of immature leaves testified to spring no less than the presence of the salmon.

Fishing boats from lordly motor boats with sun awnings, down to tiny canoes, dotted the river, some trolling as we were doing while others were anchored in long strings above favorite resting holes of the fish, with lines held taut by the current. These more leisurely fishermen trusted to the water to keep their spinners whirling—the while they waited patiently for more salmon to move upstream into their particular hole. This form of fishing is highly successful when the fish are on the move—which they decidedly were not this day.

Pleasant comment and good-natured razzing passed back and forth along the anchored lines from which every imaginable kind of tackle hung in the water. People from all classes and all places were there with an equal chance, for the salmon is not so particular as trout about the sort of tackle he goes after. In fact, the sporty New Yorker whom I met there informed us that each year he came west for the salmon run, yet with all his bewildering array of expensive tackle, he had so far failed to land a fish after two days' trial, while a little later we talked with a local farmer boy and a tourist from the middle west, with nondescript outfits and each proudly displayed salmon of fifteen to twenty pounds weight.

Full of life—fresh from salt water and with the mating fever pulsing in their veins, the salmon are exceedingly pugnacious, striking viciously at each other or any nearby moving object. It is on this pugnacity that the salmon fishermen depend, for these fish do not feed in fresh water.

My accomplice on this unexpected fishing trip had a favorite hole or two and we swung across the river in a long slant and trolled slowly up stream with our spinners sunk deep by four inches of lead. No result—so we reeled in and swung down the river in a great circle and trolled back up through the holes again. No strikes. A third trip and still no results, though we had to stand for considerable sarcastic comment from our lazier brethren as we passed the anchored lines. However, we continued to row slowly upstream through the eddies.

On the fourth trip up, we had just crossed one of the holes with perhaps a hundred feet of line out, when bang! a salmon hit my spinner just as it entered the eddy. I set the hook and prepared for battle, as with light tackle and swift water it's impossible to horse these fish the way some of the fishermen with clothes lines and shark hooks do it.

The salmon, after the first jerk, made a strategic error that shortened the fight immeasurably. When I set the hook he rushed straight for the boat, making me think he was gone. Frantically I twisted the reel and finally, with relief, felt the line tauten as I caught up with the slack. Mr. Salmon felt it also and leaped clear of the water in a mighty rush before starting head on toward the boat again. Again I reeled and again he jumped as he felt the line. Three times he did this, the last time so close to the boat that he gave us a shower bath. Then, seeing the boat, he stood off and adopted more orthodox tactics of short rushes that made the reel sing. His spectacular jumping must have tired him, for in five or six minutes he came up within gaffing distance, lying on his side, and John promptly jerked him into the boat.

He weighed 15¾ pounds, a small one as Willamette salmon go, but he was as fat as butter, so I had no complaint to make.

We had made the kill within sight of two anchored lines and the razzing promptly ceased, as that was the first salmon landed on that stretch of river since we had taken to the water. In fact, several boats quietly dropped out of line and commenced trolling over our course.

Twice more we made the circuit without anything happening, but on the third trip another salmon hit my spinner at almost the same spot as before. He behaved more after the usual run of salmon and what a fight he made! When I set the hook he first tried shaking his head until I wondered if all my back teeth were loose. Every inch of line gained was a fight, and it was a good fifteen minutes of steady battle before he was in sight of the boat. He stayed deep, battling stubbornly for every inch. I thought he was tiring, but when he sighted the boat it was different. Away he went until a good half of my gains were lost. Again I reeled, slowly winning back the line lost so quickly. The next and last rush was not so savage nor sustained, but if he were tiring so was I, and it was harder work. For another five minutes it lasted, with the salmon in sight of the boat all the time, but just out of reach of the gaff. He swam back and forth under the boat, keeping me doing a Highland fling about the bow to keep the line clear. When he finally turned on his side and came to the top of the water, I was ready to quit also, not only with him, but for the day. In other words, I was fished out and didn't bother to deny it.

He weighed just half a pound more than the first, but what a difference in the fight!

Afterword

The sun did not rise over the Sierra Madres that morning. There was no spectacle of color, no light darting across the waters, no dawn kissing the parched ground. Lake Guerrero and as far as the eye could see was an implosion of gray. Petrified trees studded the steely river bank like ancient Egyptian columns, and in the topmost branches, vultures, like gray-uniformed sentries, stood watch. Under their piercing gaze I fished for bass.

I had been to Mexico before and before it was beautiful. But on that cold January morning, secluded and far away from the world to which I belonged, I fished. I fished in a foreign place that held no beauty. It held awe.

Lake Vicente Guerrero is located in the northeast corner of Mexico. Once arid land, the huge lake is man-made and young, barely thirty years old. It is like no lake I had ever seen. Thousands upon thousands of dead tree trunks, some soaring as high as a two-story building, sprung from the water.

Pitch your lure into the water. Be fearless under the gaze of the buzzards. Sierra Madre, she is watching you, she is looking over you, and has blocked the sun from lighting your way. But this is no evil place. It is otherworldly; it is a place where you might discover something about yourself. Nothing that surrounds you can take your attention away from you and what is inside you. Nothing on the outside absorbs you in its loveliness and its charm. The Sierra Madres are not high like the Rockies. They have no peak like Mount Washington. The soil is brown and blistered, not green like New England or Kentucky meadows. The trees do not have the personality of the great pines of Michigan. There is nothing to recommend this part of Mexico.

I fished and nothing came of it. And then finally and quite suddenly, a very small bass took my lure, but I carefully returned it to the steely waters. Its home. Its place. And at that moment the sun chose to rise. It glinted over the ripples on the surface of the lake. Along the shoreline, tiny green leaves with the promise of spring and new life peaked through the dead boughs of the petrified trees. The morning rays greeted the foothills of the Sierra Madre and flooded them with brilliant color—violets and lavenders and magenta, and a crown of orange-yellow too brilliant to look upon. Suddenly everything was overpoweringly beautiful. The dawn had come to me.

This place where the sun had not risen, this place that first haunted me and made my soul kneel in awe, this splendidly unbeautiful place, Lake Guerrero, was the end of my journey. I had come where I was meant to go. There, on a lake God had no intention of making Himself, I, too, found my place. For in the great scheme of things we each have a place, and we are each of us here for reasons, perhaps, that we will never come to know. For reasons I did not know, I had embarked on a journey and went fishing. At the end I discovered my place, and was content.

And eternal delight and deliciousness will be his, who coming to lay him down, can say with his final breath—O Father!—chiefly known to me by Thy rod—mortal or immortal, here I die. I have striven to be Thine, more than to be this world's, or mine own. Yet this is nothing; I leave eternity to Thee; for what is man that he should live out the lifetime of his God?

—Herman Melville, *Moby Dick*

Directory

—

Fishing Accessories

Fishing accessories, including pliers, clippers, knives, reel bags, flies, etc.

Abel
165 Aviador Street
Camarillo, CA 93010
(805) 484-8789
Fax: (805) 482-0701
Contact: Gina Abel

Angler's World
A Division of Hunting World
16 East 53rd Street
New York, NY 10022
(212) 755-3400

Browning Fishing USA
Zebco Corporation
P.O. Box 840
Tulsa, OK 74101
(918) 836-0316
Fax: (918) 836-3542
Contact: Jim Dawson

Cortland Line Company
3736 Kellogg Road
P.O. Box 5588
Cortland, NY 13045
(607) 756-2851
Fax: (607) 753-8835
Contact: Tom McCullough

Hardy (US) Inc.
10 Godwin Plaza
Midland Park, NJ 07432
(201) 481-7557
Fax: (201) 670-7190
Contact: Jay White

Kennebec River Fly & Tackle
39 Milliken Road
North Yarmouth, ME 04097
(207) 829-4290
Fax: (207) 829-6002
Contact: John Bryan

Mayfly
P.O. Box 8307
Holland, MI 49422
(616) 393-9483
Fax: (616) 392-7070
Contact: Scott Hoffman

Orvis Company
Route 7A, Manchester, VT 05254
(800) 548-9548
Fax: (540) 343-7053
Orvis Distribution Center
1711 Blue Hills Drive
Roanoke, VA 24012-8613

Palsa Outdoor Products
P.O. Box 81336
Lincoln, NE 68501-1336
(800) 456-9281
Fax: (402) 488-2321
Contact: Bill Harder, Jr.

The Renegade Troutfitter
P.O. Box 306
Fairview, PA 16415
(814) 474-5231
Fax: (814) 474-5231
Contact: Claudia A. Kotyuk

The Royal Wulff Wristlok
3 Main Street, P.O. Box 948
Livingston Manor, NY 12758
(800) 328-3638
Contact: Doug Cummings

Dressings, Cleaners & Chemicals

Cortland Line Company
3736 Kellogg Road
P.O. Box 5588
Cortland, NY 13045
(607) 756-2851
Fax: (607) 753-8835
Contact: Tom McCullough

The Creek Company
P.O. Box 773892
Steamboat Springs, CO 80477
(800) 843-8454
Fax: (970) 879-7577
Contact: Christopher Timmerman

Kennebec River Fly & Tackle
39 Milliken Road
North Yarmouth, ME 04097
(207) 829-4290
Fax: (207) 829-6002
Contact: John Bryan

Loon Outdoors
7737 West Mossy Cup Street
Boise, ID 83709
(800) 580-3811
Fax: (800) 574-0422
Contact: Ken Smith

3M Scientific Anglers
3M Center-Building 223-4N-05
St. Paul, MN 55144-1000
(800) 525-6290

Fly Boxes

Angler Sport Group
6619 Oak Orchard Road
Elba, NY 14058
(716) 757-9958
Fax: (716) 757-9066
Contact: Paul Betters

Cortland Line Company
3736 Kellogg Road
P.O. Box 5588
Cortland, NY 13045
(607) 756-2851
Fax: (607) 753-8835
Contact: Tom McCullough

Flambeau Products Corporation
15981 Valplast Road
P.O. Box 97
Middlefield, OH 44062
(800) 457-5252
Fax: (216) 632-1581
Contact: Lauren Patton

Mill Stream
60 Buckley Avenue
Manchester, NH 03109
(800) 582-7408
Fax: (603) 647-8097
Contact: Don Dobrowski

Rose Creek Anglers
1946 Tatum Street

Roseville, MN 55113
(612) 647-1860
Fax: (612) 636-8944
Contact: Rich Femling

Sierra Pacific Products
P.O. Box 276833
Sacramento, CA 95827
(916) 369-1146
Fax: (916) 369-1564
Contact: Greg Vinci

Wheatley Fly Boxes
Distributed by Angler Sport
6619 Oak Orchard Road
Elba, NY 14058
(716) 757-9958
Fax: (716) 757-9066

Knot Tying Aids

Koehler Industries
P.O. Box 265
Hartland, MI 48353
(810) 632-5552
Fax: (810) 632-7186
Contact: Helen Koehler

Quik-Tye
S&S Manufacturing and Distribution
P.O. Box 0177
Longmont, CO 80502-0177
(800) 766-9034
Contact: Pam Bloskas

Luggage

Abel
165 Aviador Street
Camarillo, CA 93010
(805) 484-8789
Fax: (805) 482-0701
Contact: Gina Abel

C.C. Filson
P.O. Box 34020

Seattle, WA 98124
(800) 624-0201
Fax: (206) 624-4539
Contact: Steve Matson

Clear Creek Company
15 South Locust
New Hampton, IA 50659
(800) 894-0483
Fax: (515) 394-4278

Precision Flyfishing International
14109 Dartmouth Court
Fontana, CA 92336
(909) 428-2054
Fax: (909) 428-2058
Contact: Bob Montgomery

Predator Sporting Equipment
Box 1752
Sanford, ME 04073
(603) 749-0526
Fax: (603) 749-7112
Contact: Jim Coury

Sage Tech
8500 NE Day Road
Bainbridge Island, WA 98110
(206) 842-6608
Fax: (206) 842-6830

Scott Fly Rod Company
300 San Miguel Drive
P.O. Box 889
Telluride, CO 81435
(800) 728-7208
Fax: (970) 728-5031
Contact: Steve Pagano

Sportline USA
3359 Fletcher Drive
Los Angeles, CA 90065
(213) 255-8185
Fax: (213) 258-2001
Contact: John Gramatky

Rod & Reel Cases

Abel
165 Aviador Street
Camarillo, CA 93010
(805) 484-8789
Fax: (805) 482-0701
Contact: Gina Abel

Benchmark Company
179 Knapp Avenue
Clifton, NJ 07011
(201) 779-1389
Fax: (201) 773-2308
Contact: Bruce Hollowich

Boulder Landing Rod Case
3728 South Elm Place, Suite 532
Broken Arrow, OK 74011
(918) 455-3474
Fax: (918) 451-1802
Contact: Merrieann Miller

Bridgeport Landing Net Company
1104 NE 28th Avenue, #A275
Portland, OR 97232
(800) 578-6226
Fax: (503) 233-3850
Contact: Michael J. Ballis

Clear Creek Company
15 South Locust
P.O. Box 182
New Hampton, IA 50659
(800) 894-0483
Fax: (515) 394-4278
Contact: Bob Hansen

Flambeau Products Corporation
15981 Valplast Road
P.O. Box 97
Middlefield, OH 44062
(800) 457-5252
Fax: (216) 632-1581
Contact: Lauren Patton

Harding & Sons
P.O. Box 195
Evergreen Drive
Idleyld Park, OR 97447
(503) 496-3020
Contact: Etivise Harding

Landmark Company
4350 Ryan Way, #1
Carson City, NV 89706
(800) 796-2626
Fax: (702) 885-9910
Contact: Allen Putnam

Wachter Landing Nets
10238 Deermont Trail
Dallas, TX 75243

(214) 238-0823
Fax: (214) 238-1641
Contact Kathy Wachter

Wind River Inc.
3982 Rolfe Court
Wheatridge, CO 80033
(303) 378-7287
Fax: (303) 420-1522

World Gear, Inc.
24908 West Fox Trail
Lake Villa, IL 60046
(708) 356-9885
Fax: (708) 356-9886
Contact: Julie Forster

Associations

American Fisheries Society
5410 Grosvenor, Suite 110
Bethesda, MD 20814-2199
(301) 897-8616
Fax: (301) 897-8096
Contact: Paul Brouha

American Rivers
1025 Vermont Avenue NE, Suite 720
Washington, DC 20005
(202) 547-6900
Contact: Rebecca Wodder

American Sportfishing Assoc.
1033 North Fairfax Street, #200
Alexandria, VA 22314
(703) 519-9691
Fax: (703) 519-1872
Contact: Michael Hayden

Anglers for Clean Waters
P.O. Box 17900
Montgomery, AL 36141
(334) 272-9530

Fax: (334) 279-7148
Contact: Helen Sevier

Atlantic Salmon Federation
P.O. Box 807
Calais, ME 04619
(506) 529-4581
Fax: (506) 529-4438
Contact: Bill Taylor

Atlantic States Marine Fisheries Commission
1444 Eye Street NW, 6th Floor
Washington, DC 20005
(202) 289-6400
Fax: (202) 289-6051
Contact: Tina Berger

Bass'n Gals
P.O. Box 13925
Arlington, TX 76013
(817) 265-6214
Contact: Sugar Ferris
(also see page 130)

California Trout
870 Market Street, #859
San Francisco, CA 94102
(415) 392-8887
Fax: (415) 392-8895

Catch & Release Foundation
10A Midway Lane
Pound Ridge, NY 10576
(800) 63-CATCH
Fax: (914) 764-1500
Contact: Paul Carpenter

Congressional Sportsmen's
Foundation
1730 K Street, NW
Washington, DC 20006
(202) 785-9153
Fax: (202) 785-9155
Contact: Dallas Miner

Federation of Fly Fishers
502 South 19th Street, Suite 1
Box 1595
Bozeman, MT 59771
(800) 618-0808
Fax: (406) 585-7596
Contact: Jim Watkins

FFF Steelhead Committee
16430 72nd Avenue West
Edmonds, WA 98206
(206) 742-4651
Contact: Pete Soverel

Fish Unlimited
Box 1073
1 Brander Parkway
Shelter Island, NY 11965
(516) 749-FISH
Fax: (516) 749-FISH
Contact: Mark Ketcham

Fish America Foundation
1033 North Fairfax Street, #200
Alexandria, VA 22314
(703) 548-6338
Fax: (703) 519-1872
Contact: Jim Hubbard

Flyfisher Apprentice Program
407 West Seneca Street
Ithaca, NY 14850
(607) 272-0002
Fax: (607) 272-7088

Future Fisherman Foundation
1033 North Fairfax Street, #200
Alexandria, VA 22314
(703) 519-9691
Fax: (703) 519-1872

International Association of Fish
& Wildlife Agencies
444 North Capitol Street NW,
Suite 544
Washington, DC 20001
(202) 624-7890
Fax: (202) 624-7891
Contact: R. Max Peterson

International Game Fish
Association (IGFA)
1301 East Atlantic Boulevard
Pompano Beach, FL 33060
(305) 941-3474
Fax: (305) 941-5868

Izaak Walton Fly Fisherman's Club
2400 Dundas Street, West, Unit 6,
Suite 283
Mississauga
Ontario, Canada L5K 2R8
(905) 855-5420
Contact: Sheldon Seale

Izaak Walton League of America
707 Conservation Lane
Gaithersburg, MD 20878-2983
(301) 548-0150
Fax: (301) 548-0146
Contact: Paul Hansen

National Fish and Wildlife Foundation
1120 Connecticut Avenue NW,
Suite 900
Washington, DC 20036
(202) 857-0166
Fax: (202) 857-0162
Contact: Amos Eno

New England Coast Conservation Association (NECCA)
P.O. Box 552
Boothbay Harbor, ME 04538

New England Salmon Association (NESA)
33 Bedford Street
Lexington, MA 02173
(617) 862-0941
Fax: (617) 862-0952
Contact: Andrew V. Stout

North American Fishing Club
Box 3405, Minnetonka, MN 55343
(800) 843-6232 (Member Services)
Fax: (612) 936-9755
Contact: Steve Burke

Steelhead Society of BC
130-1140 Austin Avenue, Coquitlam
British Columbia, Canada V3K 3P5
(604) 931-8288
Fax: (604) 931-5074

The Theodore Gordon Flyfishers Inc.
P.O. Box 978, Murray Hill Station

New York, NY 10156-0603
Contact: Stanley Bryer

Trout Unlimited
1500 Wilson Boulevard, #310
Arlington, VA 22209
(703) 284-9411
Fax: (703) 284-9400
Contact: Charles Gauvin

Trout Unlimited Canada
P.O. Box 6270, Station D
Calgary, Alberta, Canada T2P 2C8
(403) 221-8369
Fax: (403) 221-8368
Contact: Kerry Brewin

U.S. Fish & Wildlife Service
P.O. Box 25486
Denver, CO 80225
(303) 236-7904
Fax: (303) 236-3815
Contact: Mike Smith

United Fly Tyers, Inc.
P.O. Box 2478
Woburn, MA 01888
Contact: Robert Fownes

Washington Trout
P.O. Box 402
Duvall, WA 98019
(206) 788-1167
Fax: (206) 788-9634
Contact: Kurt Beardslee

Women's Fishing Sports Foundation
2951 Marina Bay Drive
Suite 130–332
League City, TX 77573
(281) 334-1235
Contact: Gina Nesloney
(see pp. 102–105)

Books & Videos

Anglers & Shooters Bookshelf
Box 178
49 Old Middle Street
Goshen, CT 06758
(203) 491-2500

Black's Fly Fishing Directory
P.O. Box 2029
43 West Front Street
Suit 11
Red Bank, NJ 07701
(908) 224-8700
Fax: (908) 741-2827

Cortland Line Company
3736 Kellogg Road
P.O. Box 5588
Cortland, NY 13045
(607) 756-2851
Fax: (607) 753-8835
Contact: Tom McCullough

The Countryman Press
P.O. Box 175
Woodstock, VT 05091
(800) 245-4151

In-Fisherman, Inc.
2 In-Fisherman Drive
Brainerd, MN 56401
(218) 829-1648
Fax: (218) 829-3091
Contact: Al Lindner

Inter-Sports Books & Videos
790 West Tennessee
Denver, CO 80223
(800) 456-5842
Fax: (800) 279-9196
Contact: Johnny J. Jones

Judith Bowman Books
Pound Ridge Road
Bedford, NY 10506
(914) 234-7543
Contact: Judith Bowman

Lyons & Burford, Publishers
31 West 21st Street
New York, NY 10010
(800) 836-0510
Fax: (212) 929-1836
Contact: Jerry Hoffnagle or Tom
Lyons

Royal Wulff Products
3 Main Street, P.O. Box 948
Livingston Manor, NY 12758
(800) 328-3638
Contact: Doug Cummings

Stackpole Books
5067 Ritter Road
Mechanicsburg, PA 17055
(800) 732-3669 (Orders)
Fax: (717) 796-0412
Contact: Larry Johnson

Wilderness Adventures Sporting Books
P.O. Box 627
Gallatin Gateway, MT 59730-0627
(800) 925-3339
Fax: (406) 763-4911

Willow Creek Press
P.O. Box 147
9931 Highway 70 West
Minocgua, WI 54548

Clothing

L.L. Bean
1 Casco Street
Freeport, ME 04033
(207) 865-4761
Fax: (207) 865-6738

Boonena
2700 Neilson Way
Suite 421
Santa Monica, CA 90405
(800) 490-1201
Fax: (310) 399-4601
Contact: Lonnie Woodard, Jr.

Burke & Wills
P.O. Box 5222
Scottsdale, AZ 85261
(800) 532-2755
Fax: (602) 991-4651
Contact: David Michaels

"Buzzoff" Outdoor Wear
Maryed International, Inc.
5045 Lake Boulevard
Delray Beach, FL 33484
(407) 495-8258
Fax: (407) 495-8258
Contact: Mary L. Baltes

Columbia Sportswear
P.O. Box 83239
Portland, OR 97203
(800) MA-BOYLE
Fax: (503) 289-6602
Contact: Mark Bertelson

C.C. Filson
P.O. Box 34020
Seattle, WA 98124
(800) 624-0201
Fax: (206) 624-4539
Contact: Steve Matson

Eddie Bauer
P.O. Box 3700
Seattle, WA 98124-3700
(800) 426-8020
Outdoor clothing.

Flying Fisherman
P.O. Box 545
Islamorada, FL 33036
(800) 356-0607
Fax: (305) 664-8388
Contact: Michael Cleavenger

Go Fish Ltd.
618 NW Glisan #303
Portland, OR 97209
(503) 224-3474
Fax: (503) 224-0166
Contact: Bart Bonime

Goldeneye
P.O. Box 6387
Bozeman, MT 59771
(406) 586-2228
Fax: (406) 587-0478
Contact: George Foster

Griffo Gear
7909 Silverton Avenue, Suite 206
San Diego, CA 92126
(619) 566-8226
Fax: (619) 566-8250
Contact: Donna Davis

Hamilton's
P.O. Box 2672
South Vineland, NJ 08360
(800) 292-3695
Fax: (609) 691-0398
Contact: Timothy D. Hamilton

Hodgman, Incorporated
1750 Orchard Road
Montgomery, IL 60538
(800) 323-5965
Fax: (708) 897-7558
Waders.

Hook & Tackle Outfitters
6501 NE Second Court
Miami, FL 33138
(305) 754-3255
Fax: (305) 754-6559
Contact: Abe Rudman

Lewis Creek
2065 Shelburne Road
Shelburne, VT 05482
(800) 336-4884
Fax: (802) 985-1097
Contact: Kari Stolpestad

The Martin Company Flyfishing Outfitters
P.O. Box 503
Gold Beach, OR 97444
(800) 705-0367
Fax: (503) 247-7126
Contact: Greg Martin

Orvis Company
Route 7A, Manchester, VT 05254
(800) 548-9548
Fax: (540) 343-7053
Orvis Distribution Center
1711 Blue Hills Drive
Roanoke, VA 24012-8613

Outdoor Necessities
2414 NE 434th Street
Woodland, WA 98674
(360) 225-3442
Fax: (360) 225-6314
Contact: Jody Loomis-Brentin

Pacific Fly Group
730 East Huntington Drive

Monrovia, CA 91016
(818) 305-6664
Fax: (818) 305-6661
Contact: Ray Chang

Patagonia
Box 150
259 West Santa Clara
Ventura, CA 93002
(805) 643-8616
Fax: (805) 653-6355
Contact: Bill Klyn

Redball/Servus
9300 Shelbyville Road
Louisville, KY 40222
(800) 451-1806
Fax: (502) 327-6001

Sage Tech
8500 NE Day Road
Bainbridge Island, WA 98110
(206) 842-6608
Fax: (206) 842-6830

Sea Harbour Inc.
9183 Pineridge Lane
Boulder, CO 80302
(303) 823-5977
Fax: (303) 823-9066
Contact: Currie Harbour

Shoo-Bug Insect Repellent Garments
P.O. Box 81336
Lincoln, NE 68501-1336
(800) 456-9281
Fax: (402) 488-2321
Contact: Ray Clatanoff

Simms Fishing Products
P.O. Box 3645
Bozeman, MT 59772
(406) 585-3557
Fax: (406) 585-3562

Spartan-Realtree Products
1390 Box Circle
Columbus, GA 31907
(706) 569-9101
Contact: Bill Jordan

Sportif USA
1415 Greg Street, Suite 101
Sparks, NV 89431
(702) 359-6400
Fax: (702) 359-2098
Contact Diane Ducker

Sporting Lives, Inc.
1510 N.W. 17th Street
Fruitland, ID 83619
(208) 452-5780
Fax: (208) 452-5791
Contact: Janine Miller

Sportline USA
3359 Fletcher Drive
Los Angeles, CA 90065
(213) 255-8185
Fax: (213) 258-2001
Contact: John Gramatky

Stream Designs
350 Fifth Avenue, Suite 5515
New York, NY 10118
(800) 876-3366
Fax: (212) 967-2157
Contact: Janie K. Davis

Wathne
4 West 57th Street
New York, NY 10019
(212) 262-7100
Fax: (212) 262-3154

Wind River Inc.
3982 Rolfe Court
Wheatridge, CO 80033
(303) 378-7287
Fax: (303) 420-1522

Wyoming Woolens
Box 3127
Jackson, WY 83001
(800) WYO-WEAR
Fax: (307) 733-2868
Contact: Wilson Kerr

Equipment

Sunglasses

Action Optics by Smith
Box 2999
Ketchum, ID 83340
(800) 654-6428
Fax: (208) 726-9584
Contact: Peter Crow

Angler Eyes
2 Sunshine Boulevard
Ormond Beach, FL 32174
(800) 282-7696
Fax: (904) 672-8720
Contact: Jack Hewett

Costa Del Mar Sunglasses
123 North Orchard Street, Building 1
Ormond Beach, FL 32174
(800) 447-3700
Fax: (904) 677-3737
Contact: Ron Dotson

Dioptics Medical Products
51 Zaca Lane
San Luis Obispo, CA 93401
(805) 781-3300
Fax: (805) 781-3322
Contact: Cynthia Smith

Fisherman Eyewear
P.O. Box 261
Hollister, CA 95024
(408) 637-8271
Fax: (408) 636-9664
Contact: Rudy S. DeLuca

Floater Eyewear Inc.
6924 Plainfield Road
Cincinnati, OH 45236
(800) 769-3937
Fax: (513) 891 0942
Contact: Clifford A. York

Flying Fisherman
P.O. Box 545
Islamorada, FL 33036
(800) 356-0607
Fax: (305) 664-8388
Contact: Michael Cleavenger

Orvis Company
Route 7A
Manchester, VT 05254
(800) 333-1550, Ext. 844

Landing Nets

Anglers Custom Products
1 Forest Street
Hudson Falls, NY 12839
(518) 747-7458
Fax: (518) 747-6965
Contact: Marc Francato

Benchmark Company
179 Knapp Avenue
Clifton, NJ 07011
(201) 779-1389
Fax: (201) 773-2308
Contact: Bruce Hollowich

Bridgeport Landing Net Company
1104 NE 28th Avenue, #A275
Portland, OR 97232
(800) 578-6226

Fax: (503) 233-3850
Contact: Michael J. Ballis

Brodin Landing Nets
101 Spanish Peak Drive
Bozeman, MT 59715
(406) 587-8738
Fax: (406) 587-0570
Contact: Chris Brodin

Cortland Line Company
3736 Kellogg Road
P.O. Box 5588
Cortland, NY 13045
(607) 756-2851
Fax: (607) 753-8835
Contact: Tom McCullough

Hudson Woodworks
D.C. Angler Landing Nets
17744 Jones Ridge Road
Grass Valley, CA 95945
(916) 272-5606
Fax: (916) 272-5606
Contact: David Hudson

LDH Landing Nets
530 West Redwing Street
Duluth, MN 55803
(218) 724-6283
Contact: Lloyd D. Hautajarvi

Mid-Lakes Corporation (Loki Nets)
P.O. Box 5320
Knoxville, TN 37928
(423) 687-7341
Fax: (423) 687-7343
Contact: Bill Edwards

Sperrey Woodworks
P.O. Box 514
East Millinocket, ME 04430
(207) 746-5156
Fax: (207) 746-3214
Contact: Kendell Sperrey

Wachter Landing Nets
10238 Deermont Trail
Dallas, TX 75243
(214) 238-0823
Fax: (214) 238-1641
Contact: Kathy Wachter

Manufacturers of Rods & Reels

Abel Automatics, Inc.
165 Aviador Street
Camarillo, CA 93010
(805) 484-8789
Fax: (805) 482-0701

Ascent Reels
2516 Fulton Street
Berkeley, CA 94704
(510) 848-9582
Fax: (510) 548-6664

Abu Garcia
21 Law Drive
Fairfield, NJ 07004-3296
(201) 227-7666

L.L. Bean, Inc.
1 Casco Street
Freeport, ME 04033
(800) 221-4221

Berkley
One Berkley Drive
Spirit Lake, IA 51360-1041
(800) BERKLEY
Fax: (712) 336-5183

Billy Pate Reels
900 Northeast 40th Court
Oakland Park, FL 33334

Browning Fishing/Zebco Corp.
P.O. Box 840
Tulsa, OK 74101-0840
(918) 836-3542
Fax: (918) 836-0514

Charlton Outdoor Technologies
1179-A Water Tank Road
Burlington, WA 98233
(206) 757-2609
Fax: (206) 757-2610

Cortland Line Company
3736 Kellogg Road
P.O. Box 5588
Cortland, NY 13045-5588
(800) 847-6787

Daiwa
7421 Chapman Avenue
Garden Grove, CA 92641
(714) 895-6645
Fax: (714) 898-1476

Eagle Claw Fishing Tackle/Wright & McGill Company
4254 East 46 Avenue
Denver, CO 80216
(303) 321-1481
Fax: (303) 321-4750

Fenwick
5242 Argosy Avenue
Huntington Beach, CA 92649
(800) 642-7637
Fax: (714) 891-9610

Hardy (USA) Inc.
10 Goodwin Plaza
Midland Park, NJ 07432
(201) 481-7557
Fax: (201) 670-7190

HT Enterprises
P.O. Box 909
Campbellsport, WI 53010
(414) 533-5080
Fax: (414) 533-5147

JS Foster Corporation (Islander Reels)
517 Kelvin Road
Victoria, B.C. V82 1C4 Canada
(604) 384-3242
Fax: (604) 386-3177

Johnson Fishing (Mitchell)
1531 East Madison Avenue
Mankato, MT 56002
(507) 345-4623

Lamson & Goodnow Mfg. Co. (Lamson)
45 Conway Street
P.O. Box 128
Shelburne Falls, MA 01270
(800) 872-6564
Fax: (413) 625-9816

Martin/Zebco
P.O. Box 270
Tulsa, OK 74101
(918) 836-5581
Fax: (918) 836-0514

Orvis Company
Route 7A, Manchester, VT 05254
(800) 548-9548
Fax: (540) 343-7053
Orvis Distribution Center
1711 Blue Hills Drive
Roanoke, VA 24012-8613

Peerless Reel Co.
427-3 Amherst Street
Nashua, NH 03063
(603) 595-2459

Penn Fishing Tackle Manufacturing Company
3028 West Hunting Park Avenue
Philadelphia, PA 19132
(215) 229-9415
Fax: (215) 223-3017

Quantum
P.O. Box 270
Tulsa, OK 74101
(918) 836-5581
Fax: (918) 836-0514

Ross Reel USA
1 Ponderosa Court
Montrose, CO 81401
(303) 249-1212
Fax: (303) 249-1834

Sage Tech
8500 NE Day Road
Bainbridge Island, WA 98110
(206) 842-6608
Fax: (206) 842-6830

St. Croix of Park Falls Ltd.
P.O. Box 279
Highway 13 N
Park Falls, WI 54552
(715) 762-3226
Fax: (715) 762-3293

Scientific Anglers
3M Center 225-3N
St. Paul, MN 55144
(800) 525-6291
Fax: (612) 736-7479

Shakespeare
3801 Westmore Drive
Columbia, SC 29223
(800) 334-9105
Fax: (803) 754-7342

Shimano
P.O. Box 19615
Irvine, CA 92713-9615
(714) 951-5003
Fax: (714) 951-5071

Silstar
P.O. Box 6505
West Columbia, SC 29171
(803) 794-8521
Fax: (803) 794-8544

South Bend Sporting Goods
1950 Stanley Street
Northbrook, IL 60065
(800) 622-9662
Fax: (708) 564-3042

STH Reels USA Inc.
1000 15th Street
P.O. Box 816
Marathon, FL 33050
(800) 232-1359
(305) 743-3519

Valentine Fly Reels
P.O. Box 95
Chartley, MA 02712
(508) 226-0040

Zebco
P.O. Box 270
Tulsa, OK 74101
(918) 836-5581
Fax: (918) 836-0514

Manufacturers of Line

Allied Signs
P.O. Box 31
Petersburg, VA 23804
(804) 520-3242

American Fishing Wire
205 Carter Drive
West Chester, PA 19380
(800) 824-9473

Ande Inc.
1310 West 53 Street
West Palm Beach, FL 33407
(407) 842-2474

Angler Sport Group. Airflo
6619 Oak Orchard Road
Elba, NY 14058
(716) 757-9958

Berkley
One Berkley Drive
Spirit Lake, IA 51360-1041
(800) BERKLEY

Cortland Line Company
Kellogg Road
P.O. Box 5588
Cortland, NY 13045-5588
(607) 756-2851
Fax: (607) 753-8835

Fenwick (Iron Thread™)
5242 Argosy Avenue
Huntington Beach, CA 92649
(800) 237-5539

FTN Industries
P.O. Box 157
Menominee, MI 49858
(906) 863-5531

Gudbrod
P.O. Box 357
Pottstown, PA 19464
(215) 327-4050

HT Enterprises
P.O. Box 909
Campbellsport, WI 53010
(414) 533-5080

Izorline International
813 Gardena Boulevard
Gardena, CA 90247
(310) 324-1159

Mason Tackle Company
P.O. Box 56
Otisville, MI 48463
(313) 631-4571

Maxima Fishing Lines
5 Chrysler Street
Irvine, CA 92718
(213) 515-2543

New Tech Sports
7208 McNeil Drive
Suite 207
Austin, TX 78729
(512) 250-0485

Oldham Lures (Terry Oldham's
Spectra™)
Route 1, Box 94
Wimberley, TX 78676
(512) 874-2842

Orvis Company
Route 7A, Manchester, VT 05254
(800) 548-9548
Fax: (540) 343-7053
Orvis Distribution Center
1711 Blue Hills Drive
Roanoke, VA 24012-8613.

Phantom Tackle
11130 Petal Street
Suite 500
Dallas, TX 75238
(214) 349-8228

PRADCO
P.O. Box 1587
Fort Smith, AR 72902
(800) 422-FISH

R.J. Tackle, Inc.
5719 Corporation Circle
Fort Myers, FL 33905
(813) 693-7070

Royal Wulff Products
3 Main Street, P.O. Box 948
Livingston Manor, NY 12758

(800) 328-3638
Contact: Doug Cummings

Safariland Ltd. (Spectra™)
3120 East Mission Boulevard
Ontario, CA 91761
(800) 347-1200
Fax: (800) 336-1669

Scientific Anglers
3M Center 225-3N
St. Paul, MN 55144
(612) 733-6066

Stren Remington Arms Company
1011 Centre Road
Wilmington, DE 19805
(800) 537-2278

T & C Tackle (T.U.F.-Line)
P.O. Box 198
Schertz, TX 78154
(210) 659-5268

Tackle Marketing Inc.
3801 West Superior Street
Duluth, MN 55807
(218) 628-0206

Triple Fish Fishing Line
321 Enterprise Street
Ocoee, FL 34761
(407) 656-7834

U.S. Line Company
P.O. Box 531
Westfield, MA 01086
(800) 456-4665

Versitex
3545 Schuylkill Road
Spring City, PA 19475
(215) 948-4442

Western Filament
630 Hollingworth Drive
Grand Junction, CO 81505
(303) 241-8780

Manufacturers of Lures

Fred Abrogast Company
313 West North Street
Akron, OH 44303
(800) 486-4068
Jitterbug crankbaits; Hula Popper;
A.C. Plug.

Accardo Tackle
37098 Conrad
Baton Rouge, LA 70805
(504) 355-0863
Popping Minnow and Parker Minnow bass poppers.

Acme Tackle Company
P.O. Box 2771
Providence, RI 02907
(401) 331-6437

Action Plastics
3927 Valley East Industrial Drive
Birmingham, AL 35217
(800) 874-4829
Flutter Bug plastic worms; Super
Goober.

Aggravator Lure Co.
22 Cinderwood Cove
Maumelle, AR 72113
(800) 655-5873
Aggravator spoons.

American Lure Company
98 Gordon Commercial Drive
LaGrange, GA 30240
(706) 882-9099
Sugar Worm; Gator Grub.

Apex Tackle Corporation
P.O. Box 988
South Sioux City, NE 68776
(402) 494-3009

Bad Dog Lures
Snyder Co.
P.O. Box 636
Dodge Center, MN 55927
(507) 374-2955

Bait Rigs Tackle Company
P.O. Box 44153
Madison, WI 53744
Slo-Poke Jig'n Combo.

Bagley Bait Company
P.O. Box 810
Winter Haven, FL 33882
(813) 294-4271
Kill'r B's, Balsa B's, and Hustle Bug
crankbaits.

Bass Assassin Lures
Route 3, Box 248
Mayo, FL 32066
(904) 294-1049
Assassin; Lizard Assassin; Shad Assassin; Twitch Assassin.

Bass 'N Bait Company
8780 Fort Amanda Road
Spenserville, OH 45887
(419) 647-4501

Berkley
One Berkley Drive
Spirit Lake, IA 51360-1041
(800) BERKLEY
"Power" plastic worm, shad, grub,
etc., series.

Blakemore Sales Corporation
P.O. Box 1149
Branson, MO 65616

(417) 334-5340
Road Runner jighead/spinner;
Branson Bug.

Blue Fox Tackle Company
645 North Emerson
Cambridge, MN 55008
(612) 689-3402
Spinnerbaits, buzzbaits, Super Vi-
brax spinners, jigs, and skirts.

Charlie Brewer's Slider Company
P.O. Box 130
Lawrenceburg, TN 38464
(815) 762-4700
Slider lures system.

Browning/Zebco Corporation
P.O. Box 840
Tulsa, OK 74101
(918) 836-5581
Poe's Classic Super Cedar crankbaits.

Bull Dog Lures
3609-A South College
Bryan, TX 88801
(409) 846-5473
"Dog" line of buzzbaits and spinnerbaits; Tripple Rattle Back jigs.

Bumper Stumper Lures
402 East Highway 121
Lewisville, TX 75061
(214) 420-0365
Buzzbaits and spinnerbaits.

Comet Tackle
72098 Old 21 Road
Kimbolton, OH 43749
(614) 432-5550

Creme Lure Company
P.O. Box 6162
Tyler, TX 75711
(903) 561-0522
Plastic worms.

Classic Manufacturing
P.O. Box 1249
Clermont, FL 34712
(407) 656-6133
Culprit lures and soft plastics.

Coastal Lures
P.O. Box 485
Orange Park, FL 32067
(904) 272-0562
Bass Flash crankbaits.

Custom Jigs & Spins
P.O. Box 27
Glenview, IL 60025
(708) 729-9050

Daiwa
7421 Chapman Avenue
Garden Grove, CA 92641
(714) 895-6645
Team Daiwa TD Lures crankbait
series.

Double D Lures
2500 Chinook Trail
Maitland, FL 32751
(407) 628-9648

**Eppinger Manufacturing
Company**
6340 Schaefer Highway
Dearborn, MI 48126
(313) 582-3205
Dardevle™ spoons; Spinning
Wiggler.

Fenwick
5242 Argosy Drive
Huntington Beach, CA 92649
(800) 237-5539
Methods series of crankbaits; Shallow Crank crankbait.

Fish-Tek Manufacturing Company
4235 NE 27 Street
Des Moines, IA 50317
(515) 262-7419

Flow-Rite of Tennessee
107 Allen Street
Bruceton, TN 38317
(901) 586-2271
Original Formula Fish Scented Baits
series.

Freshwater Tackle Company
P.O. Box 518
Deerwood, MN 56444
(218) 534-3837

Hart Tackle Company
P.O. Box 898
Stratford, OK 74872
(800) 543-0774
"Throb" buzzbaits and spinnerbaits;
jigs and soft plastics.

Hilderbrandt
P.O. Box 50
Logansport, IN 46947
(219) 722-4455
Tin Roller spinnerbait; Headbanger
buzzbait.

Hopkins Fishing Lures
1130 Boissevain Avenue
Norfolk, VA 23507
(804) 622-0977

Horizon Lure Co.
P.O. Box 330
Huntington, TX 75949
(409) 876-3043
Ghost Minnow spinnerbait.

HT Enterprises
P.O. Box 909
Campbellsport, WI 53010
(414) 533-5080

Islander Manufacturing
9287 Horseshoe Island
Clay, NY 13041
(315) 695-2754

Jawtec Worms
P.O. Box 1181
Forney, TX 75127
(800) 544-4842

JB Lures
RR2, Box 16C
Winthrop, MN 55396
(507) 647-5696

Jig-A-Whopper Inc.
P.O. Box 3546
Mankato, MN 56001
(507) 386-1878

Johnson Worldwide Associates
222 Main Street
Racine, WI 53403
(800) 227-6432
Silver Minnow spoon.

Kalin Company
Box 1234
Brawley, CA 92227
(800) 782-2393
Hologram series.

Lake Country Products
(Lakco)
P.O. Box 367
Isle, MN 56342
(612) 676-3440

Bill Lewis Lures
P.O. Box 7959
Alexandria, LA 71304
(318) 487-0352
Rat-L-Trap Series of jerkbaits.

Lindy-Little Joe
P.O. Box C
Brainerd, MN 56401
(218) 829-1714

Luck "E" Strike USA
P.O. Box 587
Cassville, MO 65625
(417) 847-3158

Luhr-Jensen & Sons, Incorporated
P.O. Box 297
Hood River, OR 97031
(800) 366-3811
Fax: (503) 386-4917
Wooden J-Plug crankbaits; "Live Image" Dodgers crankbait; Power Dive Minnow crankbait.

Lunker City
P.O. Box 1807
Meriden, CT 06450
(203) 276-1111
Slug-o™ soft jerkbait.

Lunker Lure
115 East Illinois Avenue
Carterville, IL 62918
(618) 985-4214
Lunker Lure buzzbait; Rattle Back Jig.

Magna Strike Incorporated
224 Buffalo Avenue
P.O Box 69
Freeport, NY 10520
(516) 378-1913
Grandma™ crankbait; Equalizer™ crankbait.

Mann's Bait Company
604 State Docks Road
Eufaula, AL 36027
(205) 687-5716
Stretch and Loudmouth series of crankbaits and spinnerbaits; Mann-O-Lure™ jig-style lures.

Marble Hall, Incorporated
1426 North 27th Lane
Phoenix, AZ 85009
(602) 269-0708

Mepps
626 Center Street
Antigo, WI 54409
(715) 639-2382
Aglia®, Black Fury®, and Comer® spinners; spoons.

MirrOlure
1415 East Bay Drive
Largo, FL 34641
(813) 584-7691
Surface Popper series; twitchbaits, crankbaits; trolling lures.

Mister Twister, Incorporated
P.O. Box Drawer 996
Minden, LA 71058
(318) 377-9918
Buzzbaits and soft plastics.

Norman Lures
P.O. Box 580
Greenwood, AR 72936
(501) 996-2125
Rip-N-Ric jerkbait; Professional Edge series of crankbait.

Normark Corporation
10395 Yellow Circle Drive
Minneapolis, MN 55343
(612) 933-7060
Rapala: Shad Rap™ series of crankbaits; Rattlin' Rapala jerkbait; spoons.

Northland Fishing Tackle
3209 Mill Street NE
Bemidji, MN 56601
(218) 751-6723

Panther Martin
Harrison-Hoge Industries, Inc.
200 Wilson Street
Port Jefferson Station, NY 11776
(800) 852-0925
Panther Martin series of spinners;
Fire Tiger spinnerbait.

PRADCO
P.O. Box 1587
Fort Smith, AR 72902
(800) 422-FISH
Pro-Autograph series of PRADCO
lures; Bomber Model "A" (including
Flat "A," Fat "A," and Long "A")
crankbaits; Rebel® Pop-R series of
crankbaits and Rebel Minnows; Cotton Cordell Big-O and Wally Diver
crankbaits; Heddon Zara Spook®
surface plug, Torpedo propeller spinnerbait, and Crazy Crawler topbait;
Smithwick Rattlin' Rogue.

R.J. Tackle, Incorporated
5719 Corporation Circle
Fort Myers, FL 33905
(813) 693-7070

Reef Funner Tackle Company
P.O. Box 939
Port Clinton, OH 43452
(419) 798-9125

SAS Marketing
220 White Plains Road
Tarrytown, NY 10591
(800) 342-3838
Roland Martin's Helicopter Lure™.

Shearwater Tackle
P.O. Box 32103
Fridley, MN 55432
(612) 323-9829

**Snag Proof Manufacturing
Company**
11387 Deerfield Road
Cincinnati, OH 54242
(513) 489-6483
Weedless lures.

Southern Lure Company
P.O. Box 2244
Columbus, MS 39704
(601) 327-4557
Jerk jerkbait.

Stanley Jigs
P.O. Box 722
Huntington, TX 75949
(409) 876-5713
Jigs and spinnerbaits.

Storm Manufacturing Company
P.O. Box 720265
Norman, OK 73070
(405) 329-5894
ThunderSticks™ stickbaits; Wart se-
ries of crankbaits.

Strike King Lure Company
174 Highway 72 West
Collierville, TN 38017
(901) 853-1455
Mirage Pro series of spinnerbaits;
skirts; buzzbaits.

Tackle Marketing, Incorporated
3801 West Superior Street
Duluth, MN 55807
(218) 628-0206

Turner Jones' Micro Jigs
3514 Carriage Drive

Springfield, MO 65809
(417) 883-6723

Uncle Josh Bait Company
P.O. Box 130
Fort Atkinson, WI 53538
(414) 563-2491
Pork rind; scents.

United Brands International
1489 Market Circle
Port Charlotte, FL 33953-3804
(813) 255-0061
Flying Lure™.

Varonon Bait Company
805 Oak Ridge Drive
Birmingham, AL 35214
(205) 791-1985
Soft plastics.

Water Life, Incorporated (Rebaki)
P.O. Box 10300
Alexandria, VA 22310
(703) 960-5820

Yakima Bait Company
P.O. Box 310
Granger, WA 98932
(800) 527-2711
Worden's Lures series; Rooster Tail®
spinner with hackle tail; Poe's Ace-
In-The-Hole; Super Toad crankbait.

Zetabait, Inc.
9559 Foley Lane
Foley, AL 36535
(205) 943-1902
Soft plastics; jerkbaits.

Fishing Tackle Shops

Alabama

Fins & Feathers
975 J Airport Road
Huntsville, AL 35802
(800) 606-7603

The Hunter Collection
3000 D Zelda Road
Montgomery, AL 36106
(334) 244-9586

Werner's Trading Company
1115 4th Street, SW
Cullman, AL 35055
(800) 965-8796

Woods & Water, Incorporated
1019 McFarland Boulevard
Northport, AL 35476
(800) 484-5471

Arizona

4J's Troutfitters
10869 North Scottsdale
Road, Suite 103
Scottsdale, AZ 85254
(602) 905-1400
Fax: (602) 922-8753

Lynx Creek Unlimited
130 West Gurley, Suite #307
Prescott, AZ 86301
(520) 776-7088

Arkansas

Bancroft & Tabor
Northwest Arkansas Mall
Fayetteville, AR 72703
(501) 442-2193

California

Bob Marriott's Fly Fishing Store
2700 West Orangethorpe Avenue
Fullerton, CA 92833
(800) 535-6633

Crystal Springs Fly Fishing
2233 Grand Canal Boulevard,
Suite 202
Stockton, CA 95207
(209) 954-0963
Fax: (209) 954-0351

**Range of Light Fly Fishing
Outfitters**
2020 West Whitendale
Visalia, CA 93277
(209) 635-1500

Wind River Fly Fishing
1043 Atlas Peak Road
Napa, CA 94558
(707) 252-4900
Fax: (707) 252-4709

Orvis San Francisco
300 Grant Avenue
San Francisco, CA 94108
(415) 392-1600
Fax: (415) 391-7228

Colorado

**Breckenridge Outfitters,
Incorporated**
100 North Main Street, Suite 206
Town Square
Breckenridge, CO 80424
(970) 453-4135

Bucking Rainbow Outfitters
402 Lincoln Avenue
Steamboat Springs, CO 80477
(970) 879-4693

The Blue Quill Angler
1532 Bergen Parkway
Evergreen, CO 80439
(800) 435-5353
Fax: (303) 674-4791

Kinsley & Company
1155 13th Street
Boulder, CO 80302
(800) 442-7420
Fax: (303) 442-7286

Rod & Reel Fly Shop
P.O. Box 86, 101 Main Street
Creede, CO 81130
(719) 658-2955

Connecticut

Connecticut Outfitters
200 West Main Street, Route 44
Avon, CT 06001
(860) 678-8050

**Cubeta's Field & Stream
Incorporated**
157 Meriden Road, Route 66
Middlefield, CT 06455
(800) CUBETAS

A Sporting Tradition, Limited
71 Ethan Allen Highway, Route 7
Ridgefield, CT 06877
(203) 544-7700

Delaware

Sporting Gentleman of Delaware
Fredericks Country Center
5716 Kennett Pike, Route 52
Centreville, DE 19807
(302) 427-8110

Florida

Downeast
715 Bloom Street, Suite 140
Walt Disney's Celebration, FL 34747
(407) 566-0000

Everglades Angler
810 12th Avenue, South
Naples, FL 34102
(800) 664-8259

Pearson & Sons Outfitters, Incorporated
207 South Palafox Street
Pensacola, FL 32501
(904) 470-9626

Sanibel Light Tackle Outfitters, Incorporated
2025 Periwinkle Way
Sanibel Island, FL 33957
(941) 472-2002

Georgia

The Bedford Sportsman South
3405 Frederica Road
Saint Simons Island, GA 31522
(912) 638-5454

The Fish Hawk, Inc.
279 Buckhead Avenue
Atlanta, GA 30305-2224
404-237-3473

Orvis Atlanta
Buckhead Square
3255 Peachtree Road, NE
Atlanta, GA 30305
(404) 841-0093
Fax: (404) 841-6440

Illinois

Saturday Morning Company
126 West Main Street
Barrington, IL 60010
(847) 382-3010

Trout and Grouse
300 Happ Road
Northfield, IL 60093
(847) 501-3111

The Wildlife Refuge, Incorporated
University Mall
Carbondale, IL 62901
(618) 529-5130

Orvis Chicago
142 East Ontario Street
Chicago, IL 60611
(312) 440-0662
Fax: (312) 587-8713

Orvis Old Orchard
Old Orchard Shopping Center
Old Orchard & Skokie Boulevard
Skokie, IL 60077
(847) 677-4774
Fax: (847) 677-4793

Indiana

The Ginger Quill
328 West Cleveland Road
Granger, IN 46530
(219) 273-0996

Royal River Company
Woodfield Centre
Suite 234, 2727 East 86th Street
Indianapolis, IN 46240
(317) 253-2572

Kansas

Orvis Kansas
Town Center Plaza
4840 West 119th Street
Leawood, KS 66209
(913) 327-1600
Fax: (913) 327-1607

Kentucky

The Sporting Tradition
Civic Center Shops
410 West Vine Street
Lexington, KY 40507
(800) 303-3618

Louisiana

Louisiana Outfitters
3809 Ambassador Caffery 134C
Lafayette, LA 70503
(318) 988-9090

The Ouachita River Company
312 Trenton Street
West Monroe, LA 71291
(800) 935-3597

The Sporting Life
601 Julia Street
New Orleans, LA 70130
(504) 529-3597
Fax: (504) 529-1589

Maine

Barnes Outfitters, Inc.
184 U.S. Route #1
Freeport, ME 04032
(207) 865-1113

Fly Fishing Only
230 Main Street
Fairfield, ME 04937
(207) 453-6242

Maryland

Keepers
300 South Talbot Street
P.O. Box 1140
Saint Michaels, MD 21663
(800) 549-1872

Massachusetts

Coop's Bait & Tackle
RFD Box 19
147 West Tisbury Road
Edgartown, MA 02539
(508) 627-8202

Fishing The Cape
Harwich Commons Route 137 & 39
East Harwich, MA 02645
(508) 432-1200

Rivers Edge Trading Co.
50 Dodge Street
Junction Routes 1A & 128
Beverly, MA 01915
(508) 921-8008

RiverRun
271 Main Street
Great Barrington, MA 01230
(413) 528-9600

Wellesley Outdoors
380 Washington Street
Wellesley, MA 02181
(800) 427-9144

Michigan

Earth's Edge
222 Washington
Grand Haven, MI 49417
(616) 844-1724

Little Forks Outfitters
143 East Main Street
Midland, MI 48640

(517) 832-4100
Fax: (517) 832-1893

Paint Creek Outfitters, Limited
203 East University Drive
Rochester, MI 48307
(810) 650-0440

**The Riverbend Sport Shop,
Incorporated**
29229 Northwestern Highway
Southfield, MI 48034
(810) 350-8484

Streamside, Inc.
4440 Grand Traverse Village, E4
Traverse City, MI
(616) 938-5337
Contact: Dave Leonard

Thornapple Orvis Shop
1200 East Paris #4
Grand Rapids, MI 49546
(616) 975-3800

**Whippoorwill Fly Fishing Shop,
Inc.**
1844 M-119 Highway
Petoskey, MI 49770
(616) 348-7061

Minnesota

Bentley's Outfitters
Tower Square Shopping Center
582 Prairie Center Drive #230B
Eden Prairie, MN 55344
(612) 828-9554

Galyan's Trading Company
Tamarack Village Shopping Center
8292 Tamarack Village
Woodbury, MN 55125
(612) 731-0200

Missouri

Rainbow Fly Shop
17201 East 40 Highway
Independence, MO 64055
(816) 373-2283

Orvis Gokey Manufacturing
300 Moniteau Street
Tipton, MO 65081
(816) 433-5401
Fax: (816) 433-2391

Montana

Bighorn Fly & Tackle Shop
485 South 24th Street
West Billings, MT 59102
(406) 656-8257

Cross Currents
326 North Jackson
Helena, MT 59601
(406) 449-2292

Forresters Frontier Travels
Bighorn River, P.O. Box 470
Hardin, MT 59034
(800) 665-3799
E-Mail: www.Forrester-Travel.com

High Plains Outfitters
205 9th Avenue
South Great Falls, MT 59405
(406) 727-2119

Nevada

**"Reel Outfitters" at Rio Suite Hotel
& Casino**
3700 West Flamingo Road
Las Vegas, NV 89103
(702) 247-7883

New Hampshire

Lyme Angler
8 South Main Street
Hanover, NH 03755
(603) 643-1263

New Jersey

The Fly Fishing Shop at The Sports People
The Mall at Far Hills
Far Hills, NJ 07931
(908) 719-9100

Orvis Short Hills
Short Hills Shopping Mall
1200 Morris Turnpike
Short Hills, NJ 07078
(201) 376-4828
Fax: (201) 376-9849

New Mexico

Abe's Motel & Fly Shop, Incorporated
P.O. Box 6428
San Juan River, NM 87419
(505) 632-2194

The Reel Life
1100 San Mateo Boulevard, NE, Suite 10
Albuquerque, NM 87110
(505) 268-1693

New York

Beaverkill Angler
P.O. Box 198
Roscoe, NY 12776
(607) 498-5194
Fax: (607) 498-4740

Dixon's Sporting Life
74 Montauk Highway #9
East Hampton, NY 11937
(516) 324-7979

Jones Outfitters, Limited
37 Main Street
Lake Placid, NY 12946
(518) 523-3468

Reed's Orvis Shop
5655 Main Street
Williamsville, NY 14221
(716) 631-5131

Timber Creek Sportsman Shop
100 Rano Boulevard, Giant Plaza
Vestal, NY 13850
(607) 770-9112

Orvis New York
355 Madison Avenue
(entrance on 45th Street)
New York, NY 10017
(212) 697-3133
Fax: (212) 697-5826

Orvis Sandanona
Route 44A Sharon Turnpike
P.O. Box 450
Millbrook, NY 12545-0450
(914) 677-9701
Fax: (914) 677-0092

North Carolina

Brookings
Route 70, Box 191
Cashiers, NC 28717
(704) 743-3768

Digh's Country Sports Gallery
1988 Eastwood Road
Wrightsville Beach, NC 28403
(910) 256-2060

Fosco Fishing Company & Outfitters
9378-1 Highway 105 South
Banner Elk, NC 28604
(704) 963-7431

NC Anglers & Outfitters
714 Ninth Street
Durham, NC 27705
(800) 454-6657

Ohio

Backpackers Shop of Ohio Canoe Adventures, Incorporated
5128 Colorado Avenue
Sheffield Village, OH 44054
(216) 934-5345

Mad River Outfitters
779 Bethel Road
Columbus, OH 43214
(888) 451-0383

Valley Angler
13 North Franklin Street
Chagrin Falls, OH 44022
(216) 247-0242

Oklahoma

The Gadget Company
1702 Utica Square
Tulsa, OK 74114
(918) 749-9963

River's Edge
10904 North May Avenue, Suite A-1
Oklahoma City, OK 73120
(405) 748-3900

Oregon

Fly Country Outfitters
3400 State Street, Suite G704
Salem, OR 97301
(503) 585-4898

The Hook Fly Shop
Building 22, Sunriver Mall
Sunriver, OR 97707
(541) 593-2358

Pennsylvania

Forrest County Sports Center
311 Elm Street
Tionesta, PA 16353
(800) 458-6093

Northeast Flyfishers
923 Main Street
Honesdale, PA 18431
(717) 253-9780
E-Mail: flyfish@ptd.net

The Sporting Gentleman
306 East Baltimore Pike
Media, PA 19063
(610) 565-6140

The Wilderness Trekker
RD 1, Box 1243C, Route 61
Orwigsburg, PA 17961
(717) 366-0165

Orvis Philadelphia
1423 Walnut Street
Philadelphia, PA 19102
(215) 567-6207
Fax: (215) 567-7543

Rhode Island

Oceans and Ponds, Incorporated
271 Ocean Avenue
P.O. Box 136
Block Island, RI 02807
(800) ORVIS01 (678-4701)

South Carolina

Bay Street Outfitters
815 Bay Street
Beaufort, SC 29902
(803) 524-5250
Fax: (803) 524-9002

Luden's
Concord & Charlotte Streets
Charleston, SC 29401
(803) 723-7829

Tennessee

Angler's Trading Company
The Shops at Western Plaza
4411 Kingston Pike
Knoxville, TN 37919
(423) 558-0507

The Osprey
18 Frazier Avenue
Chattanooga, TN 37405
(423) 265-0306

The Sporting Life
3092 Poplar Avenue
Memphis, TN 38111
(901) 324-2383

Texas

Jones Creek
2301 South Broadway, #A7
Tyler, TX 75701
(903) 526-3474
Fax: (903) 592-2626

Sporting Traditions
4704 Bryce (Comer of Camp Bowie)
Fort Worth, TX 76107
(817) 377-8845

Orvis Dallas
Preston Oaks Shopping Center
10720 Preston Road, Suite 1100
Dallas, TX 75230
(214) 265-1600
Fax: (214) 265-1989

Orvis Houston
5848 Westheimer Road
Houston, TX 77057

(713) 783-2111
Fax: (713) 784-3210

Utah

Spinner Fall Fly Shop
1450 Foothill Drive
Salt Lake City, UT 84108
(800) 979-3474

Vermont

Shallowford & Company
65 Central Street
P.O. Box 520
Woodstock, VT 05091
(802) 457-4340

Taddingers
Route 100 North
(Mount Snow)
Wilmington, VT 05363
(802) 464-1223

Orvis Manchester
Route 7A
Manchester, VT 05254
(802) 362-3750
Fax: (802) 362-3525

Virginia

The Albemarle Angler
1129 Emmet Street
Barracks Road Shopping Center
Charlottesville, VA 22903
(804) 977-6882

Angler's Lab Outfitters
1554 Laskin Road, Hilltop East
Virginia Beach, VA 23451
(757) 491-2988

Mossy Creek Fly Shop
101 South Main Street
Bridgewater, VA 22812
(540) 828-0033

The Outpost
The Homestead
2 Cottage Row, Box 943
Hot Springs, VA 24445
(540) 839-5442

Orvis Tysons Corner
8334-A Leesburg Pike
Vienna, VA 22182
(703) 556-8634
Fax: (703) 556-4450

Washington

Clearwater Fly Shop
417 West 1st
Kennewick, WA 99336
(509) 582-1001

Orvis Seattle
911 Bellevue Way NE
Bellevue, WA 98004
(206) 452-9138
Fax: (206) 452-9142

West Virginia

Kate's Mountain Outfitters
300 West Main Street

White Sulphur Springs, WV 24986
(800) 624-6070, Ext. 7283
Fax: (304) 536-7854

Wisconsin

Fox Point Anglers, Limited
333 West Brown Deer Road
Fox Point, WI 53217
(414) 352-3664

Wyoming

Great Rocky Mountain Outfitters, Incorporated
216 East Walnut, Box 1636
Saratoga, WY 82331
(800) 326-5390
Fax: (307) 326-5390
E-Mail: GRMD@union-+6.com

Orvis Jackson Hole
485 West Broadway, Box 9029
Jackson, WY 83001
(307) 733-5407
Fax: (307) 733-7158

Recommended Outfitters, Guides, and Places to Fish

Alaska

The Boardwalk Wilderness Lodge
P.O. Box 19121
Thorne Bay, AK 99919
(800) 764-3918
Fax: (907) 828-3367

Bristol Bay Lodge
2422 Hunter Road
Ellensburg, WA 98926
(509) 964-2094
June-September: (lodge)
(907) 842-2500
Fax: (509) 964-2269

Crystal Creek Lodge
Box 92170
Anchorage, AK 99509-2170
(800) 525-3153
Fax: (907) 245-1946
E-Mail: http://www.CRYSTAL CREEK LODGE.com

Alaska's Valhalla Lodge
P.O. Box 190583
Anchorage, AK 99519
(907) 243-6096
Fax: (907) 243-6095
June-September: (lodge)(907) 294-2250

King Salmon Guides Expeditions, Incorporated
P.O. Box 602
King Salmon, AK 99613
May-Oct: (907) 246-3675
Nov-Apr: (847) 776-2202
Fax: (907) 246-7645 / (847) 776-9253
(800) 976-2202

Ouzel Expeditions Incorporated
P.O. Box 935
Girdwood, AK 99587
Paul & Sharon Allred
(800) 825-8196
Fax: (907) 783-3220

Alaska Trophy Fishing Safaris
Dennis Harms
P.O. Box 670071
Chugiak, AK 99567
Phone and Fax: (907) 696-2484

Arizona

Bill Schultz
HC-67 Box 2
Marble Canyon, AZ 86036
(800) 962-9755
Fax: (520) 355-2271

Arkansas

The Ozark Angler
659 Wilburn Road, Highway 110E
Heber Springs, AR 72543
(501) 362-3597
E-Mail: OzarkFlys@aol.com

John Gulley
1703 River Ridge Road
Norfork, AR 72658
(501) 499-7517

California

Clearwater House on Hat Creek
Cassel, CA 96016

Office: (415) 381-1173
House: (916) 335-5500

Captain Don Haid
2524 Fordham
Costa Mesa, CA 92626
(714) 525-5801
Fax: (714) 525-5783

Mark Pinto
1445 San Juan Avenue
Stockton, CA 95203
(209) 948-FISH

Frank R. Pisciotta
P.O. Box 10038
Truckee, CA 96162
Phone/Fax: (916) 587-7333
E-Mail: cyberfly@hooked.net

Colorado

Elk Creek Lodge
1111 Country Road 54
P.O. Box 130
Meeker, CO 81641
(970) 878-4565
Fax: (970) 878-5311
E-Mail: elk@rmi.net

Elktrout Lodge
1853 County Road #33
P.O. Box 614
Kremmling, CO 80459
(970) 724-3343

Fryingpan River Ranch
32042 Fryingpan River Road
Meredith, CO 81642
(800) 352-0980
E-Mail: area@frypan

Blue Quill Angler
1532 Bergen Parkway
Evergreen, CO 80439
(800) 435-5353
Fax: (303) 674-4791

Fly Fishing Outfitters
P.O. Box 2861
Vail, CO 81658
1060 West Beaver Creek Boulevard
Avon, CO 81620
(800) 595-8090

**Gunnison River Telluride
Flyfishers**
P.O. Box 315
Montrose, CO 81402
May-Oct: (800) 828-7547
Nov-Apr: (800) 297-4441
Year Round Phone/Fax: (970) 249-
4441

Kinsley Outfitters
1155 Thirteenth Street
Boulder, CO 80302
(800) 442-7420
Fax: (303) 442-7286

Trinchera Ranch
P.O. Box 149
Fort Garland, CO 81133
(719) 379-3263
Fax: (719) 379-3266
(also see pages 148–151)

West Fork Outfitters
Eugene Story
P.O. Box 300
Dolores, CO 81323
(888) 882-8001

Connecticut

Captain Jeff A. Northrop
P.O. Box 2540
Westport, CT 06880
(203) 226-1915
Fax: (203) 454-0857

Captain Dan Wood
6 Larson Street
Waterford, CT 06385
(860) 442-6343

Florida

Everglades Angler
810 Twelfth Avenue South
Naples, FL 34102
(800) 573-4749 (800-57-FISHY)
E-Mail: evergladesangler
@naples.com
Web site:
http://naples.com/flyfisheverglades

**Grand Slam Outfitters,
Incorporated**
Captain Bruce Miller
100 Anchor Drive, Suite 391
North Key Largo, FL 33037
(305) 367-5000
Fax: (305) 367-4340

C.B.'s Saltwater Outfitters
Aledia Tush
1249 Stickney Point Road, Siesta Key
Sarasota, FL 34242
(941) 349-4400
Fax: (941) 346-1148

**Sanibel Light Tackle Outfitters,
Incorporated**
Captains Al Helo, Tom Rizzo, John
Boardman
Forever Green Center
2025 Periwinkle Way #8
Sanibel Island, FL 33957
(941) 472-2002
Fax: (941) 472-8180

Captain Duane Baker
218 Azalea Street
Tavernier, FL 33070
(305) 852-0102

Captain Simon Becker
P.O. Box 6565
Key West, FL 33040
(305) 745-3565

Captain Frank Catino
468 Saint John's Drive
Satellite Beach, FL 32937
(Orlando Area)
(407) 777-2793

Captain Richard DeVito
3585 SE Saint Lucie Boulevard
Stuart, FL 34997
(407) 223-1300

Captain Hamilton M. Franz
4000-4th Saint Johns Avenue
Jacksonville, FL 32205
(904) 389-6252
Fax: (904) 388-9722

Captain Allen C. Kline
5590 West Oaklawn Street
Homosassa, FL 34446
(352) 628-7907
Phone/Fax: (352) 628-5381

Captain Dan Malzone
4709 Cherokee Road
Tampa, FL 33629
(813) 831-4052

Captain Larry Miniard
3733 Southside Boulevard, #9
Jacksonville, FL 32216
(904) 645-7176

Captain Terry Parsons
141 Easy Street
Sebastian, FL 32958
(Vero Beach Area)
(561) 589-7782

Captain Albert Ponzoa
203 Camino Real
Marathon, FL 33050
(305) 743-4074

Captain Danny Watkins
707 Hoover Dike Road #801

Clewiston, FL 33440
(800) 741-2517

Georgia

The Lodge at Little Saint Simons Island
P.O. Box 21078
Saint Simons Island, GA 31522
(912) 638-7472
Fax: (912) 634-1811
E-Mail: http://www.pactel.com.ouissi

The Lodge at Cabin Bluff
P.O. Box 30230
Sea Island, GA 31561
(912) 638-3611

Captain Larry Kennedy
511 Marsh Villa Road
Saint Simons Island, GA 31522
(912) 638-3214

Idaho

Three Rivers Ranch
Warm River
P.O. Box 856
Department O
Ashton, ID 83420
(208) 652-3750

Wapiti Meadow Ranch
H.C. 72
Cascade, ID 83611
(208) 633-3217
Fax: (208) 633-3219

Bill Mason Outfitters
Sun Valley Mall
P.O. Box 127
Sun Valley, ID 83353
(208) 622-9305

Will and Barbara Judge
Saint Joe Hunting & Fishing Camp

HCR 1 Box 109A
Saint Maries, ID 83861
(208) 245-4002

Solitude River Trips, Incorporated
P.O. Box 907
Merlin, OR 97532
(800) 396-1776
Fax: (541) 471-2235
(Idaho's Middle Fork of the Salmon
River)

Louisiana

Captain Gary Taylor
43207 Highway 190E
Slidell, LA 70461
(504) 641-8532

Captain Jeff Poe
141 Pelican Point Road
Lake Charles, LA 70607
(318) 598-3268
Fax: (318) 598-4499

Captain Briant Smith
1317 East Ford Street
Lake Charles, LA 70601
(318) 436-7800

Maine

Libby Sporting Camps
P.O. Box V
Department O
Ashland, ME 04732
(207) 435-8274 radio phone

**King & Bartlett Fish and Game
Club**
P.O. Box 4
Eustis, ME 04936
(207) 243-2956

Barnes' Outfitters, Incorporated
185 U.S. Route #1 South

Freeport, ME 04032
(207) 865-1113

Carroll Ware
16 Greenwood Avenue
Skowhegan, ME 04976
(207) 474-5430 Phone/Fax

Maryland

Pintail Point Farm
511 Pintail Point Farm Lane
Queenstown, MD 21658
(410) 827-7029

Captain Joe Evans
Box 3349
Annapolis, MD 21403
(410) 280-2046
E-Mail: "hamboat@aol.com

Rob Gilford
181 Thomas Johnson Drive
Frederick, MD 21702
(301) 694-6143

Captain Bo Toepfer
1410 Foxtail Lane
Prince Frederick, MD 20678
(800) 303-4950
E-Mail: qdel70a@prodigy.com

Massachusetts

Fishing the Cape
Routes 137 and 39,
Harwich Commons
East Harwich, MA 02645
(508) 432-1449

Cooper Gilkes
RFD, Box 19
Edgartown, MA 02539
(508) 627-3909

Rivers Edge Trading Company
Junction of Route 128 and 1A
50 Dodge Street
Beverly, MA 01915
(508) 921-0096

Captain Mike Bartlett
P.O. Box 122
North Pembroke, MA 02358
Phone/Fax: (617) 293-6402
E-Mail: bfast@pcix.com

Captain Rich Benson
47 Capri Lane
Chatham, MA 02633
(508) 945-1672

Tony Biski
182 Round Cove Road, Box 296
Harwich, MA 02645
(508) 432-3777

Captain Fred Christian
Goodwin's Landing
Marblehead, MA 01945
(617) 631-1879
Fax: (617) 631-6796

Captain Barry Clemson
Box 24
North Thetford, VT 05054
(802) 333-4600
Box 766
Rowley, MA 01969 (summer)
(508) 948-3750

Captain Jon Perette
113 Sedgewick Drive
Scituate, MA 02066
(617) 545-8113
Fax: (617) 545-8515

Captain Dave Tracy
P.O. Box 6041
North Plymouth, MA 02362
(800) 320-3252

Captain Chris J. Aubut
1266 Drift Road
Westport, MA 02790
(508) 636-3267

Mexico

Sports Resorts International, Inc.
1000 Louisiana
Houston, TX 77002
(713) 752-0244
Fax: (713) 650-8057
(also see pages 174–175)

Michigan

Johnson's Pere Marquette
Route 1, Box 1290S-M37
Baldwin, MI 49304
(616) 745-3972

Captain Matthew A. Supinski
7616 South Hazelwood
Newaygo, MI 49337
(616) 652-2868

Montana

Battle Creek Lodge
Box 670
Choteau, MT 59422
(406) 466-2815 or (406) 799-0499
(lodge)
Fax: (406) 466-5510

Crane Meadow Lodge
Box 303
Twin Bridges, MT 59754
(406) 684-5773
Fax: (406) 684-5772

Diamond J Guest Ranch
Box 577
Ennis, MT 59729
(406) 682-4867

Eagle Nest Lodge
Big Horn River
P.O. Box 509
Hardin, MT 59034
(406) 665-3711

Firehole Ranch
P.O. Box 686
West Yellowstone, MT 59758
(406) 646-7294
Fax: (406) 646-4728

Hubbards' Yellowstone Lodge
RR 1, Box 662
Emigrant, MT 59027
(406) 848-7755
Fax: (406) 848-7471

Lone Mountain Ranch
P.O. Box 160069
Big Sky, MT 59716
(800) 514-4644
Fax: (406) 995-4670
http://www.lonemountainranch.com

Summit Station Lodge
Forresters Frontier Travel
Glacier National Park, Montana
P.O. Box 167
East Glacier, MT 59434
(800) 665-3799
http://www.Forrester-Travel.com

Spotted Bear Ranch
2863 Foothill Road
Kalispell, MT 59901
(800) 223-4333

Beartooth Plateau Outfitters, Incorporated
Ronnie L. Wright
P.O. Box 1127
320 Main Street
Cooke City, MT 59020
June-September: (406) 838-2328
(800) 253-8545

Bighorn River Shop
Forresters Frontier Travel
Bighorn River, Montana
P.O. Box 470
Hardin, MT 59034
(800) 665-3799
http://www.Forrester-Travel .com

Paul Roos Outfitters
P.O. Box 621
326 North Jackson Street
Helena, MT 59624
(800) 858-3497
Fax: (406) 449-2293

The Tackle Shop Outfitter
P.O. Box 625
Ennis, MT 59729
(800) 808-2832
Fax: (406) 682-7729
E-Mail: tklshop@3rivers.net

Beardsley Outfitting Expeditions
Tim Beardsley
P.O. Box 360
Ennis, MT 59729
(406) 682-7292

Blackfoot River Expeditions
Paul Roos Outfitters
P.O. Box 621
Helena, MT 59624
(800) 858-3497
Fax: (406) 449-2293

Tim Linehan
472 Upper Ford Road
Troy, MT 59935
(406) 295-4872
E-Mail: http://homer.libby.org./
linehan/welcome.htm

Nevada

Captain Lex Moser
14752 Rim Rock Road
Reno, NV 89511
(702) 852-FISH (3474)

New Hampshire

Mark Ewing
8 South Main Street
Hanover, NH 03755
(603) 643-1263

New Jersey

Ed Broderick
11 Hawthorne Drive
Westfield, NJ 07090
(908) 789-3382

New Mexico

"Born 'n' Raised" on the San Juan River, Incorporated
Tim R. Chavez, Outfitter
San Juan River
Navajo Dam, NM 87419
(505) 632-2194

The Reel Life
1100 San Matco Boulevard NE,
Suite 10
Albuquerque, NM 87110
(888) 268-FISH
Fax: (505) 268-1667
E-Mail:
74724.1674@compuserve.com
http://www.thereellife.com/reellife/

New York

Beaver Brook Expeditions Outfitters
Pete Burns
P.O. Box 96
Wevertown, NY 12886

(888) 454-8433
Fax: (518) 251-3394

Captain Paul Dixon
74 Montauk Highway #9
East Hampton, NY 11937
(516) 324-7979

Captain Barry Kanavy
3944 Beacon Road
Seaford, Long Island, NY 11783
(516) 785-7171

North Carolina

Foscoe Fishing Company & Outfitters, Incorporated
9378-1 Highway 105 South
Banner Elk, NC 28604
(704) 963-7431

John Calvin
107 Brookside Avenue
Greenville, SC 29607
Home: (864) 235-4289
Business: (864) 370-0720

Oregon

Morrison's Rogue River Lodge
8500 Galice Road
Merlin, OR 97532
(800) 826-1963
Fax: (541) 476-4953

Pennsylvania

Skytop Lodge
1 Skytop
Skytop, PA 18357
(800) 345-7759
E-Mail: skytopl@ptd.net

Chuck Swartz
923 Main Street
Honesdale, PA 18431
(717) 253-9780
E-Mail: flyfish@ptd.net

South Carolina

Bay Street Outfitters
815 Bay Street
Beaufort, SC 29902
(803) 524-5250
Fax: (803) 524-9002

Captain Bramblett Bradham
P.O. Box 1248
Charleston, SC 29402
(803) 870-4688

Mike Hester
21 Orchard Park Drive
Greenville, SC 29615
Shop: (864) 297-9011
Fax: (864) 297-9085

Captain Richard Stuhr
547 Sanders Farm Lane
Charleston, SC 29492
(803) 881-3179

Tennessee

Dry Flyer Outfitter, Incorporated
Highway 411 North, P.O. Box 618
Benton, TN 37307
(423) 338-6263

Chris Nischan
2807-C West End Avenue
Nashville, TN 37203
(615) 327-0557

Larry and Emily Shaffer
358 Blazer Avenue
Smyrna, TN 37167
(615) 459-0567
(also see pages 129–134)

Texas

Gary Clouse
217 Windjammer
Rockport, TX 78382
(512) 729-1520

Judy Wong
7314 Emerald Glen Drive
Sugarland, TX 77479

Utah

Falcon's Ledge
P.O. Box 67
Altamont, UT 84001
(801) 454-3737
Fax: (801) 454-3392

Spinner Fall Fly Shop
1450 South Foothill Drive
Salt Lake City, UT 84108
(800) 959-3474
http://www.Spinner Fall.com

Vermont

David L. Deen
RFD 3, Box 800
Putney, VT 05346
(802) 869-3116
E-Mail: deenhome@sover.net

Chuck Kashner
P.O. Box 156
Pawlet, VT 05761
(800) 682-0103

Virginia

Orvis Roanoke
Market Square, 19 Campbell Avenue
Roanoke, VA 24010
(703) 345-3635

Bob Cramer
Route 3, P.O. Box 238-A
Dayton, VA 22821
(540) 867-9310

Washington

Jeff Martin
865 NW 73rd Street
Seattle, WA 98117·
(206) 781-8915

Ron Romig
4702-361 Street, S.E.
Fall City, WA 98024
(206) 222-7654

Jim Shuttleworth
4730 228th SE
Bothell, WA 98021
(888) 487-4500

Wyoming

Shirley Mountain Lodge
P.O. Box 2850
Casper, WY 82644
(307) 266-1470

Brush Creek Ranch
Star Route Box 10
Saratoga, WY 82331
(800) 726-2499
Fax (307) 327-5384

Crescent H Ranch
P.O. Box 347
Wilson, WY 83014
(307) 733-2841
Fax: (307) 733-8475

Aune's Absaroka Angler
C. Scott Aune, Outfitter
754 Yellowstone Avenue
Cody, WY 82414
(307) 587-5105
Fax: (307) 587-6341

Bressler Outfitters, Incorporated
Box 766
Wilson, WY 83014
May 1-Nov 1: (307) 733-6934
Nov 1-May 1: (307) 883-4668

Great Rocky Mountain Outfitters, Incorporated
216 East Walnut, Box 1636
Saratoga, WY 82331
(800) 326-5390
Fax: (307) 326-5390
E-Mail: grmo@union-tel.com

Lazy Boot Outfitters
Forresters Frontier Travel
Cloud Peak Wilderness, Wyoming
Box 470, Hardin, MT 59034
(800) 665-3799
http://www.Forrester-Travel.com

Yellowstone Outfitters
Lynn D. Madsen
P.O. Box 1156
Afton, WY 83110
(800) 447-4711
Fax: (307) 886-5284

George H. Hunker
Sweetwater Fishing Expeditions
Box 524
Lander, WY 82520
(307) 332-3986
E-Mail: phunker@wyoming.com

Reel Women Fly Fishing Adventures "Not Just for Women"
P.O. Box 289
Victor, ID 83455
(208) 787-2657
Fax: (208) 787-2691
E-Mail: ReelWomen1@wyoming.com
(also see Lori-Ann Murphy on pages 63–66)

Wilderness Discovery Youth Program
Randy Foster, Director
HC 63-347
Jackson Hole, WY 83001
(307) 733-7745

Index